MW00948692

Psychology of Orphans

Psychology of Orphans

Dr. Ludmila M. Shipitsyna

2005

iUniverse, Inc.
New York   Bloomington

Psychology of Orphans

Copyright © 2008 by Lyudmila M. Shipitsyna

All rights reserved. No part of this book may be used or reproduced by any means, graphic, electronic, or mechanical, including photocopying, recording, taping or by any information storage retrieval system without the written permission of the publisher except in the case of brief quotations embodied in critical articles and reviews.

The information, ideas, and suggestions in this book are not intended as a substitute for professional advice. Before following any suggestions contained in this book, you should consult your personal physician or mental health professional. Neither the author nor the publisher shall be liable or responsible for any loss or damage allegedly arising as a consequence of your use or application of any information or suggestions in this book.

iUniverse books may be ordered through booksellers or by contacting:

iUniverse
1663 Liberty Drive
Bloomington, IN 47403
www.iuniverse.com
1-800-Authors (1-800-288-4677)

Because of the dynamic nature of the Internet, any Web addresses or links contained in this book may have changed since publication and may no longer be valid. The views expressed in this work are solely those of the author and do not necessarily reflect the views of the publisher, and the publisher hereby disclaims any responsibility for them.

ISBN: 978-0-595-43018-5 (pbk)
ISBN: 978-0-595-87359-3 (ebk)

Printed in the United States of America

Contents

This current book represents an analysis of various forms of family upbringing of orphan children and children left without parental care. It makes a special accent on a description of principles, types and contents of an innovative model of patronate upbringing, as well as experience of its implementation in the City of Moscow and the Province of Vladimir, in Russia. The annexes describe various samples of legal documents, questionnaires and diagnostic resumes used in selecting of patron parents.

This book may be used for training of patron parents, undergraduate and graduate students majoring in education and psychology, as well as for professionals of specialized boarding-type educational institutions and social centers for families and children.

© Lyudmila M. Shipitsyna, 2005

© The Institute of Special Education and Special Psychology (Russia), 2005

Special Acknowledgment

Acknowledgment is given to Gordon D. Lewis for his work in bring this book to print in North America. His own addition in the knowledge and practical application of international adoptions makes a sound conclusion to the Psychology of Orphans

INTRODUCTION

The increase in the number of socially endangered children, deterioration of their physical and psychological health, increase in criminal behavior and drug addiction cases among children and adolescents are a great concern to the government and society in Russia.

The total number of children in Russia decreased by 4,289 000 over the last 10 years and this process continues. The number of children who have not yet reached the age of 18 totaled 30.5 million, by the beginning of 2003. The birth rate in Russia is less than the rate of the population's simple natural reproduction. The number of orphans, however, is increasing annually and amounted to 699,200 in 2004.

Ninety-five per cent of present-day orphans have parents, however, they have either been deprived of their parental rights, or they gave up those rights themselves.

According to statistics, in 60 per cent of all cases, parents undertake this voluntary step due to their child's serious illness. About 20 per cent of all cases are motivated by financial hardship. There is a serious contradiction in the ability of many families between the need to provide normal living conditions allowing for the proper developmental environment for their children and inadequate economic conditions of the majority of families.

The number of orphans is on the increase, due to forced population migration and economic crisis. Various data on the total number of orphans in Russia exists as shown from the low number of 2004 (699,200) to the present day official police files that state 2.5 million while it is 4 million, according to various independent sources. The criminal offense rate among adolescents is also on the increase. There were 208,000 registered criminal offenses that were committed by youngsters in the year 2000, including murders, robberies and drug-related crimes. More than 50 per cent of the young delinquents grew up in incomplete families, with over 30 per cent of psychologically unstable children who grew up without a father (18, 238).

According to statistics, Russia occupies First place in the world, by the number of orphans per each 10,000 children. Nearly 50 per cent of this country's children, (about 18 million), belong to the social risk zone. There are 422 baby foster homes for 35,000 children, 745 foster homes for 84,000 children and 237 boarding schools for 71,000 children in Russia. More than 100,000 children who need guardianship are discovered in Russia annually.

Currently children do not have solid legal protection against cruelty and domestic violence. Domestic violence is the reason that approximately 2,000 children and adolescents commit suicide annually, 50,000 leave their homes and 6,000 run away from foster homes and boarding schools. Twenty-five to twenty-six thousand minors become victims of a crime annually. Over 2,500 sexual offenses are registered in Russia each year, including sexual offenses against minors. Cases of rape of minors are on the increase.

We are used to explaining an increase in the number of "social" orphans through various social problems, i.e. poverty, unemployment, parental alcoholism, etc. However, many nations while undergoing similar economic crisis, do not have such numbers of children abandoned by their parents.

Many socio-economic measures have been taken in Russia over the recent years to prevent child abandonment. The Russian government regularly passes decrees which adopt various measures to combat abandonment and crime among minors. New types of assistance to children and families are being developed, with new regional centers for family support now opening to advance this assistance.

However positive these actions are, they have not led to a decrease in social abandonment. This lack of positive results reveals that the new measures taken do not take into account some of the more important aspects of the problem of abandoned children. As long as the government looks only to the socio-economic conditions of the family as the major cause of abandonment, any measures taken will prove to be ineffective. At the same time, a lot of families have managed to keep their children, despite having undergone serious economic and psychological crisis.

There are four major factors that influence the solution of the abandonment problem: socio-economic, psychological, educational and health-related. Currently, main government efforts are concentrated in the socio-economic area. They provide wide assistance to various population strati instead of assistance aimed precisely at those families at risk of abandonment. There are almost no efforts aimed at resolving psychological and health-related causes. The Ministry of Education has had the responsibility of orphan issues including education for some time in Russia. The activities of various social and psychological services are aimed, not at prevention of abandonment, but at assisting those who have already become orphans.

It is a historical fact traced back even to ancient times that active discussions were held regarding the specifics of child development in orphanages and the goals of their upbringing. Up until the 20th century these discussions were primarily held by therapists, teachers and philosophers. Psychologists entered the scene much later. The first psychological researches of children in orphanages were performed in the 1920's. Under the influence of the theory of psychoanalysis, there was an opinion of psychology at the time (that is shared by many even up to the present) being that the first years in the life of a child are critical in affecting the development of his or her personality. Consequently, researchers paid major attention to babies and little children.

It has been convincingly demonstrated that the loss of the parental family and primarily the loss of communication with a mother, influences a child's development quite negatively. This influence becomes even more acute the earlier the loss of maternal communication occurs. The first detailed data had been obtained by the group of researchers from the Vienna School of Child Psychology, led by Sh. Buler.

The later famous research by R. Spitz, J. Bowlby and K. Goldfarb that determined the direction for research of the problem of psychological deprivation in childhood clearly relied heavily on the Vienna School data.

It is the research of orphanages and the specific impairments in personality development of children within orphanages that led J. Bowlby to propose the attachment theory. It is shown in psychological research of attachment that only intimate, emotional and stable relationships with an 'object of attachment' resulted in normal psychological development and the development of a healthy, active and socially adaptable personality.

The ability to love and to attach is the fundamental characteristic of a normal development, which is called a criterion of psychological health by all major psychologists and psychotherapists, beginning with Sigmund Freud. The inevitable instability and multi-polarity of a social environment that surrounds a child in an orphanage is clear. The absence of a key caregiver (person who takes care of a child) and mentor (one who guides him or her throughout their life) and lack of adult supervision in providing feelings of stability, reliability and protection, creates extremely unfavorable conditions for the formation of attachment and emotional development for a child. Moreover, it contributes to the destruction of the natural instinct of a child for intimacy and love. These children do not form the most important foundation for their further psychological development and for feelings of trust to the world.

A series of Russian psychological research had been undertaken in the 1980s and 1990s that have convincingly shown negative consequences of an institutionalized upbringing.

The major theme of this research is the idea that children's upbringing in the conditions of an orphanage does not take into account adequate psychological conditions of providing for full personality development and inevitably includes factors slowing down psychological development.

This present book, *Psychology of Orphans* is devoted, not only to psychological aspects of the development of "social" orphans, but also to multidisciplinary issues associated with the development, education and upbringing of children in their natural families, as well as in the alternative families and boarding institutions.

In this book we have tried to analyze the results obtained from the Russian and foreign researchers, as well as the results from our own research in issues of psychological and educational causes of the existence of problem families and children, possibilities for psychological rehabilitation and correction of the orphans' upbringing within foster or patron families, as well as within centers for family upbringing and various other types of family placement.

One of the new types of family placement of orphans is a patron family. *Patronate upbringing* is the type of placement of a child who requires government assistance, into the families of 'patron parents', under the mandatory condition of separation of the rights and responsibilities and the protection of the legal interests of a child, between the child's parents, the institution and the patron parents.

The Patronate upbringing was known since ancient times, though it only started to spread in Europe and the USA since the middle of the 19th century.

The development of patronate upbringing started in various countries of the world in the 20th century, especially after the end of World War II. Throughout the first post-war decades, the development of this form of upbringing allowed closure of large children's homes almost everywhere. Family upbringing appeared to be much cheaper for the states' budgets and more suitable to the needs of children. As a result 75% of children in the USA were returned to their biological parents, while the other 25% were placed into advantageous family environments.

The Buckner Foundation has the most significant experience in organization of patron families and training patrons for children in the USA. The Buckner Foundation has over 100 years of experience in executing social programs aimed at reduction of the number of institutionalized children and finding a family for a child where he or she would be getting an individualized approach and attention.

In 1995, The Buckner Foundation organized the Department of International Assistance to Orphans in the USA. It also began organizing assistance programs in Russia as well. According to an agreement with the Russian Federation's Department of Education, the Buckner Foundation and the governments of several Russian provinces, including the Province of Vladimir and the City of St.Petersburg, are working on establishing models of patron families using foreign experiences and adjusting those to Russian reality. The analysis of the results of implementation of this new form of family placement for orphans has shown efficiency and opportunities for development of patronate system in conditions of modern Russia in both large urban centers and small towns. There are, however, a lot of difficulties in implementation of system of patronate families in Russia. They are associated in the first place with the lack of

■ Proper legislation;

■ Psychological and educational criteria for selection of patron parents;

■ Complex system of guidance for patron families;

■ Preparation, training and consulting of patron parents etc.

The present textbook is the fruit of common efforts of the professionals from the Buckner Foundation and the Institute of Special Education and Special Psychology of the Raoul Wallenberg International University for Family and Child. Its main goal is assistance in preparation and training of patron parents and children's home professionals in selecting orphans for the system of patronate care and subsequent guidance.

The textbook touches upon main problems and causes of disadvantaged childhood in Russia, features of psychological development of institutionalized orphans with emphasis on causes of their socialization, emotional development and communication area. Various types of family upbringing of orphans and children left without parental care in historical and modern aspects are considered. The book pays its main attention to the development of a system of patronate care, its principles, methods and models.

Separate chapters are devoted to the description of current legislation providing for the rights and guarantees given to children left without parental care, as well as providing for the rights, duties and responsibilities of parents with respect to education and upbringing of their children.

This book may be useful to undergraduate and graduate students majoring in education and psychology, as well as to professionals of specialized institutions, teachers, psychologists, speech therapists and social workers. It may also be used for the education process of parents wishing to adopt a child or to become a foster parent or a patron.

1

THE MAIN CHARACTERISTICS OF PROBLEM CHILDHOOD IN RUSSIA

1.1. The Reasons for Children becoming «Social» Orphans

Some of the main categories of problem children in Russia is comprised of children without parents, children with parents whose parental rights have been taken away, children of incarcerated parents, as well as children of those parents who are incapable of performing their parental duties due to the social and moral specifics of their lifestyles.

The major increase in the numbers of «social» orphans and development of some new features of this phenomenon has become a serious challenge for Russia over the recent years. The so-called «hidden social orphans» can be found due to deterioration in living conditions of a lot of families. The number of children belonging to the above-mentioned category is constantly increasing due to instability of socio-political situation, inflation, unemployment, forced population migration, decrease in the level of families' living conditions and weakening of their infrastructure.

The known numbers of children without parental care is on a constant increase.

This number was 59,000 in 1991; 102,000 in 1994, 113,000 in 1998 and 123, 600 in 2000 (an 8% increase).

The number of institutionalized children amounted to 272,700 as of January 1, 2000. That means an increase of almost 120,000 over the three years. The number of institutions for children is also on the increase. The increase amounted to 182 institutions for normally developing children and 18 institutions for children with various developmental disabilities over a three-year period. Around 30% of known «social» orphans are institutionalized. Around 50% of «social» orphans are transferred to their relatives' care, while about 0.9% to the guardian families. Various families foster around 7% of all children here and abroad.

The number of orphans and children without parental care is constantly growing in spite of the sharp decline in birth rates. This number was 572,000 in 1996; 597,000 in 1997; 620,000 in 1998; 662,000 in 2000 and 700,000 in 2001.

The number of full orphans is increasing because of the early parental deaths mostly due to unnatural causes. The full orphans' share among the total number of orphans amounted to only 5% of the total number of orphans only 5-7 years ago. Nowadays this indicator reaches 25 to 30% in some of the provinces.

The phenomenon of «social» orphans has gained recently an acute socio-economic and moral importance. There is a need for deep analysis of social, psychological and educational aspects of this problem. What are the causes for the children to be left alone while their parents are still alive?

This is not just a Russian problem. Intensive urbanization of modern society, enormous social changes and intensive population migration in many countries is accompanied by the increase in the numbers of children abandon parentally. However, the nature of such an abnormal form of mothers' behavior still remains unknown and incompletely researched. Some practical research involving these women, as well as the analysis of existing sources of scientific information regarding this problem is found in the following. These mothers have extreme difficulty of counteraction between various social, psychological and pathological factors that negatively influence the feelings of motherhood, which represents the most important form of women's social behavior.

The Belgian committee on women's social issues has described three main categories of women leaving their children upon extensive study of all reasons for leaving children by their mothers. The first and the most frequent is when a child's father leaves a future mother while pregnant. The second is when a child is born out of wedlock. The third category consists of women with low levels of social and moral adaptability and responsibility.

Russia is experiencing the third wave of increase in the number of orphans over the last 100 years. The first wave occurred after the communist takeover and World War I, the second wave happened after World War II. There had been 678,000 orphans in Russia in 1945 and about 700,000 at the end of 2001. Nowadays the increase amounts to 100,000 children per year. The reasons for existence of orphans in 1945 are understandable. At the same time it is difficult to recognize and accept as natural the following causes of orphans' existence at the present time:

- The leading cause in the recent years is alcoholism and drug addiction that lead to cruelty towards children in the family, neglect of their needs and interests. Over 100,000 children annually are taken away from such families, partially through taking away parental rights (43,000 in the year 2000).
- The number of full orphans increases due to early deaths among the population due mostly to unnatural causes.
- There is an increase in parental incompetence due mostly to psychological illnesses.
- The number of incarcerated parents does not decrease.
- The number of children born out of wedlock is on the increase
- The social disorganization of families, financial difficulties and difficulties in living conditions are increasing, as well as unhealthy relations between parents and degradation in family morals.

The reasons for children becoming social orphans mentioned above are only describing the consequences, the final point in a complex way of degradation of a human. The consequence of this degradation is incapability to bring up one's own children, decrease in parental responsibility and even premeditated refusal to perform parental duties.

1.2. Implications of "Social" Orphan hood for the Children

The implications of becoming «social» orphans early in their lives are very negative for the children. They include: heavy and often irreversible consequences for their physical and psychological well-being, which started showing up even prior to the official loss of their families such as;

■ abnormal fetus development during an unwanted pregnancy;

■ negative social experiences during early and pre-school childhood.

Being an orphan has a destructive effect upon the emotional connection of a child with his or her social environment, with the world of adults and peers, who are developing in more advantageous conditions and causes serious secondary disturbances of his or her physical, psychological and social development.

The most dramatic implication of «social» orphanhood is the direct threat to the physical health, as well as psychological and social development of a child who is left without parental care. Up to 60% of all children's homes patients are children with various chronic diseases, primarily those of their central nervous system and those belonging to the 3rd through 5th health groups (the lowest health groups). Over 55% of patients lack in their physical development. Only 4.7% of all patients may be characterized as completely healthy.

The reasons of physical and psychological disorders of orphan-children vary. First of all, most institutionalized children have hereditary disorders caused by alcoholism, as well as by drug addiction over the recent years. The number of orphans suffering from hereditary psychological and neurological disorders is constantly increasing. It is the abandoned children who most often have inherent physical and psychological abnormalities as a result of their parents being intoxicated during the ovulation process or due to the use by the future mother of various chemicals that are allegedly supposed to stop pregnancy. Moreover, the institutionalized children are genetically presupposed to various psychological disorders, including mental disabilities and schizophrenia.

Second, the unwanted pregnancies are dangerous by it self when a future mother is predisposed to abandon a newborn right in the maternity ward. The effects of stress during such a pregnancy represent the causes of deviations of vital interactions between a mother and a fetus and disruptions of various sensor, exchange and gummoral connections between them. The majority of future mothers who are inclined to abandon their newborns experience various psychological disorders during their pregnancies, such as hysterical reactions, depression, psychic disorders etc. Psychological disorders lead to abnormal behaviors of these women during pregnancy, such as hyperactivity, unsuccessful attempts to abort, use of tobacco, alcohol, narcotic drugs etc. The majority of them are unprepared to give birth, which is evidenced by extremely high rates of premature births (37.5% as compared to 4.7% in the general population), as well as high rates of various disorders during the birth process it self (59.2%). Two-thirds of all newborns have weights of less than 3 kg. Almost half of those born upon maturity have signs of morphological functional immaturity. 43.7% of newborns showed clear signs of brain damage. 46.9% of all newborns are in need of intensive care as compared to 14.8% of the general population newborns.

Premature births, small weight of newborns and cerebral disorders that accompany them often lead to various neural and psychological disorders in approximately 47 to 60% of all cases. If we combine all of the above with the negative influence of the early break up with the mother upon the newborn's psychological development inevitably accompanied by the newborn's psychological deprivation, as well as hereditary influence of parental psychological disorders, it becomes evident that children born out of unwanted pregnancies comprise a special psychological risk group and require extreme attention and extensive medical, social, educational and psychological prevention measures right from the time of their birth.

The majority of child abandonment cases are associated mostly with temporary personality, social, psychological and financial crises rather than with specific social needs or serious moral degradation of a particular woman. In many countries of the world that do not have «social» orphanhood there exist various social, medical and psychological support services that actively cater for women and families in crisis situations. Unfortunately, it must be noted that in this country similar services are only beginning to emerge over the recent years.

The third factor that leads to various disorders in elder orphans is the variety of social, educational and psychological bad habits in the former parental families. The forms of improper upbringing characteristic of «social» orphanhood are complete absence of care and the so-called hyper-care. The majority of families where children are lacking any kind of care may be characterized as socially disadvantaged families with low standard of living, unacceptable nutrition levels, parents' alcohol addiction, immoral ways of life, assaults and abuses within the families, as well as common habitation with relatives having serious psychological disorders.

Various forms of physical, sexual and emotional abuse of children are typical for those families. The absence of parental love, lack of proper nutrition, lack of schooling, various forms of abuse lead the children to leave such families. All of these become the reason for sensor and social deprivation and lack in psychological development in 2/3 of all cases, as well as the reason for brain malfunctions associated with neural disorders, enuresis, learning disabilities, slow reaction times, emotional instability, habitual lying, pathological fantasies and expression of neurotic reactions.

The fourth and definitely one of the most important factors for children's disabilities and lack of their proper social adjustment is his or her forced taking out of a native family and institutionalization. The parental family with its natural form of life organization and its communication level with relatives and especially with a child's mother represents the main condition of full-valued psychological and emotional development of a child. Taking a child from his or her parents facilitates the development of so-called deprivational psychological disabilities, which become more serious the longer the period of a child losing contact with his or her mother and the longer the influence of this break up upon a child. In early childhood such deprivation causes such disabilities characteristic of early development stage as lack of general and speech development, lack in development of fine movement and mimics. Later various emotional disabilities may be observed, such as lack of expression of emotions, inclinations to fear and worries, behavior deviations like frequent reactions of active and passive protest and refusals, lack of distancing feeling in communications or vice versa difficulties in communication.

Isolation of a child from his or her mother usually causes serious consequences in his or her intellectual development and formation of personality that are not subject to correction. Starting from the second year of life isolation from a mother also leads to negative results for a child's personality that are not subject to correction, though his or her intellectual development may become completely normal.

Orphanages usually get those children who already suffer from psychological deprivation and lack of parental care. Stopping lengthy deprivation in the early childhood obviously leads to normalization in development. It concerns, however, only visible behavior and general functions of intellect. As for the speech development it may be delayed even if deprivation ended prior to a child achieving the age of 12 months. In general, the earlier the deprivation of a baby that is less than a year old ends the more close to a norm his or her further development will be. It has to be noted however, that speech and learning disabilities, as well as abilities to form long-term and serious interpersonal relationships are considered to be less reversible.

Consequently, «social» orphan hood makes its most serious mark upon the psychological life of a child. The earlier a child is taken out of a parental family the longer and more isolated they stay at an institution, the more visible disabilities in his or her psychological development become. The delayed and improper intellectual and personal development becomes the main disability. In many cases (85 to 92%) the institutionalized children are incapable to successfully absorb the general school program while the share of children with delays in psychological development among the general population of children does not exceed 8 to 10%.

1.3.   The Main Groups of «Social» Orphans.

There are three main categories that can be distinguished among «social» orphans:

1. Children having no parents, as well as those children with parents whose parental rights are taken away, whose parents are incarcerated or whose parents are incapable to perform their parental duties due to their personal social and moral characteristics.

The «social» orphanhood is growing in scale and the number of children from disadvantaged families, as well as from low-income families is constantly on the increase.

The deep social crisis in this country has affected both financial and moral state of a family as the chief institution of natural and essential biological and social protection of a child. For the first time since the end of World War II the death rate exceeds the birth rate and every third marriage ends up in divorce.

Due to the high divorce rate approximately 470,000 children are left without one of the parents annually. The number of children born out of wedlock is also increasing with 354,000 children born out of wedlock in the year 2000. Almost 22,000 out of wedlock children were born by underaged mothers.

Currently about 2.8 thousand women give birth to their children at the age of 15; 13,000 - at the age of 16 and 36.7 thousand at the age of 17. The share of children born by the underaged mothers comprises on average around 3.8% of all children being born. It is within this group of incomplete families of underaged mothers that the highest level of deprivation from a mother is observed. Around 1% of all newborns to such mothers become orphans during the first days of their lives by their abandonment of their mothers in the maternity wards.

The number of children, whose parents parental rights are taken away remains at a high rate. In 1995 their number was 20,000 while in 2000 it already amounted to 43,400.

The increase in the numbers of incomplete families occupies considerable place among the factors disadvantageous for decreasing «social» orphanhood.

Financial difficulties, as well as a narrowed circle of intra-family communications within an incomplete family have a negative impact upon children. They frequently experience communicational difficulties with their peers, as well as (especially the boys) some neurotic symptoms. According to various polls over 50% of young delinquents were brought up in incomplete families and over 30% of children with psychological disorders were brought up in fatherless families.

Parents' unemployment becomes an additional risk factor for their children's development.

The number of children becoming orphans at an early age is also on the increase.

2. *Orphan children and children deprived of parental cares that have*

physical and psychological developmental disabilities.

Based on the statistics the health levels of children accepted into the children's homes is continually deteriorating. In 1980 the share of children with psychological and hereditary disabilities comprised 40% of all those admitted to the children's homes, compared to 1998 when it already comprised 81%. As per above-mentioned there are multiple reasons of various physical and psychological disabilities of orphan children. The majority of those are hereditary due to parental alcoholism and narcotic drug addictions. Abandoned children have a higher rate of physical and psychological developmental irregularities.

The number of children's homes and special schools for orphan children with limited health-related abilities is on the increase. In the year 2000 there were 56,000 orphan children or children deprived of parental care receiving their education in special schools, primarily designed for mentally disabled children.

As well there were 33,000 handicapped children, more than half of them being orphans that were institutionalized in 150 children's homes for the mentally disabled or the 6 children's homes for the physically disabled belonging to the Russian Federation Department of Labor.

3. *Orphan children and children deprived of parental care with behavior problems leading to susceptibility to the criminal environments and lack of self-protection.*

Children deprived of parental care are more inclined to vagrancy and danger to become victims of violence and crime (they may become objects of sexual victimization and subjects of sexual trade), as well as to danger of becoming involved in criminal activity. They become early tobacco and alcohol addicts or acquire addictions to various toxic materials and narcotic drugs.

The following are the current state of family environments producing the majority of children with aberrant behaviors:

- Negative socio-demographic;

- Dysfunctional psychological;

- criminal;

- Parental unemployment etc.

Children's and adolescents' behavior is negatively influenced by the unresolved issues of the minors' lack of school adjustment and lack of activities while out of school.

The majority of children and adolescents with aberrant behaviors come from various government institutions for children. The number of children absent without leave from children's homes and special boarding schools is increasing each year. The reason for absence mentioned most frequently is inability to live there due to cruelty on the part of teachers and other personnel members.

The majority of students in special boarding schools (around 70%) are 13 to 15-year old minors with 18% of them orphans and children deprived of parental care.

In the next chapters we are going to review in detail the consequences of problems arising within families that lead to the increase of orphan children and children deprived of parental care, as well as children with deviant and addictive behaviors that have been deprived of parental care.

2

DEVELOPMENT OF A CHILD'S PERSONALITY UNDER THE CONDITIONS OF INSTITUTIONALIZATION

2.1. Psychological Development of Orphan Children and Children Deprived of Parental Care

Psychological development of children brought up outside the family, that is, within different types of institutions for children represents currently a very acute problem.

It is always undesirable and unnatural for a child to be brought up outside of his or her own family. While the financial conditions of the majority of the Russian society still remain quite poor it leads to a lot of children being voluntarily institutionalized, that is, transferred into the government's care at the will of their parents. Still the majority of children in the children's homes are those whose parents' parental rights have been taken away. This represents evidence (in Russian society) of low morals of thousands of mothers and fathers who have refused their care and love to their children.

As a rule, institutionalized children are lacking in psychological development from their peers brought up within families. The rate of these children's development is slow. Their psychological and physical health has a number of negative features at all stages of their development. Many institutionalized preschoolers are passive in all types of activities; their vocabulary, attention span and memory are poor.

School students of early age have specific deviations in the development of intellect. It expresses itself in delays or absence of any developed visual thinking, which requires some internalized active planning. This leads to increased difficulties in studying the school program successfully. Children lack spontaneity in their behavior, self-control, activities planning. Poor speech, as well as delays in mastering writing, reading and arithmetic must be mentioned. Most of the children have to attend special schools even during their first years of study.

Numerous researches have shown that psychological development of the majority of institutionalized children is more delayed as compared to normal for their age group.

Children's communications opportunities are narrowed down by their institutionalization, their lives are strictly organized, and they experience shortages of communications with adults. The same age peers constantly surround children, and collectivism dominates individualism.

Specific features of development of institutionalized children are studied in the research by psychologists and education professionals, such as I.V.Dubrovina, A.G.Ruzskaya, M.I.Lisina, Y.O.Smirnova, A.M.Prikhozhan, N.N.Tolstykh, N.N.Denisovich and others.

The research mentioned above has shown that institutionalized children experience communication shortages that cause them to be in a state of psychological deprivation.

Some researchers undertake attempts to classify the most typical behaviors of children in the conditions of limited main life stimuli. They distinguish between different types of children that suffer the consequences of psychological deprivation.

N.N.Denisovich has noted the critical consequences to a child's development when considering the situation where assistance and support are limited and a child's need for love and acceptance remains unsatisfied. He has distinguished 3 types of child character can be classified from this background with psychological deprivation of personality:

a)   striving for compensation;

b)   well adjusted;

c)   Latent.

A.Yarulov in developing a program for psychological and educational assistance aimed at developing the personality of children deprived of parental care has taken a different focus. He pays most of his attention to individual approaches to each child taking into account the reasons for their orphanhood. He conditionally divides orphan children into 4 groups.

The first group – are immature almost primitive children that have been admitted from the residential centers for abandoned babies at the age of 3 or 4. The majority of them do not know how to play, have difficulty speaking, and have fear when encountering unknown people. They show little psychological activity, they are fearful to everything new and engage in passive behavior within the society.

The second group – are children poorly developed socially, those coming from extremely disadvantaged family conditions. They are fast moving, know how to speak, however, they are loaded with negative life experiences. They often use swear words in their speech, they show early sexual curiosity. While playing they often reproduce the actions and attitudes observed by them seeing the parent drunk.

The third group are- children whose parents are dead. As a rule, they are superior to their peers in their development and do not require special correctional efforts.

The fourth group - mentally disabled children and children with delays in psychological development that are admitted from the residential centers for abandoned babies and disadvantaged families. They require specific medical, psychological and educational assistance.

Specific conditions of institutionalized living often lead to delays in psychological development of children in some significant areas. Apathy is noted in the early age children. It is expressed through absence of emotions in children. They start to speak later in life, which creates disadvantage for development of early forms of thinking. It also hinders social interaction with the people who surround them. Institutionalized children have narrow general knowledge; they are not acquainted with the environment and with various subjects typical of regular living. Visual thinking that is supposed to become complete during the preschool age and is the foundation of successful education is below that which is regular for their age due to poor development of feelings. Moreover, a number of children have shown underdevelopment of an ability to spontaneously control their behaviors, to independently adhere to the rules in the absence of any adult control, which leads to lack of independence and self-organization. The children can easily get anxious and tired, which is explained by their constantly being surrounded by their peers and their free time being planned and organized by adults.

Significant delays can also be found in the communications area. It is reflected by low initiative on the part of children to try and communicate due to the lack in necessary ability and means of communication.

Communication is not the only area where substantial differences are found in respect to a child's upbringing within and outside a family. Communication represents a factor that determines many secondary differences. Shortage of communication leads to delays and deviations in psychological development. Communication shortages prevent children being brought up outside a family setting to learn how to speak in their due time. Institutionalized children have low levels of curiosity, are slow and indifferent when encountered with new impressions. Preschoolers living outside a family move slowly, are impulsive and unable to plan their actions, they are unable to concentrate on any one activity. In other words, they can barely control their own behaviors and are lacking in the level of spontaneity as well. Insufficient levels of self-consciousness may explain the low level of spontaneous self-control. During their preschool years normal children already start to realize the internal aspects of their existence that are independent of any exact situations and they can start to distinguish themselves individually from any exact (corporate) situations. This process occurs in two main directions - as comprehension of a child's relationship to his or her surroundings (his or her preferences, desires, and intentions individually attended to in a family environment) and as establishment of connection between the past, present and future events and actions of a routine household. However, the institutionalized preschoolers comprehend their actions through those moments that are organized and predetermined (mealtime, bedtime). These moments are repetitive and primitive and do not become personal for each child since they are common for a group as a whole. Because of this the institutionalized preschoolers do not distinguish and consciously establish their own actions, they do not remember what they have done, they are not aware of what they are going to be doing. They are not developing any schedule for their own actions.

It must be said therefore that the psychological development of preschoolers being brought up outside of the families is substantially different from that of those living within families. The main difference is high dependence on the situation context that can be seen in various types of activity. In learning this is exhibited in inability to resolve problems requiring some abstract thinking without relying upon any practical actions. In behavior it is exhibited in impulsiveness and inability to control one's own actions. In the sphere of self-consciousness it is dependent on the desires of the situation that is taking place and absence of time schedule for a child's own actions. High dependence on the exact situations may become a serious personality disability that could slow down the development of intellect, willpower and emotional sphere.

Institutionalized primary school students lack in ability to purposefully research various subjects and occurrences and determine their features. Observational disability may have consequences not only for school learning, but for the general psychological development of a child as well. An ability to be guided by some definite general action mode while performing a certain task represents the core of learning activities. Institutionalized children lack such ability. Moreover, these children have an underdeveloped visual thinking and a reverse logical thinking process. Classification thinking is predominant.

First graders living outside a family can perform direct and elementary instructions of an adult. Their actions have a step-by-step nature. Action and self-control directly follow teacher's instruction. A child is incapable of performing those tasks where instructions are not given step-by-step, but are dependent on them being established prior to the beginning of an activity. This is the consequence of low development of behavioral self-regulation characteristic of institutionalized children.

While in primary school they still suffer a lack of imagination and visual thinking. Motivational preferences are determined through communications with adults. The main desire is to get attention, approval or a reward of some kind from a teacher. Institutionalized primary schoolchildren are lacking in peer-to-peer communications skills. They are unable to have an equal basis communication with an unknown child, as well as adequately estimate those qualities that are needed for friendly communication. The need in such a communication shows up as a tension in communicating with adults. Extreme desire for communication with adults and simultaneous excess dependence on adults causes aggressiveness in these children.

The features of psychological development of institutionalized children shown above may play a vital role in the whole development of a child's personality.

22. Development of a Child's Personality in the Conditions of Deprivation from his or her Mother

Attachment to an adult is a biological necessity and primary psychological condition for a child's development. Mother is the most important adult for a newborn when the primary interpersonal contact is established. Recently researchers view newborns as a creature capable of exhibiting initiatives that can play an active role in interacting with its environment and that is capable of learning in this environment and interacting in it.

A child who is deprived of parental love has less chances to develop high self-esteem, warm and friendly relations with others and stable positive self-image.(Kon, 1989). Unfriendliness or inattentiveness on the part of parents

...es children's animosity. This animosity may be exhibited either directly
...inst the parents themselves, or indirectly.

Even daily correctional therapy with children of an early age in the
homes for abandoned babies (either individual or group) did not help to
establish close emotional ties or form attachments. All attempts to improve
the process of children's development through short-term educational
influence have not had any positive impact upon their social and emotional
spheres. This emphasizes impossibility to open up children's abilities without
ongoing communication with a sensitive and emotionally close person. This
proves the necessity to radically change the whole social environment for
children in the homes for abandoned babies (Mukhamedrakhimov, 1999).
The presence of a peer by itself just provides for development and promotion
of communications in the early age, however, the adult determines and
organizes the process.

A baby itself actively «chooses» mother from out of the environment.
Existence of an attachment between the mother and the child by the end of
the first year of baby's life is proven by the experiments with «strangers» that
have been going on starting from 1970s. (Cited from A.S.Batuyev and others
). A team of US psychologists led by K.Rubin is researching the types of early
children's social isolation, mechanisms of its evolving and its connection with
further socio-emotional development, especially for forecasting any future
difficulties in children's communications with others. This research also
analyzes the difficulties of a child's interrelationships with the outside world.
They are associated with a child's temper features, his or her experience of
communicating with parents, financial status of a family, parents' education
level and general state of intra-family relationships.

It is well known that the first feeling in a life of any living creature is love
for its mother. For this reason the full-valued development of a child may be
exercised only in coordination with the mother.

Currently there are over 700,000 children in our country growing up in
children's homes and boarding schools without parental love. The problem
of orphans with living parents has not disappeared, but has catastrophically
increased due to rise in alcoholism and loss of moral values.

As a result the children's homes and boarding schools contain a very
specific group of children whose hereditary features are not quite clear and
who suffer from a clear deprivation syndrome.

It is difficult to clearly determine a notion of «motherhood deprivation»
since it combines a variety of different terms. It includes a child's
institutionalization, insufficient care for a child on the part of a mother,
temporary deprivation of a child from his or her mother due to the mother's

illness, and finally, insufficient love or a loss of love of a child to a certain person acting in a role of a mother in regards to him or her.

Most of researchers consider a lack of basic trust in the world as the first, the foremost and the most difficult consequence of the»motherhood deprivation». It causes fear, aggressiveness, and absence of trust to other people and to him- or herself with the lack of desire to learn and study.

Two elements are essential conditions for formation of a child's trust towards outside world: a mother's love and care and their continuity.

It is strange to note that everyone does not recognize the need for emotional care. It is quite often that even the loving mothers believe it necessary to be stern to their children so that not to spoil them and have them fail to become independent. The mothers like this try not to hug their children, feed them on a strict schedule and not approach there children while they are crying. These are the consequences of such an approach: when children are age 7 or 8 they often become clients of physicians and psychologists complaining about emotional problems. However, the reason is that during the first year of its life a child does not need a stern mother or his or her own independence, but continuing and conditional mother's love, warmth and care.

These are the general characteristics of a child growing up in the conditions of «motherhood deprivation» since his or her birth: lack of intellectual development, inability to form meaningful relationships with others, slow emotional reactions, aggressiveness, or unassertiveness. In the opinion of some researchers this personality type is different from the one that is deprived a care of a mother not right from the very birth, but later when the close emotional ties have already been established. In those cases a break-up with a mother begins as a heavy emotional stress for a child.

Even a six-month old is crying during the first month of a break-up demanding a mother and looking for someone capable to substitute her. The second month of a break-up may be characterized by the reaction of avoidance, that is, if somebody approaches a child it starts yelling. The third month is characterized by avoidance of any contact with an outside world and development of apathy and autistic stimuless (concentration upon itself).

This is characteristic not only of institutionalized children, but of those in hospitals, sanatoriums and other similar institutions. Usually the consequences of deprivation gradually fade away upon a child's return to a family, however, some special research has established that the changes occurring as the result of more than 5 or 6 months break-up (separation) with the mother can become irreversible.

Unlike a child deprived a care of a mother from its very birth, the development of a personality of a child who had had a mother at one point, but later became deprived of her can be characterized as that of a neurotic type when certain defense mechanisms show themselves up at the forefront. The children after having been deprived of a mother have to adjust to the new conditions in their lives. It is not rare that they act as if having forgotten their mother, they began to act negatively towards her, they do not want to recognize her, and they break the toys given by her.

Such neurotic reactions may be clearly observed in pictures drawn by the abandoned children. Lithuanian psychologist G.T.Khomentauskas analyzed drawings by 7-year olds who had been living in there families, but later found themselves placed in boarding schools. He believes the drawings showed that the first thing a child has to cope with in a situation of such an abandonment are harassing thoughts that he or she has been deceived by the parents as well as other adults. That he or she is not needed by anyone and not loved by anyone anymore and that he or she is completely alone in this world. Such thoughts by the child provoke outbreaks of protest and reactive behavior and subsequent complete depression. At this period of time a child may either express puzzlement or complete distrust to an adult. «They all are like that. They may deceive you and abandon you at any moment.» Children become absorbed in themselves, they do not share their feelings with adults, and they keep what they were offended with inside themselves.

If one were to ask a child to draw a picture of a family at such a moment, he or she would refuse under any pretexts trying to unconsciously avoid a traumatic feeling. A child would ask various defensive questions like «What for?», «What is it - a family?» or just would say «I can't draw people.» Even after he or she would agree to start doing drawing it they would sit silently looking around for a subject. They would start depicting some things that show somebody who is not alive or things that are not really human unlike a child having good emotional relations within a family. It is a paradox at first glance that family members are absent from the drawings of abandoned children. It is not that a child does not remember them or that they are not significant for him or her. Family members or to be precise what he or she remembers about them are associated with negative emotions like a feeling of being abandoned or unloved. So a child would be trying to avoid the subject. At the same time children lose trust in those people that were previously close to them, as well as to any other adults. They do not feel safe or comfortable in the world that surrounds them.

G.T.Khomentauskas research looked for various ways a child may act or think to overcome this situation, to live through it in his or her mind. He sees two ways of this. A child believes that his or her abandonment is a punishment for being bad, so he or she loses self-respect as the result and starts feeling guilty, which becomes their main personality feature. This is the first way. The second way is recognizing that family and parents are responsible for everything. The internal condition of such a child may be characterized as a mixture of anger, hurt and love towards the parents that leads to a break-up with the family and rise in the child's aggressiveness.

There is a hypothesis that institutionalized children are not just lacking in their development and certain personality characteristics but are extensively forming several mechanisms different in principle that help them adjust to institutionalized life. The reason for this is not the break up of early emotional connections with the mother or other adult relatives, but the fact that the institutionalized life does not require performing some of the personality functions that are indispensable in normal life.

Unfortunately, institutionalized children are psychologically different from their peers growing up within families. Their rate of development is slower. Moreover, they possess certain qualitative negative features that are different for each stage of their development - from early childhood to adolescence and so on.

Psychological development features show up differently and not to a similar degree at each age. However, all of them have quite serious consequences for the development of a child's personality.

Even institutionalized babies in the first year of life evolve different from their peers growing up in families. They are slow, indifferent, and not quite happy, they have low drive for new knowledge and their emotions are simplified mostly to crying. Their pre-personality features that evolve during the first year of a child's life and later become the personality foundation are abrogated. They do not form any attachments to adults, they do not trust anyone, and they are self-absorbed, sad and passive.

The two and three year olds that are institutionalized add new features to those mentioned above. They have low curiosity, lack in speech development, delays in working with various subjects and absence of independence. Institutionalized 3 to 7 year old preschoolers are noted for being passive in all types of activities, their speech skills are poor and they do not show much attentiveness having constant conflicts in relations with their peers.

Primary schoolchildren have specific deviations in intellectual and motivational development. Those are expressed in delays of their visual thinking that requires for an internal plan of action to be thought out. This lack leads to increasing difficulties in studies that require a progressive line of cognitive thinking. Because of this issue we find that during the first three years of schooling the majority of institutionalized children (up to 50%) are transferred into special schools. The children are not independent in their behaviors, lack self-control and planning of their actions and this environment only adds to the negative behaviors and development of the child's personality.

In adolescence the specific features of psychological development of institutionalized children cause their difficulties in relations with other people. When they are 10 or 11 the adolescents form their attitudes towards adults and peers based on their practical utility for a child's needs. They make themselves able not to form any attachments or any deep feelings. This leads to them becoming morally dependent on others and getting into the habit of living by the orders from others which later in life create many difficulties for them. They experience difficulties in forming their self-conscience (they start realizing their own lack of development) and a lot more.

Institutionalized children experience a lot of deviations in their communications with adults. On one hand they have a great need for attention and acceptance on the part of the adults around them. They require human warmth, care and positive emotional contacts. On the other hand, they experience complete dissatisfaction in feeling this need. This dissatisfaction comes as the child experiences only a small amount of attention on the part of adults and not enough to relate it to genuine acceptance or love. The low level of personal, intimate and genuine contact by adults only feeds their emotional poverty. The repetitiveness of adult content in the child's life in an institutional setting is mostly aimed at behavioral regulation. The frequent change of adult care givers involved also does not help and only reinforces negative perceptions.

The adult-child communicational features mentioned above deprive children, firstly, of realization of their own importance and value that is necessary for their psychological well-being. The second realization lost here is of the value of having another person in their life or of the need in forming any deep or lasting attachments to people.

That is why today even with the modern conditions of children's upbringing in the homes for abandoned babies, children's homes and institutions for social welfare still have the same results with the children as did the old institutionalized hospitals from our past.

Unfortunately, the methods and ways of dealing with abandoned children cannot compensate for their disadvantageous life circumstances and deviations formed early in their development of intellect, emotions, willpower and personality. These deviations have as their consequence that institutionalized children are much less prepared for various real life situations. These consequences can be seen even in their adult lives making it harder for the former institutionalized children to adapt as adults.

The institutionalized children require specially organized psychological help from the earliest ages. Such assistance should be provided for upbringing of each one according to specific features of their age, personality and behaviors. This may be achieved today through permanent employment of a professional psychologists within those institutions who would be responsible for studying and diagnosing children individually. Cooperation with trainers and teachers who work daily with the child could lead to the development and implementation of a prevention and correctional program. These measures would go a long way to compensate disadvantageous experiences and circumstances of life experienced by the children and provide for progress in their personality developments.

2.3. Development of Communication in Institutionalized Children within the Children's Homes

In each human community, be it a kindergarten, a classroom, among friends, within various formal and informal gatherings, an individual exhibits a personality. This provides an opportunity to evaluate oneself within a system of relationships with others. The process of learning the environment and human types of activity is a collective process, which initially evolves in an «adult-child» system.

All types of a child's individual activity including various forms of play, and skills displayed in arts or other knowledge are only secondary forms of childhood. These activities are established initially during joint interaction with adults and peers and are a measure of the child's social adjustment. Existence of a social group is impossible without common activities, thus, it is impossible for a group of children to be established and exist without those. A common activity in a group of children is that «field of gravity» where interpersonal relationships are established. These relationships are formed, become close and unbreakable through the activities. The process of a child's involvement into any social group for play, study or any other activity represents his or her recognition of the type of common activity, its structure and his or her inclusion into it as a participant .

Relationships of children with each other (including friendship) are exercised through common activities, information exchange, and mutual assistance. Communication with peers influences the development of a child's personality. It becomes the learning process on how to coordinate his or her actions with that of other children. Through play and in real life, during their communications with peers children reproduce relationships of adults while practicing various behavior patterns and evaluations of their peers and themselves. While communicating with their peers the children utilize and check the validity of all those types and norms of human relations that they have learnt while communicating with adults. The nature of interpersonal relations is quite complex in any society. They include both individual features of a personality like its emotions and willpower, intellectual capabilities, as well as societal norms and values learned by a person. It is an active position of each person and his or her actions that constitute the most important link in a system of interpersonal relations. An individual makes themselves acceptable in a system of interpersonal relationships by acting within the framework of these relationships. Within these various human communities the social cues and rules are defined for all to adhere to. Even though the communities are different in form and content the behavioral values and structure exist in them all, be it kindergarten, a classroom, a circle of friends or various formal and informal communities. A child lives, grows up and develops within the interconnection of various relationships. Personal inter actions such as shared sympathies, attachments and antipathies wind through the group like invisible threads making a very strong impact upon the lives of every child and the group as a whole. It is the personal interrelations that are the most important factors of the group's emotional climate and emotional welfare of each of its members. Each child within a group occupies a specific place in a system of personal relations. Personal relations are not specifically set up by anyone. They get established accidentally due to some complex psychological circumstances. A student's situation may be advantageous; he or she feels accepted by a group, feels sympathy from his or her co-students and in turn shows sympathy towards them. This psychological situation is felt by the students as a unity within a group, which in turn makes them sure of themselves. Lack of understanding in relationships with classmates, the feeling of not belonging to a group may become a source of psychological disability in the development of a personality. The state of psychological isolation has a heavy negative impact both on the development of human personality and his or her activities. This kind of student most often becomes a gang member, they study badly and they are ineffective and rude in communications.

If you take a look at any class or any kindergarten group you will notice that each person is in their own micro-group or individual micro-environment there. This particular microenvironment largely determines personal development, personal successes and general emotional well-being of a person. Each group member occupies some specific place within it having a unique system of interrelationships with the rest of the members. This may be advantageous or disadvantageous for them. Existence of subgroups within a more general group may be explained by selectivity of human communications. The features of children's communications are determined by the individual features of each person (type of a nervous system, character, personal experience, levels of development of interests and needs etc.). Some of the students are seeking company of faster and livelier peers, while quiet and passive children attract others. Some children are more assured near the strong and decisive ones. The others, in their turn, prefer to befriend those who are weak and shy getting satisfaction in protecting them. It is within a group that a child can find the behaviors satisfying for him or her. It is through communication s within a group that they obtain an experience in communicating that is so important for the development of their personality. While attempting to figure out the reasons making communications one of the strongest factors of a personality development, it would be an oversimplification to see the educational importance of communications only in obtaining particular ends. To view this simply as an opportunity for children to exchange information about what surrounds them is too basic or if only as a means for acquiring knowledge and skills for future need in obtaining successful employment as an adult.

An educational importance of communication is not limited only to increasing human knowledge about the outside world or in stimulating the psychological development that is necessary for his or her labor activities.

An educational importance of communication also involves it being a mandatory condition of general intellectual development of a human, especially their characteristics in perception, expressive and thinking processes.

Communication has no lesser importance as a form of activity for the development of a person's emotional sphere and in particular the development of feelings. All feelings that people communicating with each other are primarily invoking in one another are used for evaluating each person's actions, appearance and response from that exchange. As well as those feelings that a person is experiencing upon observing the others' actions and deeds there are other concluding emotions that arise during communication. All those feelings make the strongest impact upon development of stable emotional responses towards various sides of reality when socializing with a group. It leads to a more natural exchange during group or social events.

Communication is no less important for the development of human willpower. The development of character habits in concentration, persistency, decisiveness, bravery, being goal-oriented or those of a reverse nature are to a large extent determined by how day-to-day communication situations influence the development of the qualities mentioned above.

In order to be able to communicate with other people a person must have a certain psychological culture, which consists of three main elements:

- to be able to correctly evaluate other people and their psychology;

- to be able to give adequate emotional responses to other people's behavior and actions;

■ to be able to choose with respect to each individual a way of communicating with them that would best suite that persons characteristics in a way that would not contradict any moral requirements.

A person who is psychologically prepared for communicating is the one who has learned what, when, where and with what purpose something may need to be said. Also, a decision on not only the right verbal response but also the right physical one to be returned in order to leave a good impression and exude the necessary influence upon a communication partner needs to be understood. When speaking about the communication means of institutionalized children we must emphasize that they do not correspond to their actual motives and needs. Their expressions and mimics are poor and the dominating way of communication is their speech. However, their speech is poor in content and grammar. Also the contact between children in the institutions is much weaker than those between children at school. There is far less individual communication in orphanages and more group interaction but in a very controlled environment. Institutionalized children lack opportunity in learning more social cues in communication because of less interaction with adults. This leads to weaker relationships in communication between peers. A great opportunity of peer-to-peer communication that exists in an institution is not exercised in development of more mature concise and emotional contacts. Children brought up in families usually are taught to share their experiences in curiosity, amusement, joy or other feelings and necessarily involve their peers of all ages into sharing their feelings. Institutionalized children are less attentive and more immature towards actions and feelings of their partners. Often they do not notice when their counterparts get offended, ignore them when they ask for something or even when they start crying. Although being together in an institution they often behave independently of each other.

Within an institution a child always has to communicate with one and the same narrow group of peers with no power of changing it and no opportunity to be excluded from it. Any other child in a regular family or school is capable to change his or her communication circle. Belonging to a certain peer group becomes unconditional within an institution. As a consequence peer relationships become more of a relative-to-relative type rather than a friend-to-friend type. On one hand this may be considered as a positive factor enhancing emotional stability and protection when a peer group becomes an analogue of a family. On the other hand there are certain negative sides since contacts of this type do not enhance peer-to-peer communication skills. As an example there is a lack in skills to befriend a previously unknown child simply because the institutionalized child does not know how or were to begin such a thing. There is a lack to adequately estimate one's own qualities that are needed for selective friendships. These children have plenty of problems of which the children in regular families are completely unaware. Each institutionalized child has to adapt to a large number of peers. Their contacts are superfluous, nervous and done as if in a hurry. A child seeks attention and rejects it at the same time, becoming aggressive or passively abstaining from communication. While in need of love and attention he or she is not capable to behave in a way appropriate to gain them. Negative development of communication experiences leads to a child's negative attitude towards others.

Subsequently when a group rates him or her negatively (below his or her self-rating) a child becomes disappointed and dissatisfied.

The primary school age institutionalized children easily attaches to any adult who shows even a minimal level of kindness towards them. They are ready to fulfil any task given by that adult and do anything possible to receive attention from them. Indirectly one can observe the same with adolescents. At the same time institutionalized children can often be rude when interacting with adults, become aggressive or offended with no apparent reason. Even the most superfluous observation leads to a conclusion that a need in communicating with adults is unsatisfied in them and this causes several behavioral problems.

The above is also proven through the results of programmed observations performed by R. Burns using the Stotg Card. Teachers and trainers who know a child quite well fill out the Stotg Card. Based on descriptions and evaluations of various children's behaviors it allows the degree of a child's lack of adjustment and those complexes of symptoms that dominate in the lack of adjustment, to be determined.

It appeared that there were two leading complexes of symptoms for primary school age institutionalized children: worries about adults and animosity towards adults. The latter one evidences various forms of rejection of adults by a child and may become a beginning of animosity, depression, aggressiveness and antisocial behavior. The animosity can be shown by extremely impatient actions on the part of the child relating to any directive from the adult. For the occasions when the child is in a good mood there is sometimes a hello said to a teacher. If however the adult takes the lead to say hello first the child may express anger or suspicion when responding to a hello being said to him or her. They become very moody in there behaviors and sometimes it seems that they deliberately try to fail any task asked of them. They are unsympathetic, especially when they try to defend themselfs from any perceived accusations. They are always pretentious and always think that they have been punished unjustly. Subsequently, difficulties in communications with adults can be characterized as a leading factor of lack of adjustment of institutionalized children.

During a study of psychological preparedness of institutionalized children for school education one positive area was determined. Those children from institutions were leading the children who grew up in families in at least one of the indicators. That of expressing a desire to accept and fulfill a task given by a teacher. However, the analysis has shown that this desire of institutionalized children is a reflection of a child's inability to regard an adult as a teacher. To fulfill a task as a learning exercise, in other words, is a reflection of an unsatisfied need in communication with adults. This unsatisfied state is expressed in a desire by whatever means to obtain the positive acceptance and attention of the adult, not the teacher.

Consequently, these results let us discover that communications of institutionalized children with adults are two-fold: on one hand, the need is very acute; on the other hand, the forms of communications are primitive, immature and underdeveloped. According to the Stogt Card these two dominating complexes of symptoms evidence the same as above: worries are the expression of dissatisfaction of the need to be accepted by adults and animosity evidences inadequacy of the types of interaction with adults.

In adolescence the specifics of psychological development of institutionalized children mainly show up in the system of their interactions with people surrounding them. These interactions are associated with some stable and determined characteristics of these children's personalities. By the age of 10 to 11 the attitudes towards adults and peers is based on their practical utility for a child. Children form an ability not to get too attached to somebody, superfluous feelings, a habit to live without taking responsibility; they experience difficulties in developing self-conscience and so on. They become very pushy in their interactions with other people constantly requiring love and attention. They do not show a wide range of feelings while the feelings they do show are quite affectionate. They can show outbursts of emotions like joy or anger while at the same time lacking deep and stable feelings. They are almost completely lacking the conscious inward feelings associated with understanding of arts and moral collisions. They are very touchy emotionally, when even a short remark of dissatisfaction may cause an outburst of emotions, not to mention actual situations that create real emotional tension and loss of control in internal stability. Psychologists call it a low tolerance for frustration.

At the same time the presence of a heightened need in attention and kindness of adults observed with institutionalized children is evidence of their openness and eagerness for any contacts with adults with a desire for adult approval and attention. Openness and sensitivity of those children to any appeal from adults may become a reason for efficiency of impact of any training. By showing attention and kindness to a child an adult may satisfy this acute need. It is worth remembering, however, that a need in attention and kindness of an adult must not remain the only communicative need of a child. It is essential to develop on its basis more complex needs in cooperation, respect, sharing in feelings of another and mutual understanding. All of these needs develop through common activities of adults and children, in the process of their educational and personal conversations. Consequently, a need in attention and kindness must become a basis for building training programs for children growing up without families.

2.4.   Development of an Emotional Sphere of Institutionalized Children

Family is a concentration of human relationships and at the same time a specific societal instrument. Family upbringing is more emotional in its character than any other type of upbringing since it is conducted through parental love towards children, which in turn causes similar feelings in children towards their parents.

Initially the basis for emotional attachment of children to their parents is dependence from them, and a mother is closer in this respect to children than a father. A child deprived of parental love has less chances for high self-respect, warm and friendly relationships with other people and stable positive self-image. Unkindness or inattention on the part of parents causes children's animosity. This animosity may be directed either towards parents themselves or show itself up indirectly. Unmotivated violence may show up with respect to other people. If the aggression is turned inside it causes feelings of guilt and worry.

The main reason of emotional deprivation is disruption in emotional connection of a child with his or her mother. Permanent care of a mother is reason for the development of a child's feeling of trust to the world that is imperative for a normal personality development.

It is obvious that any disruption of an emotional connection with a mother substantially disrupts a child's personality development. Discontinuance of an emotional impact from a mother causes a child to have a primary worry, which becomes stronger as the time passes. Further development of a child's personality continues in the conditions of highly expressed anxiety. Subsequently this development becomes more and more disharmonious.

In the conditions of emotional deprivation a child is incapable of constructive social contacts. Shortage of communication experience strengthens emotional and social deprivation of a child.

Observation of children from disadvantaged families evidences that those children considerably lack in physical and psychological development as compared to their peers from good families.

Children from disadvantaged families experience a strong dissatisfaction of their main psychological needs. Some researchers believe that the degree of deprivation of children from disadvantaged families is stronger than of institutionalized children.

Disruption of the connection between mother and child constitutes deprivation of the mother from her child and causes a child to have emotional problems. There exists an opinion that the absence of a father hurts a child less than an absence of a mother. However, a fatherless child does not have an example of behavioral regulation and suffers from lack of authority and control.

These children become aggressive and undisciplined. If a mother gives a child an opportunity to feel human love and care, a father opens for a child a way into a human society. A mother teaches to give, a father teaches to give back.

Parental love causes a child to develop and strengthen feelings of self-respect. A child deprived of parental love feels dissatisfied, unworthy, and offended by unkindness or inattention by the parents.

When a father is absent from a family a mother' time and attentions are directed mostly to the economical well-being of a family. She has less quality time or attention to her child for this reason. Subsequently, a child's psychological development does not take a constructive direction. A new person within a family who would take upon himself a duty of a responsible parent may diminish the probability of deprivation.

Deprivation may evolve even in the conditions of a complete family. The reasons could include alcohol abuse by the parents, relationship dissatisfaction, the emotional immaturity of parents or cruelty and absence of love with respect to a child. Our children found in such families, are completely unprotected. They are unprotected, first of all, from a criminal environment, both at home and on the street.

«Social» orphans are most hurt by that. These are orphan children, whose parents are still alive, but morally degraded, who leave their children to the will of fate.

Observations of children suffering from psycho-physiological and psychosomatic malfunctions, nervous disruptions, and difficulties in communication, thinking or learning activities show that all of the above is mostly characteristic for those children who were lacking parental love and affection.

There is plenty of research on the subjects of personality development of institutionalized children or children left without parental care.

The majority of researchers have an opinion that social isolation negatively influences development process. The reason for deviations in the child's character is felt to be in the absence of a child's emotional contact with parents, in particular a mother and communication with adults that would suit a child's nature. It has already been shown that in the case for institutionalized children their contacts are superfluous, nervous and done as if in a hurry. A child seeks attention and rejects it at the same time, becoming aggressive or passively abstaining from communication. It is also true here in children from families that are dysfunctional or degenerate.

Children's negative attitude towards other people is associated with difficulties in understanding any emotional condition of another person, which then leads to mistakes in attempts for social interaction.

Unsatisfied need in love and recognition and emotional instability of a child opens a pathway for a child thinking they have a right to be delinquent. Children intuitively understand that they can rely only upon themselves in this life and thus assure themselves by all possible means in that believe. They violate the rules, become rude and try to dominate others even by violence. This is a demonstration of need for independence.

Life experiences of institutionalized children are limited. The main source of information is limited to a few adults such as a teacher, trainer or caregiver at the children's orphanages. Movies featuring supermen and situations far from standard do not give children an adequate understanding of real situations awaiting them in regular life.

A lot of researchers who studied individual differences in the emotional lives of such children mention a number of times a radical change in character in the emotional state such as immediate joy or beginning of sudden anxiety and worry.

K.Y.Izard believes that the main emotional features of human character are worries, depression, love and animosity.

When a person is anxious or concerned that means a consistent inclination is to perceive a lot of situations as threatening and to react with worry when those situations are encountered. High levels of anxiety directly correlate with the presence of some nervous conflict and with various emotional and nervous outbursts.

The type of personality developing in the conditions of deprivation from a mother is called unemotional. Such a child has slow emotional behaviors, is unable to establish meaningful social contacts with either his or her peers or adults. Disruption of emotional contacts leads to a feeling that he or she is weaker than everyone else around them and they go on to develop a low self-esteem. Such children mostly believe that the whole world is seemingly against them.

It is essential to take into account the fact of how institutionalized children view the notion of «we». It represents a specific psychological notion. The whole world appears to be divided into «our own» and «the rest». «Our own» and «the rest» are subject to different standards of attitude that mostly do not correspond to societal standards. It is important to understand this when we observe children's cruelty towards their peers or preschoolers.

There are reasons a child starts to behave unpredictably in a difficult situation. L. S. Vygotskiy noted the existence of specific patterns of abnormal development and difficulties in interactions with people in these children based on there perceptions of "us and them".

For example the development of an emotional unhappiness can occur in various situations such as experiencing feelings of hurt after having failed to achieve success in a task particularly when this is noted by an adult. Despise for certain types of food can be formed under conditions of strict control and the demand for it to be eaten as often is the case in institutions. Actual hatred of any type of control is common. When tired or during a general bodily weakness children react with outbursts of anger to every little thing. You can well observe aggressiveness and the intent to accuse others for this behavior. The inability and absence of will to acknowledge there own guilt results in the child's use of domination of defensive behavior in conflict situations. The child cannot and will not admit wrong on there part despite all efforts to reason with them which does not help to solve the conflict in a constructive fashion. Instead of dealing with difficult situations on there own we observe a trend towards affective reaction including, defensiveness and trying to hold others responsible.

The research has shown the main reason of children's emotional problems lie in various deviations in psychological development. We do not speak here about serious psychological deviations, but more about those that are temporary, less noticeable, borderline level deviations.

Children with delayed development only have either positive or negative feelings. They almost never have any shades in their feelings like normal children do. Their feelings are often inadequate, disproportionate in their dynamics to impacts from the environment. Their feelings about serious life events are often light and superfluous while feelings about unimportant events may be very strong and long lasting.

Basic emotions of joy, anger, sadness, suffering and so on are more understandable. Research shows that institutionalized children are considerably lacking in their knowledge regarding these emotions as compared with children having a family.

The impact of egocentric emotions upon their opinions is regarded as immaturity of personality when children with delays in mental development are considered. A child gives highest ratings to those who he or she likes, those that are close to him or her. They rate life events in the same fashion: whatever is pleasant is good. L. S. Vygotskiy has mentioned the existence of specific rules or patterns of abnormal development and difficulties in interactions with other people leads to other perceptions in the children.

It is typical for a child to actually be a prisoner of their own emotions since he or she is unable to control them. It is this mental disability of having the inability to control one's own actions for the reason of broken life relationships, sufferings and conflicts within the child's environment.

Emotions of a mentally retarded child are in general insufficiently differentiated. In this regard he or she is reminiscent of a baby. It is known that little children do not possess a wide range of feelings - they are either glad with something and enjoy it, or are disappointed and cry. A normal older child has a wider range of feelings.

Feelings of a mentally retarded schoolchild are more primitive, he or she feels either satisfaction or dissatisfaction and almost no intermediary feelings.

Emotions of mentally retarded children are often inadequate and disproportionate to the impact from an outside world. Some children show extreme superfluity and lightness in perception of serious live events and are moody, the other children (observed quite frequently) show extremely strong and long-lasting feelings in regard to insufficient events and causes. Something insignificant may cause a very strong and long-lasting emotional reaction.

A transition from low to high forms of emotional life, in other words, development of feelings of a higher level is directly associated with changes of ratio between emotionality and intellect.

The weakness of intellectual feelings can be found in a fact that children do not correlate their feelings with respect to a new situation; they can not find satisfaction of their need in some action that is a substitute of what has been initially planned. For instance, they are unable to console themselves after being offended in some way.

Weakness of intellectual regulation in emotions also leads to a fact that special school students have difficulties with the so-called high spiritual values like feelings of shame and responsibility. Mentally retarded children have to be specifically taught these feelings. Unless the high values are taught as a child grows, satisfaction of elementary needs and emotions starts to take place more and more.

It is the timely work of a teacher and a family aimed at both intellectual and high spiritual values to be developed in the child that not only causes these values to be developed but also to assume a leading position in the child's life.

A lot of children with intellectual disabilities have so called disphorias (periodic negative mood swings) They are often anxious and show aggression against themselves and adults. It may show up like in the example below. A student who has been calm and obedient for a long period of time suddenly appears in the classroom in a bad mood and reacts with anger to any objections. In a day or two the bad mood suddenly disappears by itself. If a teacher understands that a child is in a state of disphoria, it is best not to talk to him or her and ask about anything.

Sometimes a different mood swing called euphoria can be observed. This is when a child unexplainably has a very good mood. In this state children become insensitive to surrounding reality. They continue laughing and enjoying themselves even after getting a bad grade. Euphoria may be a symptom in the beginning of an acute period of a disease.

Apathy may be another type of a mood swing. Sometimes special school students express the thoughts that are completely inadequate to their age like indifference to life and people or loss of any usual child's interests.

When becoming long lasting the dominant feelings gradually form various personality features (insensitivity, nervousness, anger, indifference, liveliness, light-mindedness etc.)

Anxiety occupies a special place within the context of differentiated emotion theories the term used for any combination of fear and other affects. Fear is the dominant emotion in the syndrome of anxiety.

Many researchers consider anxiety as a generalized feature in humans that is neither associated with nor related to any other specific area. Even so they correctly emphasize the connection of anxiety with affecting some definite areas of activity in communication or situational circumstances between humans.

For proper perspective on this, one needs to distinguish a state of worry and anxiety as a personality feature. It is assumed that emotional state is more intensive than an emotional personality feature.

Anxiety is often connected with sensitivity and defenselessness. Words used by an adult in correcting a normal child (who takes no exceptions to this type of correction) can cause an acute reaction with an anxious child because they experience deeper feelings of guilt. More than what the adult correcting a child had been counting on.

As a rule, worry is caused by emotional break up with a close person. Anxiety may be divided into a number of factors. They are presumed to be: fears, suffering, shame, anger and interest. Fear, interest, guilt and anger are the ones most likely to appear in profiling.

Institutionalized children have a poor vision of an outside world and do not develop a system of views corresponding to a higher level of personality development. When a child's most important needs remain unsatisfied he or she experiences an on going negative emotional state that is expressed in expectations of permanent lack of success. Such children are unsure in the correctness of their own behavior and decisions and show this by being afraid of everything, very touchy, full of superstitions and highly sensitive etc.

Worry is an emotion that evolves during a general evaluation of a situation deemed disadvantageous and represents a frequent emotional phenomenon. For this reason some researchers consider it "our guardian" and a certain level of it as necessity that is required for a harmonious full-value life. A constructive worry mobilizes us to overcome obstacles and solve problems. The criteria of a constructive worry represent an ability to find out its causes, not to become desperate in a difficult situation and to indicate reasonable ways for resolution of a problem that caused it.

It is easy to recognize a person in a state of worry. They are puzzled and hurried at the same time. The activity level is practically equal to zero. Anxiety as a personality feature may become a symptom of neurosis development. Anxiety may become independent from whatever has caused it. It may become a type of a fixed personal reaction.

Various feelings and results can be observed within different age groups. Preschoolers who suffer anxiety from the possibility of having to leave home are enable to control their bodily functions. Older students at school worry because of their relations with peers.

The difficulty lies in the fact that anxiety contradicts basic personal needs like a need in emotional stability and feeling of personal security.

Anxious children have specific attitudes towards success (they want to be successful) but also maintain an absence to properly evaluate there results as successful or not. The basis then for worries is a traumatic probability of there lack of success leading to low self-esteem and excess dependence upon an adult confirmation. Within an institution dependence of a child's emotional well-being is based on an adult's attitude and that determines the great value of this relationship.

Some researchers feel it is important to understand the real reason for some children's worries like being excessively touchy, getting offended easily or starting to cry is based on genetics. These are the consequences of hypersocial and superstitious features of their parents' personalities and their neurotic state.

In the opinions of Y.V.Novikova and N.I.Nayenko the level of anxiety starts to rise sharply after 11 years of age reaching its peak at the age of 20. It comes down by the age of 30. The second peak can be observed after the age of 60. It has been observed that in the preschool and primary school age boys there is more worries than girls seem to present and vice versa after the age of 12.

In the conditions of an institution worries can show up as a wide range of fears, offensiveness and deviant behavior. Fear can be observed in an individual by its consistent nature of indicators such as a high level of anxiety, low drive for life, lack of sufficient bodily strength and lack of trust. It is most difficult to overcome fears of children with no parents. Fear is the result of worries and fearful thinking and represents one of the most dangerous emotions since a person may be scared to death. A person is not born with fear; fear is often unrecognized and takes various shapes. Children with emotional difficulties do not associate their fears with anything specific and show them in a form of anxiety that has no apparent causes. Anxiety is indeliberately spread upon various objects or situations and a child starts to fear those objects and situations.

Thus, we observe delayed mental development of institutionalized children, which often is caused by emotional disturbances like instability, contradictory emotions, excessive anxiety, excessive sympathies and animosities towards people, impulsiveness of actions, excessive anger, excessive fears, pessimism or joy without cause, indifference etc. It is important to note that each case is very specific and evolves as a result of a combination of emotional and mental behaviors of a child and his or her actions, reactions, or perceptions to circumstances around them.

2.5.   Development of Self-Conscience (I-Concept) of Orphan Children

2.5.1.   Genesis of Self-Conscience

Development of a human personality includes development of his or her con-science and self-conscience as an inalienable part of the whole being. Human personality is nothing else but his or her self-conscience. Self-conscience and self-esteem is the central link in the structure and development of a personality. The totality of human behavior, his or her experiences, further development and personality structure correlate with his or her self-esteem.

A transition from one age-based period of development to the next can be described by changes in leading activity and development of new personality features in a child. Based on this knowledge the cause and effect of some personality changes can be connected with other developmental features as well.

The age-related contradictions in conscience that evolve due to deprivation of institutionalized children from satisfying their most essential needs provoke and worsen all latent and obvious communication conflicts and promote children's anxiety development.

The absence of positive family influence, considered the parental image, is that critical factor that determines the development of self-conscience and an "I-concept" of institutionalized children.

Consequently, self-conscience is that area of psychological development that on one hand remains the key one for the development of a child's personality. On the other hand it is subject to the most harm in the conditions of growing up without any positive family influence.

For this reason the area of self-conscience development is the most important in overcoming the negative consequences of institutionalization. It is also the most important in preparing an institution's graduates to an adult life in the outside world.

Self-image represents the structural development of self-conscience and the final product of interconnected activity of three of its sides - the cognitive, the affective and the behavioral ones.

The more time spent by an early and pre-school childhood being influenced in the institution or in a disadvantaged family obviously has an impact on the development of a child's personality. Communications with adults and between other peers works in developing self image. Contents and forms of interrelationships within an institution have a major impact upon how the development of one of the most central personality features, a child's self-image, may turn out. Communications between adult and child or within peer groups develops within an individual the attitude toward themselves and lays the foundations of how they think of themselves

The development of self-image in institutionalized children is for this reason an important and necessary factor for understanding problems and peculiarities in the behavior of each individual child. Understanding the internal forces that creates the development of self-image can lend to the approach of a corrective program for each individual child in the process of his or her training and upbringing.

According to many researchers a positive self-image is determined by the following three factors; being completely convinced in the necessity to be liked by other people, being sure in one's ability to perform some type of an activity and feeling of self-importance.

If a positive self-image is established in the process of interpersonal interaction in a certain socio-cultural environment then a person has been found to develop better social skills. They are more likely to respect other people encountered in there future, not use or allow indecent words or actions, be more self assured and not second-guess the necessity of there own productive activity.

The modern view on the peculiarities in the development of self-image in institutionalized children has an extremely abstract and undifferentiated character. The most important factor agreed on in self-image development of a child is the image of or relationship with parents. In the conditions of an institution the determining factor of self-conscience development is growing up outside a family's positive impact.

The term of *self-conscience* is mostly used in domestic psychology while a term of an "*I-concept*" has only recently been introduced into research.

R.Burns defines "I-concept" as a sum of all the individuals' self-concepts associated with one's self-esteem. The descriptive part of an "I-concept" is often called self-image or an "I-picture". *An ingredient that determines an attitude towards oneself or one's qualities is called* **self-esteem** *or acceptance of oneself.*

In essence an "I-concept" determines not only what an individual is, but also what he or she thinks about him or herself, how he or she evaluates his or her abilities and possibilities of future development.

The "I-concept" includes three main elements if viewed as a sum of attitudes towards oneself:

- self-image - what an individual thinks about him or herself;

- self-esteem - an affective evaluation of one's self-image that may have various degree' of intensity since some features of a self-image may trigger stronger or weaker emotions associated with their acceptance or blame;

- Potential behavioral reactions, i.e. some real actions that may be caused by self-image and self-esteem.

It has been established in the research of parental impact upon children's and adolescents' self-esteem that parental support has an important impact upon self-esteem while parental control does not have such an impact. It has also been discovered that a mother's spiritual warmth and support is a primarily cause in the development of a child's self-value while these coming from a father mainly influence positive self-esteem in the areas of proficiency and efficiency.

There is a lot of research in domestic psychology devoted to the problem of development in self-conscience. The research of self-esteem from the point of view of its role and functions in the total personality structure in domestic psychology has been given a start by works of L.S.Vygotskiy and L.I.Bozhovich

Applied research works by M.S.Neumark and L.S.Slavina was devoted to studying of children's aspirations level based on their being sure or unsure of themselves. Observation of how self-esteem affected their outlook to aspire confirmed the development of self-esteem concept as one of the most important factors in understanding how children formed personalities. Another important conclusion was reached as the result of this research. It was clear that the older a child is the more important their own evaluation becomes for him or her as compared to evaluation from adults. This evaluation becomes more and more stable, and at a certain developmental stage a need in preservation of self-evaluation that has been formed becomes no less and sometimes even more important than a need in evaluation on a part of others.

Research notes from L.I.Bozhovich on specific age influencing character development concludes; "By learning the requirements of the environment and by establishing their own evaluation of the environment and self-evaluation the children gradually become independent of the direct impact of a situation. As they become older a need to conform to their own requirements towards themselves and the goals that they establish for themselves and not just a need to obtain an approval from those who surround them become the main incentive of children's mental development".

All theories of an "I-concept" development concentrate on the features characteristic of a specific age period. In this respect E .Ericsson's theory of personality development is very interesting. E.Ericsson is considered to be one of the leading researchers in Western psychology. E.Ericsson views the development of a personality and its self-conscience as a gradual change of stages, each of them having its own somatic and qualitative emotional features. Inescapably an individual experiences a certain crisis at each stage of psychosocial development, which means a new turning point in his or her development as a member of society. The prospects of advantageous personal development undoubtfully depend upon what psychological "baggage" a child or an adolescent carries on with him or her into a next stage of his or her life.

According to E. Ericsson's theory the foundation of a personality development is created at *the first stage* that lasts from the moment of birth until the age of 18 months. During this period a child must gain a feeling of trust towards the outside world. This is the basis of establishing a positive self-esteem. A feeling of trust to the world serves as a basis for a child to acquire new experience, a guarantee of correct transition to other stages of development. In an environment that he or she trusts a child feels love and acceptance, a firm basis for future interactions with other people and establishing of positive attitude towards him- or herself is formed then.

The second stage of a child's development lasts from the age of 18 months until three or four years of age. During this period a child recognizes his or her personality and him or herself as an active living creature. The main positive result of development at this stage is an attainment of feeling of independence. In other words, a child must undergo a transition from a state of complete dependency from adults to relative independence when he or she starts recognizing oneself as a separate person that is capable of performing certain activities.

It is during this period that a child needs understanding support and inspiration the most. The developing feeling of autonomy must be supported to such a degree, so that conflicts arising due to prohibitions on the part of adults would not lead to excessive shyness and doubts in efficiency of one's own efforts. The development of self-control must not be harmful for the development of positive self-esteem.

The main criterion of self-esteem at this level of development is a degree of curiosity towards the outside world and a so-called drive to more firmly stand on one's own feet.

The third stage of development starts approximately at the age of four years. It is at this time that a child receives some first impressions on what kind of person he or she may become. Simultaneously he or she defines for him or herself the boundaries of what is permitted. The learning activities of a child become extremely energetic and persistent, curiosity being the chief driving force here. Parents' reaction on a child's curious behavior is very important for all further development. Ericsson considers the main danger of this period to be a possibility of a child's feeling of guilt for their curiosity and activity that may suppress a feeling of initiative. To establish a child's positive self-esteem it is vital not to cause in them feelings of guilt and punishment in respect to themselves.

The fourth stage of development includes the school years when a child gets involved into a systematic organized activity and performs it either independently or in interaction with other people. Ericsson mentions that psychologically a child is already ready to perform the roles of his or her parents, but before children reach biological capability they must learn a working ethic and show an ability to support themselves. Subsequently, during this period a child attempts to gain recognition and win approval by performing various productive activities. As a result they develop enjoyment out of work and ability of self-expression in productive work.

The fifth stage of development, the stage of establishing a feeling of identity, which E. Ericsson defines as "that subjective feeling of continuous self-understanding" that gives a person his or her mental energy. This stage encompasses the age of senior adolescence. In general this youthful age can be described as a transitional period from childhood to adulthood. Ericsson believes that the main task of individual development in the period of senior adolescence is self-determination and establishment of self-identity as a counterbalance to the absence of any role definition of a personality. The bodily changes (associated with puberty), changes in relations with parents and peers, in the area of learning capabilities and in an attitude to a society in general unite in a single process of revaluation of oneself by a young person. This finds its expression in development and transformation of an "I-concept" in the period of senior adolescence.

R.Burns as if repeating E.Ericsson also emphasizes the significance of parental psychological impact upon development of a child's personality that is determined by at least two factors. One is the individual psychological characteristics of parents and the other is their style of bringing up a child. At the same time the issue of social, ethical, cultural and spiritual content of parental feelings and views in upbringing remains beyond the scope of research.

Most of psychological research in the area of self-conscience genesis concentrates around four problems.

1. transition of a baby from reactivity to activity stage and associated establishment of various mechanisms of mental self-regulation;

2. recognition of its own image by a child and learning personal pronouns;

3. evolution of children's self-evaluation and establishment of conscious self

4. Social self-determination of a personality.

2.5.2.   Development of Children's Self-Conscience in a Family and within an Institution

The problems of deprivation from a mother and its influence upon development of a child's personality are widely researched by scholars in various countries. However, the use of results obtained in this research in theory and practice of domestic psychology and educational science is highly inefficient for various reasons.

First, the results of research vary from one another due to use of different techniques and just for this reason are incomparable.

Second, the comparative analysis of research convinces that its results are mainly determined by existing social and cultural conditions.

Finally, most of the research on the issue of mental deprivation has been done with children of early and preschool age. There is very little research in existence devoted to adolescents, while this age is the most important for self-conscience development.

Czech researchers I.Langmeyer and Z. Mateicek who studied mental deprivation noted an absence of the feeling of being sure in oneself as one of the serious consequences of institutionalized children being deprived of satisfying their need in parental love. The absence in the feeling of being sure of oneself in the early stages of childhood development can become a stable characteristic in the personality of an institutionalized child.

Domestically (in Russia) the mental features of children brought up outside a family have been researched by L .I. Bozhovich's. The goal of this research has been to locate "the area of the least resistance" that becomes subject to maximum destruction in the absence of family upbringing. The very personality of orphans has appeared to be such an area.

The researchers have come to a conclusion that institutionalized children are not only lacking in development of various personality traits but extensively develop some distinguished mechanisms that allow a child to get used to life in an institution that in fact substitutes a personality per se. It seems that the reason for this lies not only in deprivation of early emotional contacts with a mother and other closely related adults, but also because of the institutional environment itself. Institutionalized life does not require any personality development in those functions that a child performs compared with performing the same functions when in a normal life setting in a community away from the institution.

Observation from very early ages in the development of all aspects of institutionalized children's personality shows a lack. With self-esteem it is not just lacking, but has a qualitatively different form and develops in a different fashion. Particularly they develop a stable negative view of themselves that leads to low self-esteem, while the majority of preschoolers brought up in families develop high self-esteem. Children from families develop a stable super positive attitude towards themselves that is most productive for personality development during this formative age stage.

A child brought up in a family has a highly developed emotional attitude towards them self, most frequently positive. Such a child accepts and loves them self independently of others' opinions. Institutionalized children primarily evaluate themselves and they mainly do not have any emotional attitude, be it love or hate, towards themselves. If not negative they maintain indifference.

Comparative research into the self-image of institutionalized children and students of regular schools has shown only one thing in common between them. Each had interactive relations with other people. The differences are seen in that regular school students, as a rule, emphasize those qualities that guide them in developing friendships. They as well use the social skills that allow them to understand other people, as well as their ability in recognizing the absence of the same skills within themselves that create difficulties in understanding others. Emphasizing qualities that are important for overcoming the most difficult obstacles in one another for communication is evidence to a key recognition of another's personality. It allows for others to have their own, universal and sovereign, multifaceted internal world different from ours.

These subjects are completely unpopular with institutionalized children. Most often they just express their attitude to other people in the simplest and uncomplicated form possible. Statements such as "out of everybody I like Petya the most, I always get into fights with Kolya" express relationship symptoms without solutions. If I like him I do not have to fight with him. Institutionalized children pay a lot of attention to their ability to get along with other people as the key to interactions "I know how to behave in order to be left alone".

The most important for institutionalized children is their own ability to adapt to a situation. Children raised in a family setting even at an early school age try to establish themselves through counteracting the situation with the established rules and requirements expected by adults. Institutionalized children try to adapt to the same situation by taking a protective or defensive nature in their behavior that is founded in their own self-evaluation and self-image.

Comparison of self-images in this respect may create an impression that institutionalized children are more sociable and can better adapt to a situation and use it for their own good. In reality this is far from being so. They are far more infantile and dependent in their behaviors and self-evaluation coming from others. In the institution children except and want control over them and it is recognized as giving them value. The completely opposite is true when regular school students openly express their drive for independence and protest against excessive care and control placed on them by the educational institution or other family members as devaluing their individuality.

When comparing self-images it is worth noting that those of institutionalized children are mostly negative and relate to a person as a whole. The basis for such self-image usually represents itself in negative moral qualities such as uncaring, rudeness, lying etc. If the self-evaluation is not openly one-sided, it still can be seen here in the child as a contradiction between their own opinion and the opinion of others.

In M .I. Lisina's opinion the development of this complicated system is a result of a child's learning from two different levels in adult attitude towards them. It starts from parental attitudes at the very early stages of development.

On one hand, parents unconditionally love them independent of any behavior and personality traits. On the other hand, they objectively (good or bad) evaluate him or her depending on the situation. Of course this unconditional love and objectivity is possible only in those families where a child is completely accepted. A child growing up outside of a family is deprived of at least one of those levels and this lack supports the development in the child of the simple, one-sided attitude towards themselves that is mostly negative.

Psychologists often notice that institutionalized children have developed a negative self-image and are not sure of themselves. One may think that a negative self-image and low level of self-respect in institutionalized children evolves only as a result of hearing numerous negative comments of surrounding adults. Any child can hear plenty of those. In some case's a situation can be easily improved by expressing approval, support and emphasizing successes. However, the research shows that when a person has reached a stable negative self-image he or she adopts the so-called discomfort of success when they feel uncomfortable and even bad when receiving praise.

The discomfort of success can be explained by the fact that it is more important for a person to keep a usual, even negative, attitude towards oneself rather than an indeterminate and undefined self-image. In this there exists a notion of self-identity. This means a feeling of continuity in one's own self. Self-identity also includes acceptance and love of a person by him or herself. A person perceives any sharp contrast or change in attitudes of others toward them as a threat to their own self-identity.

A feeling or sense of self-identity is established quite early during the first months of life. This process is different for institutionalized children as compared to children growing up in families.

The main reason for the development of a negative self-image and indeterminate self-identity of institutionalized children is seen by most researchers in one common factor. From early childhood institutionalized children have had to deal not with just one loving and caring adult unit or mother, but with a number of constantly changing adults that are very different in their behaviors and emotional attitudes towards a child.

It is assumed that an early childhood self-image develops on a basis of a person's reflection in a "social mirror" i.e. on a basis of other people's attitudes towards him or her. For this reason, if such a reflection is multiple, if there are many of those "mirrors" and the reflections do not conform to one another, a child does not develop a feeling of self-identity.

Replacing and distributing of a mother's responsibilities between various trainers or caregivers is seen by many researchers not only as a source of incorrectly developing self-identity, but also as a determining factor in all other deviations of mental development of institutionalized children. Some researchers have shown the results of constant changes in people taking care of a child in the following outcomes. The multiple caregivers coming in and out of the life of the child can create attachment disorders later in life. Depending on whom the child forms attachments with and how those attachments were disrupted a child starts to behave in similar manner. They act as if they do not care about being accepted or cared for, or of any future need to build contacts with other people. They trust adults less and less as time goes by and attachments or ability to love become weaker and weaker. A child becomes egocentric and uninterested in social interactions. Their contacts with people become aggressive and full of animosity since they do not receive any love and care. A child develops a feeling of abandonment, which may not correspond to reality, but becomes a basis for a negative self-image. This, in its turn, leads to strained relations with people and to the real inability to accept or trust another individual. As a result a negative attitude towards themselves and others becomes stronger.

A.I.Lipkina, Y.I. Savenko and others have researched self-image in children with delayed mental development. They have been researching self-images of school students with similar degrees of delayed mental development and who have shown similar adequacy in their classes. There has been established a positive correlation between adequate negative low or high self-image being maintained based on the efficiency of the student in the learning process.

Children with lengthy periods of low grades established ongoing low evaluation of their abilities, which, in turn, makes further studying more difficult and their position within a class more disadvantageous. A.I.Lipkina and V. I. Lubovskiy believe that children with delayed mental development often have low self-esteem, caused not only by objective difficulties in learning, but also in an on going disadvantageous emotional atmosphere. The child continues to maintain and further develop a low self image in a learning environment when they are placed with other children having low grades at school.

Children with delayed mental development experience difficulties communicating with others. This reflects in dysfunctional development of learning activities, emotional and willpower processes, as well as personality traits. They show a predominant contrast to the extreme in the evaluation of other persons' qualities. They express their opinions leaving no room for any doubt and they are lacking in vocabulary for describing people's personal characteristics so are perceived as rude and impolite. This lack in understanding of social interaction also extends to the process in development of moral and ethical values of these children. It also impedes the development of social and emotional maturity in a wider social context such as the realization of the effect their attitudes toward other people and themselves has and their understanding of their place among peers. Evaluation of their peers to themselves in children with delayed mental development is often determined by the situation. Teachers' opinions often significantly influence these children's self-image development.

Consequently, the content of self-image and how it was established, is often the most important result of upbringing and training. A child's self-image and their attitude towards themselves mainly determine their behavior and academic success. Plenty of research shows that negative self-image results in poor academic success, disinterest in learning, low motivation and bad behavior. Therefore, children struggling with difficulties in learning are more hindered by their view of themselves making them more incapable of serious studying than any effect of their actual mental or physical disability. That is why when working with children having low grades it is not enough just to eliminate gaps in their knowledge. It is imperative to have special classes on increasing a child's self-esteem to achieve success. Nothing facilitates success more as being sure of it and nothing facilitates failure more than expectation of it.

Parents play a major role in development of self-esteem in early childhood. Later a school joins in, and its influence becomes crucial. If a child comes to school already with an established negative self-image the teachers may unknowingly add to it and the classroom environment strengthen it. On the other hand, they may also develop a child's more positive image of themselves and of their abilities.

Many researchers point out that positive self-image is determined by three factors;

1.   belief in being liked by other people

2.   belief in the ability to perform various activities

3.   belief or feeling of self-importance (this is a derivative of a general intuitive self-evaluation by an individual when they determine whether they are liked by others and their level of proficiency).

All these three factors are developed in the process of interpersonal relationships and in a certain social and cultural environment (parents, teachers, peers etc.). The most important part in the process for transferring of knowledge and experience gained by our civilization is in the recognition of the natural and continuous value of each individual and the importance of interpersonal relationships in the process of upbringing.

Recognition of the primary value for each person as an individual stimulates their personnel development, liberates individuality and creates conditions for the recognition of inalienable human rights. If family, school and environment have established a positive self-image in a child it would guarantee that they would respect others in the future and would avoid indecent words or actions. This child would be sufficiently sure of them self so as not to doubt the necessity of their own creative activity.

3

DEVIATIONS OF A CHILD'S SOCIAL AND EMOTIONAL DEVELOPMENT WITHIN INSTITUTIONS.

3.1. Causes of Deviations in the Socialization Process

Socialization is defined as acceptance of a child within a system of social relationships and as a part of this system while the child is still becoming a socialized member in the society by learning the elements of its culture, societal norms and values. The complicated socialization process presupposes the solution of the main problems in education and upbringing of a child, i.e.:

- development of his or her personality and interpersonal communication
- preparation for independent living
- vocational training

This process is quite complicated enough for children brought up in normal families let alone those in the conditions of institutionalization or disadvantaged families. Here the issue of preparing children with adjustment malfunctions for independent living and work (their integration into society) becomes vital. This may be achieved through special measures of psychological and educational guidance in the process of training and upbringing.

Societal integration of orphans includes:

- influence of a society and social environment upon a child's personality

- active participation of a child in this process

- Improvement of a society itself and its system of social relationships (often unavailable for children deprived of parental care due to rigidity of its requirements to its potential subjects).

An orphan's personality develops in the process of integration. It is determined by a place that he or she would take in a system of social relations such as relations of friendship, family relations, relations at work etc. A variety of means are used during a child's socialization that are specific to a societies issues and dependent upon the child's age.

The main goal of any children's institution is for the transitional development of the children for socialization and integration into a modern society.

Several factors influence a process of socialization (Kon, 1967). **The first** group represents macro-factors (space, planet, the world, the country, society, government); **the second** group represents meso-factors (province, city, town, and village). These factors exude their influence both directly and indirectly through micro-factors like family, peer groups, micro-society where a child grows up. Micro-factors influence human development through socialization agents, i.e. those people who a particular person interacts throughout his or her life (parents, brothers and sisters, relatives, peers, neighbors, teachers etc.) (Bayborodova, 1997).

Socialization micro-factors have a different hierarchy for an institutionalized child as compared to a child growing up in a traditional family. The most important agents of socialization here are groups of peers and the institution's trainers and teachers...(Bayborodova, 1997, Kugan, 1995).

Orphans often have incorrect visions of societal roles. Subsequently learning of any societal role by a child or adolescent deprived of parental care becomes difficult and requires individual educational influence. It must also be taken into account that institutionalized children not only exhibit lack of personality development, but they have also extensively developed some completely different mechanisms, especially in social and emotional areas to help themselves better adjust to institutional living. Naturally, this is not only a consequence of disruption of emotional and communicative connections with mother and relatives, but because the very life within an institution often does not require of a child's personality to perform those functions that it does or must perform within a regular family (Shipitsyna et al., 1997).

The most difficult task for an orphan is learning responsibilities of having a family (Dubrovina, Ruzskaya, 1990; Langmeyer, Mateicek, 1994; Shipitsyna et al., 1997).

G.S.Krasnitskaya (1997) believes that family as a value remains completely undisturbed within an orphans' system of values. Moreover, a desire to have close relatives, a need to have a family and development of an ideal of a family are much more acute in orphans than in children brought up in normal conditions. Lack of or insufficient experience of family life enhances idealization of family relations and an image of a person having a family. This ideal is often abstract and is deprived of everyday details of living.

Orphans often imagine two family models - a positive and a negative one. A child associates his or her joyful emotional state like expectation of a holiday with a positive family model. A child idealizes his or her experience of family living, but does not have an exact understanding of his or her feelings and understanding of a positive family model (Krasnitskaya, 1997).

In spite of the fact that 90% of children are orphans with living parents and that their parents either on their own free will or by court decision do not take care of their children, some orphans are still inclined to get back to their parents or to create a family.

In spite of the disadvantaged situation in the family, bad morality of the parents and voluntary abandonment by parents, children often miss their living parents and family. Children often run away to their parents and when coming back to an institution later bring back and securely keep those things that remind them of a family (pictures, personal belongings from the home, toys, and letters). Many children attempt to find their families or relatives if they do not know the address.

Some orphans have a negative family model with very exact contents and exact images of what qualities should not be characteristic of a husband, wife, mother or father and what features should not be present in their relationships or in their attitude towards children. Most often this group of orphans rejects their bad parents and expresses a desire to never be like them. There is also a distinguished group of orphans who feel sorry for their mothers and dream of helping them to change their behaviors after becoming adults (Krasnitskaya, 1997).

The data mentioned above convincingly proves that it is necessary to make radical changes in the institutions' position as to the children's families.

The thinking of protecting or preventing a child from the "bad influence of bad parents" must transition to getting parents and relatives involved in a child's upbringing during his or her stay at an institution. The very period of a child's stay at an institution must be regarded as a temporary support to a family in a state of crisis. It is probably necessary "to soften" a negative image of a child's biological family by accepting this type of stand.

Experiences of several institutions shows that keeping in place strong ties of a child with biological relatives (such as meeting relatives over the weekends and during vacation time or keeping family albums and other things reminding of a family and involving relatives and parents into the everyday issues of the institution's and child's living) not only brings significant changes into the social and emotional development of a child, but also brings changes in parents' and relatives' attitude towards a child and influences relationships between them.

One of the most complicated and under researched issues of socialization is in attitudes held within a society and most critical within schools, towards children deprived of parental care and living in an institution.

This problem starts from a principle in the make up of classes within boarding schools and classes in regular schools for institutional children. Let us consider various types of education for orphans.

1) **Children deprived of parental care live and study in a boarding school. Two types of such schools may be distinguished:**

- A boarding school where classes are made up of boys and girls of the same age. This make-up causes limitations in communications of orphans that undoubtfully leads to considerable underdevelopment of communication skills of orphaned children.

- A boarding school where classes are made up of boys and girls of different ages according to a principle of "a family substitute" one class or group unites children from several "family substitutes".

  Both types of class make-up and the very education of orphans in boarding schools do not create advantages for their social and emotional development. With living environment being limited and social experience of establishing communications beyond a specific age realm not available all the children (especially those formerly brought up in a family) now face a substantially narrowed interactive environment to develop in.

  The practice of education suggests several ways of overcoming this type of situation:

■ Active participation of orphans in establishments for additional education outside boarding schools. This enriches their emotional and communicative experiences and gives an opportunity to determine their position in various micro-social groups. It would be better if a child attends not just one establishment for additional education (studio, school of arts), but two or three where he or she would interact with various groups of children.

■ Quite often a boarding school becomes a cultural center for children in a neighborhood, small town or village. Children brought up in families also study at the boarding school. This situation is more advantageous for the orphans both for their communicative relations and emotional development. They develop a feeling of being the host, not a guest, a feeling of self-dignity and desire to show the best side of themselves and their boarding school.

■ Visits of children to their relatives, guardians and foster families over the weekends, holidays and vacations. This way of social and emotional development is important since a child finds him self or her self, in real and not role-played conditions of a family, thus, gaining skills of family relationships and everyday family living.

2) **Orphans live in an institution, but attend a regular neighborhood school.**
Presently we can observe two principles of class make-up in schools attended by institutionalized orphans:

■ Orphan classes are established at school which consists completely of institutionalized children. Artificial segregation often leads to aggressiveness in those children caused by the attitude exhibited towards them from children brought up in families and by teachers.

■ The situation of common studying in one class with peers from regular families appears more advantageous for orphans. In these conditions an orphan may find themselves to be in two different social positions. One is among peers in a class and the other among peers within an institution. Each of those situations may lead to various emotions ranging from a state of aggressiveness and untruthful behavior in order to adjust to good and friendly relations with children from families to being docile at the institution.

A school's attitude towards children deprived of parental care is best exhibited within a triad of "student-teacher-trainer".

As I. S. Bardyshevskaya's research (1995) shows institutionalized children more often appear in a category of the so-called "inconvenient" children having adjustment problems. Teachers characterize these children as causing conflicts and irritating the majority of teachers. Their behavior is perceived as defensive, stupid, independent and aggressive. Their grades constantly vary. They lose interest in learning somewhere by the 3rd or the 5th grade. They always have some problems in relationships with their classmates.

More than often a school tries to get rid of these students. The children feel an unfriendly attitude towards them by the teachers and that adds to the wound of "abandonment by adults" not heeling. Instead of a child's right to respect, dignity, fair attitude and the need to be understood from teachers, they more often receive negative reinforcement of their self worth.

There is a completely different relationship picture between trainees and trainers working in the special regime boarding schools and institutions with children.

A principle of "substitute family" is a basis for their activity, which means:

■ elimination of age-based groups;

■ small groups of children living together like families where a trainer takes on the role of head of a family, a safe-keeper of the family comfort and welfare;

■ open type of an institution stimulating wide contacts of children with society, a practice of attracting foster families;

■ making conditions of living as close to the ones at home as possible where the house chores are not role-played but are for real

A trainer's role changes also in assisting a child's development. Help is given for the child in realizing that an outside world exists and how to live in it. Friendly participation in all normal events lived through by children becomes the main thing here. The task of a trainer is to create social and emotional comfort for a child, an atmosphere of friendliness, interaction and mutual assistance. The institution's regime also changes to take into account the rights of children for:

■ free time;

■ voluntary participation in joint activities;

■ voluntary communication of choice;

■ participation in resolution of internal issues of a group-family and an institution as a whole

A trainer is more concerned with creating advantageous conditions for development of each of the trainees rather than with controlling their lives. He or she is not just a trainer, but "a substitute mother" in "a substitute family". Under these conditions the orphans' attitudes towards a trainer become warmer and more trusting like towards a relative.

Two issues may be distinguished in the relationship of "trainee-trainer" type: on one hand a need in communicating with adults and on the other hand, primitive and underdeveloped forms of communications based on dominating complex symptoms of anxiety and animosity.

Consequently, it is important to establish an atmosphere of psychological comfort in the communication of a child with "a significant adult". It is important to surround a child with attention and care while also providing for emotional communication required in the development for a healthy range of emotions. Assisting a child in this manner helps them obtain some new and different impressions on life outside of a home or institution. Building a system of complex educational training in the most simplistic way so as to stimulate development of personality and of a child's socialization demonstrates true concern for there self worth from the adults around them.

3.2.   Causes of Deviations in Adjustment at School

The problem of deviations in adjustment at school is very acute for orphans. This acuteness is highlighted in the society as a whole by the deviant behavior arising from maladjustment in the schools due to the learning problems in the children.

On one hand, social and emotional deviations that are often the direct cause of adjustment deviations can be explained by an impact of various factors. These range from a difference in their natural make up biologically, genetically, psychologically, socially and in education. On the other hand, social and emotional deviations cause the most disharmonies of a person's interactions with the surrounding environment.

Students with deviant behaviors and difficulties in learning and communication prevail among institutionalized children with adjustment problems. Adjustment problems evolve as a result of long-term influence of traumatic situations upon a child, disruption of interpersonal relations with adults and peers, which in its turn, creates internal tension, anxiety, aggressiveness, inclination towards conflicts, feelings of incompleteness and abandonment.

A lot of institutionalized children have delays in emotional, mental and intellectual development. All of it increases a problem of school adjustment and is expressed in a range of defined factors mostly consisting specifics in emotional and personality areas.

These children deserve special study due to various specific factors in individual and interpersonal relations. In general they comprise a risk group due to their deviant behavior at an institution. If 20 years ago children with delays in intellectual and mental development comprised 0.3-0.5% of all school age children and adolescents, now this figure reaches 3-5%. Due to their personality features and lack in necessary social programs to assist these children and adolescents in adjusting to life outside the institutions they commit around 15-20% of all crimes and violations of law.

Problems in school adjustment may be caused by social, medical, psychological and educational reasons (see Table 1).

Social reasons are those that stem from the social status of an orphan in an institution, where they are in reality "nobody's child". At regular schools orphans receive social assistance and support from teachers, trainers and administration. However the problems in the school for the orphan may be caused by a prejudice or negative attitude toward them on the part of regular children brought up in families and their parents. No matter the cause, it is necessary to foresee these social reasons and resolve them in a timely manner especially in the conditions of integrated education of orphans at regular schools.

Medical reasons are those that stem from various disabilities that orphans might have. The most frequent and more serious causes of disabilities among orphans are brain traumas received prior to birth as a result of a mother's intoxication, traumas during birth, neural viral infections during early childhood etc. Almost all children show signs of nervous system deviations, including expressed neurosis, that are caused by psychological traumas received in a former disadvantaged family or due to a loss of parents.

Psychological reasons most frequently stem from a lack of parental love and care and early deprivation from informal communication with adults. It is known that this factor leaves its trace during all further period of personality development. Underdevelopment of self-identity as a result of this deprivation becomes a reason for emotional frigidity, aggressiveness and at the same time excessive defenselessness of institutionalized children.

Some of the children have emotional problems of a different nature. That is when after having an emotionally warm family childhood they find themselves in a state institution without parental care. These children are constantly frustrated and are predisposed to neurotic reactions.

Educational reasons are most frequently associated with the lack of social education of children who become orphans before they are admitted into an institution coupled with their deviant behaviors prior to admittance. Usually this deviant behavior is continued by the child in the first months after admittance with 70% of all children and adolescents exhibiting such deviant behaviors regularly. Along with psychological disabilities more than half of admitted children also have general mental underdevelopment, which makes a process of rehabilitation more difficult (Shipitsyna, 1996).

Table 1.

Medical	Social
developmental disabilities	deprivation from mother and family
health problems	lack of acceptance of orphans by peers

Reasons for poor school adjustment

Psychological	Educational
-general mental underdevelopment	-lack of proper social education
-emotional deprivation	-deviant behaviors
--communicative deprivation	

Thus, poor social and psychological adjustment causes disharmony of relations with a person and their surrounding environment. This is exhibited in low socialization of institutionalized children, their incapability of independent living, poor school adjustment and often in deviant behaviors.

The system that focuses on providing development programs to orphans other than just the study aimed at their diagnostics and labeling, will require a complex mix in disciplines. Finding the corresponding mentally developing correctional and rehabilitation programs to fit conditions for their education and communication will be challenging. However, there preparation for future independent living and integration into society depends on those who will do just that. There right to join a community of peers who have parents and enter an environment of normally developing children is an inalienable part of social adjustment and the reason for providing complex assistance to orphans with problems in development.

3.3. Causes of Disruptions in Interpersonal

Relations

Some specifics in development of communications with adults and peers can be noticed even in preschool age orphans. All of the following are causes for disruption in interpersonal communications even in the very young orphans:

- Frequent changes of adults in institutions

- different patterns of their (adult) behavior

- decrease in intensity of trusting relations between adults and children

- absence of emotional closeness with adults

- adults inclination to suppress and impose their opinions upon children

- primitive style of emotional communications

- prevalence of group responsibility

- inclination to control children

In the opinion of several researchers (Mukhina, 1991; Prikhozhan,, Tolstykh, 1991), when institutionalized children experience a shortage of communication with adults they become more spontaneous when in contact with adult strangers preferring more direct physical contact with them. I. V. Dubrovina and A. G. Ruzskaya consider direct physical contacts (hugging, touching and holding) as a special type of personal communication where the means of communication does not correspond to motives and needs.

Orphan preschoolers do not exhibit activity in cooperation, inclination and ability for common interactions with adults. Advanced interactions or communication with adults become more business like later in life for these orphans taking on a more primitive form.

A child's dysfunctional communication with adults can be seen from the first days of there admittance into an institution. Thus, it may be considered as a consequence of a preschool childhood spent outside a family.

Two complexes of symptoms are leading in institutionalized early age school students - anxiety and animosity in respect to adults. (Mukhina, 1991; Prikhozhan, Tolstykh, 1991).

The first complex reflects the child's anxiety and is an indicator that they are unsure in whether a trainer is really interested, accepting and loving of them. This complex is observed in such symptoms as excessive tardiness in performing their duties or excessive talking and need to say "Hello" to a trainer. A child often brings and shows a trainer various pictures and subjects, always finds an excuse to occupy a trainer with their presence and always requires assistance. This results in the child receiving the attention and control of a trainer being focused just on them.

The second complex is animosity and it is evident in various forms of non-acceptance of adults by a child. Including animosity other symptoms shown are depression, aggressiveness, and antisocial behavior. As an example, a child becomes extremely impatient unless the circumstances are in there favor and they are then in a good mood. These subjective mood swings sometimes have them desiring to say "Hello" to a trainer while other times avoiding any response other than expressions of anger. Or they become suspicion in a non solicited "Hello" addressed to them by a teacher or trainer and their behavior will instantly change to defensiveness. Sometimes it seems that they deliberately perform a task badly then always think that they are being punished unfairly for it. There attitude is unsympathetic, especially when being defensive if they think they are being accused of something.

We can distinguish two issues in communications of institutionalized children with adults. One is when the seriousness of the circumstances creates the communication to be very tense, while on the other hand, the forms for communications are too primitive and underdeveloped to allow for problem solving. The two dominating complexes of symptoms essentially evidence the same - anxiety evidences dissatisfaction in a need to be accepted by adults, (Shipitsyna et al.,1997; Strebeleva, 1998)

The above facts of communication difficulties between the children and adults may be associated with the fact that an institutionalized child encounters a greater number of adult people than most children. This begins from their very early years with the adults being from various backgrounds and as a result no stable emotional relationship is establish or was intended. Because of this a personality is developing in the child being one of egocentrism and disinterest in social interactions.

Excessive need in communication with adults and its complete dissatisfaction leads to the complex fact that young orphan school students show aggressiveness towards adults while expressly desiring communications with them. A child's need for a kind attitude on the part of an adult is combined with a deeply frustrated need in intimate and personal communication with an adult (Minkova, 1995).

Interpersonal communications of institutionalized children with each other are also different from those growing up within families (Prikhozhan, Tolstykh, 1990; Shipitsyna et al., 1997).

In both groups a conflict with other children most often causes defensive reaction in the form of accusation of this type "you're stupid yourself." However, if in an institution defensive reactions in the form of accusations are more prevailing while other reactions of a different type are quite rare what about actions in regular schools? Here we observe fewer defensive type reactions overall but more intropunitive reactions of a type aimed at getting a satisfactory result or need out of the conflict. It is noticed, however, that both in an institution and at a regular school during conflicts with other children one may almost never observe intropunitive protective reactions of a type "I'm sorry, this'll never happen again".

Institutionalized children are less successful in resolving conflicts in communications with adults and peers than regular school students for several reasons. Aggressiveness, accusations against others, inability and absence of desire to confess one's own fault are some. The inability to recognize their own faults is a main problem leading to domination of defensive behaviors and failure to constructively resolve conflicts.

In an institution a child constantly comes in touch with the same narrow group of peers. It is not within his or her power to change this group and find another one, while this is available to any regular school student. At the same time a child cannot be excluded from this set group.

Belonging to a certain peer group becomes unconditional within an institution. As a consequence peer relationships become more of a relative-to-relative type rather than a friend-to-friend type.

On one hand this may be considered as a positive factor enhancing emotional stability and protection when a peer group becomes an analogue of a family. On the other hand there are certain negative sides since contacts of this type do not enhance peer-to-peer communication skills. Essential skills to befriend a previously unknown child or to adequately estimate one's own qualities that are needed for selective friendships are not developed.

Institutionalized preschoolers have much weaker contacts than their kindergarten peers. The contacts are one-sided, have little emotion in them and mostly consist of simple questions and directions. The basis of underdevelopment lies in a lack of empathy, i.e. ability and need to share one's own feelings with the others (Dubrovina, Lisina, 19820.

It may be noticed that institutionalized children do not form full emotional contacts even with their own brothers and sisters. Observations of institutionalized children with no prior experience of communication with elder brothers and sisters show that these children are not attached to them as relatives and have very low level of communications with them (they do not know what to do when they get together, they do not show kindness, care or interest in each other).

Concluding research shows that difficulties in peer-to-peer communications are caused by:

- unsatisfactory level of communications with adults

- absence of skills of practical and verbal communication

- inadequacy of emotional reactions

- dependence of behaviors upon situations

- inability to constructively solve problems

Disruptions in the communications area have an impact upon an orphan's personality development, influencing his or her self-image, attitude towards them selves and making harder the development of self-identity.

3.4. Causes of Deviations in the Development of Morality

Research has shown that life outside a family in the conditions of long-term social isolation and in a narrow closed group damages the moral development of a child's personality.

The unsatisfied need in love or acceptance and the emotional instability of a child's situation makes them vulnerable for the so called "right to violate the law". Children intuitively understand that they can rely only upon themselves and for this reason try to establish themselves by all available means. They violate ethical norms, becoming rude, dominating, lying or lazy.

Foreign research (H.Heartshorn, M.May) shows that unadjusted children lie 2.5 times more than their peers brought up in families.

It is established that children from incomplete families have more problems than children from complete families since an incomplete family is comprised, as a rule, out of a mother and a child. The control is weaker there, thus, a child appears in a company of his or her peers, were authority is higher than that of a family. Children mostly follow a leader. Abandoned children lie mostly to attract attention to them selves. Thus, disadvantaged adolescents have more reason to lie than those from good families do.

A lie represents a specific way of protection in the process of adjustment to an environment. Moreover, our society is in difficult conditions nowadays. The old rules are crumbling, life is changing rapidly, the anthropo-ecological tension is increasing and a person has to adjust to all of it by developing mechanisms of protection. One of which is to lie. A person lies not necessarily because this is their nature, not because they are a liar, but because they are weak. In face of the circumstances and this constantly changing world it becomes a developed survival technique. Thus, a lie may be considered a socio-psychological phenomenon used to protect oneself in the process of adjustment to requirements of social environment and regulating the norms in behavior of a person.

In order to find out what institutionalized teenagers aged 13 through 15 think about lies (as compared to teenagers from good families) we used the following procedures. An interview format with the subject of "What is a lie?" was done. Then an associative experiment in a form of a composition with the subject topic of "Lies in your life" was added. As well a drawing experiment where teenagers were asked to draw a lie was included. The teenagers' emotional reaction during the interviews and their liveliness during the process of drawing showed an importance of this subject to them and a desire to share something vital or worrisome.

The results obtained in this experiment have been analyzed using content analysis, which allowed discovering the main elements of individualized sense of lying.

The analysis has shown that conditions of upbringing and features of social and emotional experiences had more influence on expression of visual and sensual components than on their contents. We found the same way of thinking about lies in both groups that reflected moral, interpersonal and reflexive aspects. The drawings depicting some bad act making a person worse and making them look low in the eyes of the rest reflected the moral side of lying. The reflexive side of lying has appeared in drawings where the main hero was the drawings author that meant a possibility of identity between a person being drawn and an author. Interpersonal side of lying has been reflected in those images of communicative situations where people important for a child were included.

The differences between groups in comparison have been that for institutionalized children the sense of lying was mostly in the area of interpersonal relations. 40% of drawings touched upon a subject of family and school. The main heroes of drawings have been relatives (mother, father or both). Lies have been associated either with money, or with lack of academic success. Contents of 20% of drawings have reflected the way of life within an institution with trainers and teachers as their main heroes.

The reflexive side of lying has been reflected rarely. A teenager him- or herself has been a main hero of a drawing, but a lie has been presented as a bad act (steeling, a broken glass, aggressive behavior towards other children). For a small part of institutionalized children a lie has been something abstract, not real an indeterminate black or gray spot with almost no structure. In this group lies have been thought of something primarily associated with some context or real life interests and situations important for teenagers.

Analysis of most frequent motives for lying has shown that their contents and hierarchy have some common traits for teenagers brought up in different conditions. Fear of punishment, protection of oneself and escaping punishment, as well a desire to become more important in the eyes of other peers or close relatives make teenagers lie independently of their living conditions (see Table 3).

One of the main reasons for lying was a fear of punishment. In particular the desire to escape verbal or physical impact on the part of parents, trainers or an elder sibling. When mentioning in an interview that lying to adults is a more frequent occurrence than lying to peers the teenagers considered adults at fault for the lies committed by teenagers. In the teenagers' opinion adults do not want to notice changes occurring in teenagers. "Our parents do not want to consider us adults already, we're still little obedient kids for them, but we wanna be ourselves. They don't wish to understand this, so we have to hide some things, so not to worry mother".

Prohibitions from adults represent a serious problem for teenagers. The majority of prohibitions are perceived by teenagers as suppression of their freedom, independence and self-identity. That is why lying among teenagers is not only possible, but completely acceptable if it is used to escape punishment, prohibitions or suppression on the part of adults.

One of the motives uniting the two groups of teenagers is a motive of self-defense. Most frequently teenagers defend themselves again from adults, especially the closest adults - their parents. This is one of the typical expressions of teenagers protecting themselves with lies, "Sometimes one has to lie to adults since they don't understand us. When you come home late, you'll be accused in all possible sins, so you have to think of some excuses in order to defend yourself and lie. These lies don't hurt anybody, just saves us from swearing and punishment".

The unique feature of teenagers is considerable increase in understanding of one's physical, psychological and spiritual self. This explains bolstering by teenagers in order to increase one's own value. According to polled teenagers they consider bolstering also as a lie, though harmless.

Table 2.

Comparison of motives for lying of teenagers brought up in different conditions (according to the results of interview and composition), %

Motives for lying of institutionalized children (n=20)	Number of answers	Motives for lying of regular school students brought up in complete families (n=20)	Number of answers
1. Fear of punishment	100	1. Escaping prohibitions	90
2. Self-defense	90	2. Fear of punishment	80
3. Escaping prohibitions	80	3. Protection of friend from trouble	75
4. Preservation	60	4. Self-defense	40
5. Desire not to make somebody sad	40	5. Tool of adjustment to environment	30
6. Increasing one's own significance	35	6. Increasing one's own significance	20
7. Escaping being ashamed	20	7. Tool for obtaining power	20

Social and psychological conditions of the teenagers' upbringing allow us to make certain corrections in understanding their motives for lying. For institutionalized children the motive of preservation of their internal world from the intervention of others' is very important. During an interview the teenagers would tell us that their environment does not allow them an opportunity to be left alone so they have to pretend being sick or simply miss classes at school in order to be alone or to meet a friend. Institutionalized teenagers have to act within a rigid disciplinary framework. However, there are situations when one wants to be alone and to do whatever they want. These situations turn into situations of forced lying. "Even when we want to watch a movie on TV very much, and they put us to bed, we pretend as if we go to bed, and then quietly go back and watch the TV".

When outside the walls of an institution teenagers are ashamed of their orphan status. They often ask others not to disclose their origin. They are ashamed that they are nobody's. That is why a motive of escaping being ashamed is quite important for institutionalized teenagers. During an interview teenagers would remember, "its awful when you're told in front of everybody that you're from a children's home, everybody's looking at you".

Lying provides teenagers with internal and partially external freedom and keeps their internal world whole and untouched.

For teenagers brought up in families and having wider opportunities for emotional contacts and communication lying may serve as a tool of conforming to the requirements of an environment or of adjusting to it. A small group of teenagers uses lying to gain power and leadership.

The results of research as to what teenagers ages 14 through 17 think about laziness have shown that institutionalized teenagers consider themselves to be more lazy than teenagers brought up in families (the differences are true).

The associative experiment has discovered the most common traits and differences in perceptions of the laziness phenomenon of institutionalized teenagers and those brought up in families. Three elements with most associations have been discovered (see Tables 3 and 4).

The commonality between the groups has been found only in one aspect that became one of the three dominant definitions for both groups. This is in the aspect of "absence of incentive". Independent of conditions of upbringing teenagers are associating laziness with the absence of desire to do anything (see Table 5).

Almost the same number of teenagers from both groups is associating laziness with a desire to sleep or by sleep in itself.

Table 3
Contents of the laziness definition for institutionalized teenagers

Aspects	Examples of associations	Number of answers
Absence of incentive	to go(2); not to go anywhere; to go somewhere; not to go; going to walk somewhere; to walk(2); not to go walking; I don't want; I want nothing; I don't want to do anything(2); not to do anything(2); when you don't want to do anything; to do something; I don't want to do anything; to do nothing that is asked; I don't want to talk; no dancing; don't want to get dressed; to sit in the same place; to get up from bed; to get up for morning exercises; I don't want to get up	28
Decrease in incentive to study	to do homework; not to study(3); no studies; not to do homework; not to learn lessons; to study; I don't want to study; don't want to learn; don't want to write; to write; to miss school; talking during class; getting Ds; at school(2)	17
Areas of executing laziness	not to clean the room; don't want to clean; make bed; to clean up; not to wash dishes; not to wash clothes; when I don't wash clothes; to sew; don't want to help friends; not to take transportation; to go to the children's home; to go visit somebody; to take transportation; children's home; do nothing what is asked	16

The aspect of "decrease in incentive to study" occupies a second spot in popularity for institutionalized teenagers and twice exceeding the same indicator for teenagers brought up in families.

Institutionalized teenagers do not have associations for "relaxation" while this aspect is the main one for teenagers brought up in families. The aspect of "emptiness" has been discovered for institutionalized teenagers (an example:

I do not know what to occupy myself with). Such examples have not been discovered for family brought up teenagers. One might suppose that orphans with rigid schedule in an institution do not have any free time. At the same time family brought up teenagers are aware of a variety of ways of how to occupy themselves when "they become lazy". Institutionalized teenagers do not have such an aspect as "being tired". Quite often family brought up teenagers use such definitions as "tiredness" or "sickness" as a pretext to refuse to work. It is quite possible that due to an emphasis on a "have to" feeling in their upbringing these definitions are insufficient for institutionalized teenagers to refuse to work.

Table 4.
Contents of the laziness definition for family brought up teenagers

Aspects	Examples of associations	Number of answers
Relaxation	rest(4); to rest(2); to relax; to do nothing: to take care of nothing; entertainment; to lay down(6); to sit down; to smoke(2); music(2)	21
Absence of incentive	to do as little as possible; to do nothing(2); no desire(3); doing nothing; to do nothing; don't want to do anything; to send everything to hell; whatever will be will be; doing nothing; being involved in nothing; no interest; to get up; to go home; to go walk somewhere	18
Personal traits of a lazy person	lazy: the one doing nothing; to do nothing; not to be accurate; inaccurate(2); making mistakes in writing; not understanding; not being smart; having no abilities; to understand nothing; unmoving; unstable; unreliable; fat	15

Institutionalized teenagers associate the phenomenon of laziness with various household chores and social activities twice as often as regular teenagers (see Table 5).

When interpreting a drawing of laziness 10% of both institutionalized teenagers and those brought up in families have depicted it in a form of some fairy tail creature. In all other aspects there appeared to be differences. Institutionalized children never depict laziness as something abstract unlike family brought up ones. There are noticeable differences in using verbal descriptions of laziness in drawings of orphans.

Self-identification with laziness is encountered two times less in institutionalized teenagers than in family brought up teenagers. Institutionalized teenagers depict laziness in a form of interaction of a human and some abstract creature unlike regular teenagers who usually depict a lazy person.

Institutionalized teenagers perceive laziness in a form of some unfinished duty unlike family brought up teenagers. The associative test shows the same. 15% of institutionalized children refused to make a drawing explaining it as follows – "I don't know how to draw laziness", "This is stupid" - or they would just plainly refuse to draw saying "I'm not going to do it!"

Table 5
Representation of a laziness definition in a conscience of a teenager, %

Aspects of laziness definition	Number of associations for institutionalized teenagers	Number of associations for family brought up teenagers
Absence of incentive	24%	13%
Decrease in incentives to study	14%	7%
Areas of executing laziness: -household chores	13%	7%
-interpersonal contacts, social activity, personal traits of a lazy person	12%	11%
Sleep	9%	9%
-absence of incentive to work	6%	2%
-being in a virtual reality	5%	7%
-emptiness	4%	0%
-symbolic	3%	2%
-emotionality	2%	1%
-physiological pleasures	2%	5%
-relaxation	1%	5%
-tiredness	1%	5%
-subculture thinking	0	5%
-other	3%	9%
Total number of associations	118	134

Thus, the research conducted has shown a negative impact for the institutionalized upbringing of teenagers leading to furthering deviations of socio-emotional areas on the development of an orphans' personality, including their morality and ethics. This can be vividly seen in a comparative analysis of motives for lying and laziness of institutionalized teenagers and those brought up in families.

3.5.   Socio-Emotional Deviations in Orphans with Sensorial Disabilities

Training and upbringing of orphans having sensorial, intellectual and physical disabilities takes place, as a rule, within a special boarding school.

Each boarding school holds about 10 to 30 orphans deprived of parental care.

For instance, the boarding school for the blind and visually disabled in Krasnogvardeyskiy district of St.Petersburg holds annually up to 30 orphans. 300 to 320 visually disabled study simultaneously at this school going back to their families for the weekend and every day in their senior grades.

Obviously, orphans at boarding schools become isolated from their peers during the time free of classes, especially during summers.

This forced isolation causes emotional outbursts since children realize their abandonment and that it is because they are somewhat "special". The emotion is there even though the school organizes good conditions of rest for them that sometimes even exceed those that other handicapped children get within their families.

The majority of handicapped orphans already have had some negative life experience prior to being admitted to the boarding school.

The problems of socialization of handicapped orphans (in the boarding school scenario as defined in the example case at St. Petersburg) are created by the double negative influence of their heavy handicap and the conditions of upbringing in the environment of peers having the same handicap but those peers also having families to return to. The peers with family are being taken care of by a family that gives them love and establishes emotional and intimate connections between them and their parents outside of the boarding school environment. A true handicapped orphan is usually surrendered at birth and is deprived of love and care by their family or relatives during the early sensitive period in their development. By the time of being admitted to school he or she realizes that they are not needed or wanted and that no one including them can change their fate. This makes a substantial negative impact upon a child's mentality and establishment of their status within the society.

As a rule, handicapped orphans are physically weak and have serious disruptions in their emotional area, which adds to developmental problems caused by the primary disability. Handicapped orphans are claustrophobic and suffer autism-type communication difficulties.

Being deprived of any family life experience orphans are unable to adjust to conditions of independent living among healthy people upon their graduation from boarding school. A lot of them have to live in social welfare institutions. In spite of being provided with accommodation, government and school financial support they are unable, as a rule, to adjust to independent living conditions. Many come back into a permanent institutional lifestyle structure just to survive.

It is most likely that the society and the government have to provide social protection not only for handicapped children, but also for young people that have graduated and who are deprived of parental care. Inability to control their personal budgets or not to have problems with neighbors in apartments and houses (the majority obtain accommodations in shared apartments) are serious issues. Along with that is the failure of the orphans to work along with colleagues or other students. This causes the young handicapped in particular, to find them selves outside of mainstream life and not welcomed in society.

Disruptions in the emotional area of development for a handicapped person deprived of parental care have long term consequences. Their negative and limited life experience makes psychological, medical and educational guidance necessary not only in preschool years, but also during the first years of independent living. During a stay of a handicapped orphan in a boarding school they must be taught those types of activities that would enhance their socialization in society. In particular, the main tasks in a boarding school for the visually impaired should be their education in necessary cultural and everyday living skills. As well there is a crucial need for communication skills in line and accounting for those difficulties that are caused by the degree and character of sensorial disability in development.

Vision impairments or blindness significantly complicate communication of a child or an adult with the rest of the people. Difficulties in communication are even more complicated for handicapped orphans with their negative life experiences. These difficulties are compounded for them by there lack in ability of interacting with any accuracy in the world of real life issues because of their dependency on a poorly developed and narrow sensorial base.

Disruptions in communication cause complications in work, studying, learning, orientation in space etc.

Development of verbal and non-verbal communications in the conditions of a specific school organized for the visually impaired should be done in a very effective fashion in consideration of those with this disability. Since spontaneous learning of communication skills up to the level of free utilization by students with serious impairments of vision is unreal and significantly complicates their orientation among people with normal vision, this form of non effective communication would not be administered.

This type of social and emotional development within boarding schools for impaired children must be a priority since ignoring it reflects upon any possible normal activity and independence and causes severe long term problems of separation from society in a person. A specific system of correctional work aimed at developing communication skills of visually-impaired orphans was developed by researchers from the Institute of Special Education and Special Psychology (St. Petersburg). It was modified in order to suit the conditions of special boarding schools and taking into account the specifics of learning activity of the blind and visually-impaired.

Execution of a system in communication development guidance for handicapped visually impaired orphans has a step-by-step nature that corresponds to the structure of learning and skills mastered by a child and in accordance with their age.

Efficiency in educational guidance for communication activities with social orphan students (visually handicapped) was achieved with the participation from all the professionals who share a part of the educational process in rehabilitation, correction and development in the boarding school.

3.6.   Socio-Emotional Deviations in Orphans with Delays in Psychological Development

Studies of children suffering from any of the following disorders such as psycho-physiological and psychosomatic disabilities, nervous-based diseases, and difficulties in communication, mental activity or education showed that all of those disorders can be most frequently observed in children deprived of parental attention and care.

A child starts to behave unpredictably in a difficult situation. L.S.Vygotskiy (1983) pointed out the difficulties in communication in a child by noting the existence of specific rules of abnormal development.

It has been shown that children with delays in psychological development have either overly positive or overly negative feelings. They practically do not show any differentiated shades of feelings like normal children do. Feelings are often inadequate and disproportionate to an outside world impact in their dynamics. They vary from extreme lightness and superfluity of feelings associated with serious life events to extreme force and longevity of feelings associated with insignificant events.

Immaturity of personality of orphans with delays in psychological development shows itself in the influence of egocentric emotions upon evaluating conclusions. A child most highly values those who are close to them and who they like. They evaluate life events in the same fashion - good is what is pleasant.

Observations of activity of orphans with delays in psychological development during classes at school, as well as outside of class allowed seeing problems that children encounter - frequent conflicts, aggressiveness, inability to be sure in oneself and deviant behavior. The problem is also in that teachers and trainers have no idea of how to correctly evaluate various children's behavioral reactions, specifics of their development and emotional state in a process of communication. Very few of them associate those with a child's state of anxiety. Though quite often a child's behavior does not reflect his or her real condition, but is aimed exclusively at bringing an adults' attention. This is evidenced by research made by T.A.Vlasova, M.S.Pevzner (1973), A.M.Prikhozhan, N.N.Tolstykh (1990) and others.

Our research attempted to study the specifics of emotional area and level of anxiety in orphans with delayed psychological development as well as their ability to adequately evaluate and interpret various life situations and their ability to interact with adults and peers (see Table 6).

It has been established that students with delays in psychological development have a high anxiety index. Communication problems of these children are associated with negative experiences, inability to adequately evaluate situations and difficulties in distinguishing various emotions. Communications with adults and peers are influenced by excessive inclination towards conflicts, animosity, destructive aggression and feelings of guilt. Inadequate behavior from a child depends on a state of anxiety, feeling of loneliness, defenselessness and depression, as well as various fears. All these conditions cause a child to be unsure in them self's creating feelings of being unfit and complicating any social adjustment.

We have obtained some interesting data within the control group of normally developing family children as well. These children have the most difficulties when communicating with peers. We may suppose that this is associated with inability to correctly evaluate life situations, defenselessness and presence of various fears. Normal children have shown more jealousy, feeling they are being deprived of attention and in competition for attention from parents as compared with children having delays in psychological development. It has been discovered that boys' anxiety index is higher than the one for girls.

Primary school students independently of development of their psychology and conditions of upbringing (within a family or in an institution) have common difficulties in communication with peers, general communicative difficulties, difficulties in evaluating real life situations and presence of anxiety and fears of indeterminate nature.

Table 6
Main problems discovered in the research of primary school age orphans with normal and delayed development, %

Main problems	Description of problems	Normally developing children (n=30)	Children with delays in psychological development (n=30)
COMMUNICATION PROBLEMS	Traumatic experience	45	80
	Incorrect evaluation of life situations	55	95
	difficulties in interactions with adults	20	40
	-with children	80	85
BEHAVIORAL PROBLEMS	Inclination towards conflicts	15	60
	Aggressiveness	35	80
	Guilt	35	70
	Being unsure in oneself	20	40
	Animosity	20	30
STATES OF ANXIETY	Defenselessness	40	70
	Loneliness	25	45
	Depression	25	40
FEARS	Of death	80	80
	Social and spatial	50	70
	Nightmares, fairy tail heroes	40	55
	Medical	30	40
	Physical harm	40	40

3.7.   Socio-Emotional Deviations in Orphans with Mental Retardation

Emotions of mentally retarded children are often inadequate and dispro-portionate to the impact from an outside world. Some children show extreme superfluity and lightness in perception of serious live events and are moody while other children (observed quite frequently) show extremely strong and long-lasting feelings in regard to insufficient events and causes. Something insignificant may cause a very strong and long-lasting emotional reaction.

Table 7
Anxiety indices of children with mental retardation from families compared to those brought up institutionalized children, %

Evaluation of anxiety index	Family brought up children (n=20)	Institutionalized children (n=27)
Average	54.8	50.8
High	40.0	33.3
Medium	60.0	60.0
Low	-	6.7

A lot of children with intellectual disabilities have so called disphorias (periodic negative mood swings), they are often anxious and show aggression against themselves and adults. It may show up like in the example below. A student who has been calm and obedient for a long period of time suddenly appears in the classroom in a bad mood and reacts with anger to any objections of them or there behavior. In a day or two the bad mood suddenly disappears by itself. If a teacher understands that a child is in a state of disphoria, it is best not to talk to him or her and ask about anything.

Sometimes a different mood swing called euphoria can be observed. This is when a child unexplainably has a very good mood. In this state children become insensitive to surrounding reality. They continue laughing and enjoying themselves even after getting a bad grade etc.

Apathy may be another type of a mood swing. Sometimes special school students express the thoughts that are completely inadequate to their age like indifference to life and people, loss of any usual child's interests.

Changes in emotional reactions are noticeable in institutionalized children with mental retardation in the conditions of deprivation from a mother, which may express itself in growing feelings of anxiety and aggressiveness. To check this hypothesis we have studied emotional features of institutionalized mentally retarded children and family brought up mentally retarded children studying at a special (correctional) school.

We have studied two groups of children ages 7 to 9. One group came from an institutionalized setting (17 people) and the other of those growing up in families (20 people). Children from both groups have been students of 1st and 2nd grades of a special school of an 8th type.

Comparative analysis of anxiety indices from the two groups of mentally retarded children has shown no distinguishable differences between the two groups (see Table 7).

We have noted a trend for a high anxiety index (through its average indicator) of family children in comparison to institutionalized children.

Probably the reason for this is that institutionalized children grow up in more stable atmosphere with a strict constant day schedule. This circumstance is important for mentally retarded children since they have stereotypical ways of thinking that is difficult to change.

Table 8
The structure of anxieties of mentally retarded family and institutionalized children, %

Situation	Group of family children (n=20)	Group of institutionalized children (n=27)
Child to child	61.2	68.2
Child to adult	47.2	55.7
Alone	71.0	35.9

Family children studied originated from complete but disadvantaged families due to alcoholism and conflict relationships between parents. Children from such disadvantaged families often experience situations of emotional stress and for this reason they have a level of anxiety that is higher than that of institutionalized children.

It has been interesting to study the structure of anxiety of family and institutionalized mentally retarded children. Anxiety structure has been studied in three types of situations - child to child, child to adult and being alone (see Table 8).

We can see that family children have high anxiety levels in situations of being alone and child to child while institutionalized children exhibit higher anxiety levels in situations child to child and child to adult.

Anxiety level in the situation of being alone is two times less for institutionalized children. Being in a state of constant peer interaction within an institution a child has no opportunity to be alone. Institutionalized children do not think about the future. They have difficulties adjusting to a lot of situations upon leaving an institution. However, while in an institution they do not have a problem of loneliness and losing oneself within a social environment. Adults make all the decisions for them. That is why they rarely fear loneliness.

Family children fear loneliness and losing oneself in a social environment. Children observe hard economic conditions and conflicts within a family. All of it enhances a feeling of anxiety and the fear that they may have to deal with or remain one on one with the difficulties of life.

Thus, it is not only those children who are placed in institutions due to various circumstances that are deprived of conditions that are extremely important for personality development. The lose of emotional contact with a mother and parental care can leave all children subject to emotional deprivation even family children who come from dysfunctional household settings and lacked proper parental attention.

Analysis of questionnaire "Difficulties in communication" for primary school students that are mentally retarded has shown that 9.3% of all orphans never experience communication difficulties in their trainer's opinion, while parents believe that only 7.6% of their children never experience difficulties in communications.

Table 9
Research results of communication difficulties as per the questionnaire
What is an obstacle for us?

	Frequency of indicators	Never	Never	Rarely	Rarely	Frequently	Frequently	Always	Always
	Indicators	Orphans	Family children	Orphans	Family children	Orphans	Family children	Orphans	Family children
	Absence of communication skills	14.8	Number	31.5	62.5	29.6	6.2	24.1	-
2	Frequent sickness and rare communications with peers	46.3		35.2	62.5	16.6	6.2	1.9	-
3	High self-opinion	35.2	1	25.9	-	27.8	6.2	11.1	-
4	Negative attitude towards others	33.3	75.0	31.5	25.0	25.9	-	9.3	-
5	Inclination to physical fights	20.4	56.3	31.5	18.7	29.6	25	18.5	-
6	Shyness	33.3	18.7	40.7	25	20.4	12.5	5.6	43.8
7	Being unsure in oneself	25.9	18.7	44.4	37.5	20.4	43.8	9.3	-
8	Getting offended easily	14.8	6.2	37.1	25	35.2	56.3	12.9	12.5
9	Starting crying easily	20.4	18.7	48.2	37.5	16.6	31.3	14.8	12.5
10	Inclination towards communicating	53.7	75	27.8	12.5	11.1	12.5	7.4	-

Difficulties are experienced rarely but when they do occur it is in 44.4% of institutionalized children compared to 61.6% family children.

Difficulties in communication are experienced more frequently and almost always by orphans 46.3% but only by 30.8% family children

Let us discuss the results of the questionnaire "What is an obstacle for us?" (see Table 9).

The table shows that institutionalized children more often than family children have the inclination to be left alone. Opinions for this are that orphans more often exhibit negative attitude towards others, have independently developed a high opinion of them selves over others and are inclined to physical fights if challenged in any way. At the same time many of them are never unsure in themselves (25.9% of orphans and 18.7% of family children), shy (33.3% and 18.7% correspondingly) or easily offended (14.8% and 6.2%). These differences in attitude and actions may be explained by insufficient attention that a trainer pays when working with children and participating in various activities together (education, play, work etc.) and by different conditions of children's living and upbringing. Quite often parents instead of trying to understand the psychology of a mentally retarded child feel guilty towards them and do not always adequately react to their behavior. This leads to a child getting easily offended (56.3%), starts crying easily (37.5%) while an orphan reacts in such a way in less of the situations (37.1% and 48.2% correspondingly).

Thus, the research of various emotional and personal qualities of mentally retarded children growing up in different conditions has shown that social and psychological deprivation in both families and institutions disrupts a child's mental development and becomes the cause of deviant personality.

Disruptions in family relations and family influence upon a child's development are one main source in the spreading of "social orphan hood" when a child loses parental care and assistance while parents are still alive.

When children are neglected in a family, when they are verbally, physically and sexually abused there, it not only causes emotional outbursts, but aggressive and destructive behavior as well (Vostroknutov, 1996; Gor'kovaya, 1996; Brutman, Severnyy, 1998).

Conditions creating the early lack in socialization among a large and growing group of children and adolescents begins from the disruption within family conditions leading to deprivation and lose of the mothers care in the first place even before a child becomes institutionalized. This is accompanied by serious and chronic stressful situations for many of them that are at risk already of producing psychological and physical violence. Many children will also be vulnerable for development of nervous system disabilities with all the various deviations in behavior that accompany those neurological dysfunctions. For other children abnormal conditions of early socialization are accompanied by criminal environments with a real risk of the child starting to commit crimes and develop antisocial personality keeping consistent forms of delinquent criminal activities in their daily routines.

Diagnostics of the consequences to socio-emotional deprivation and deprivation of a mother becomes crucial for institutionalized children. Development of guidelines for prevention and correction of behaviors of children and adolescents brought up in institutions or disadvantaged families is a serious issue having a multi-disciplinary nature and requiring heightened attention on the part of various governments, social and scholastic bodies.

The high level of anxiety and aggressiveness of institutionalized children gives reason for the development of psychological and educational programs aimed at decreasing those concerns and to the organization of psychological therapy.

Organization of psychological therapy is hindered by the lack of systematic approach to the problem. Also there is insufficient psychological and educational knowledge on the nature of school adjustment problems now in use for deviant behavior and ways used for its prevention. Incorrect interaction of teachers with orphans may lead to conflicts. This incorrectness may be provoked by negative societal attitudes and lack of knowledge of specifics of psychology of mentally retarded children. The unkind attitude of a teacher is a serious obstacle for a child's adjustment to an institution's conditions and represents a serious danger of continued negative development of behavioral deviations.

The main road of assistance to unadjusted orphans having difficulties in learning, communication and behavior must be the one of their steady social integration into an environment of normally developing peers.

The interests of a student, a teacher, a school and an institution must be interconnected and correlated within this process. Creation of a micro-society ready to understand and accept a problem child may not be done without specially organized assistance and support. To organize them it is vital to implement systems of psychological, educational, medical and social guidance for each child from the moment of his or her admittance into an institution. This guidance includes complex diagnostics of a child's problems in development. This would lead to the establishment of an individual plan that would include not only correctional activities for a child, but simultaneous assistance to teachers and trainers. The basis of this plan must include correction of psychological functions and emotions of a child's development and of self-evaluation and skills for adequate communications with adults and peers within a society.

The outlined measures would without doubt enhance the socialization of orphans making their relations with any environment more harmonious. This would allow for a decreased risk of encountering problems in adjustment at school and reduce deviant behaviors of institutionalized children.

4

DEVELOPMENT OF SYSTEMS AND OF INSTITUTIONS FOR THE CARE OF ORPHANS AND CHILDREN ABANDONED BY THEIR PARENTS

4.1.   The History of Care for Orphans

The process in historical development of the care for orphans and their social and educational protection (when considered within a social and cultural framework) allows us to trace various connections and contradictions between societal norms and the needs in protection of children deprived of family-type care and the conditions of their practical execution.

The problem of assistance and support for children left for some reasons without parents has a long lasting history. It was first mentioned in the 4th century BC.

It is known that in the era before Christ a child's right to life was unprotected. It was completely dependent upon a fathers or mother's will. Murder of a child was not punishable by law and was accepted in morality. It was only in the beginning of a Christian era the Emperor Constantine issued his first decree in 312 AD that would prohibit children's murder and abandonment, and it was only in 767 AD when the first home for abandoned children was opened in Milan, the so called "home for upbringing".

In Russia the history of care for orphans starts during the period of establishment of a feudal government, since 988 AD. Since then the government decrees primarily were devoted to institutional forms of caring for those children.

There have been 4 main periods in the development of systems of orphan care and social and educational protection of abandoned children.

One of the criteria determining each period is societal attitudes to this category of children, their social status, which is mainly determined by reasons for their orphanhood and belonging to some class of people (nobility, church nobility, common folk, peasants etc.).

The other criterion that is inseparable from the first one is the level of scientific knowledge about personality development and socialization of children deprived of parental care, which mainly determines the contents and forms of the organization of social and educational process of care for orphans.

4.1.1.   The First Period of Development in the System of Care for Orphans

The first period (patriarchal - 10th-17th centuries) is characterized by non-acceptance by society of a child abandoned by patriarchal family. Family type here (patriarchal) is what had been established in the early stages of civilization development during the times of slave ownership and feudalism. We can mention a big psychological distance between parents and children within a patriarchal family (L.G.Morgan. The Ancient Society. St.Petersburg, 1935).

During this period in Russia there have been several groups of children outside the children-parents relationship system such as children born out of wedlock, orphans and children paupers (street children). In the conditions of a non existent or weak development in systems of social orphan care, children from the first two groups eventually comprised the majority of the third one. The boundaries between them were quite relative. The problem of life preservation was most acute for children born out of wedlock. Early history shows an orphan's only home was the streets and the only way to sustain life was to beg.

A special situation was created during the period of acceptance of Christianity. On one hand, religion developed a more caring attitude towards a child and brought attention to its purity and innocents. Christianity promoted a slogan "to be like children are" that refers to the child's purity and innocents as an example for adults to follow and made child murder a sin. Thus Christianity became a guarantor of a child's life. On the other hand, Christianity rejected the equality of all children and accepted legitimate children over those children born out of wedlock. An attitude towards a woman bearing a child out of wedlock outlawed her own life and the lives of all categories of these children. The legitimate status of children born out of wedlock was extremely different as compared with all other children. Children born out of wedlock became a risk group in respect of their lives quite early.

The legitimate status of a child born out of wedlock may be described as catastrophic up to the beginning of the 18th century. The very fact that the definition of born out of wedlock was a stamp of shame and use of this definition with respect to a persons birth situation was considered as swearing requiring punishment says a lot.

First of all, we see a great difference in legitimate status of children born in and out of wedlock. Consequently the government exhibited different attitudes to the facts of murder of these children. The Law of 1649 for the first time prohibited murdering a child born out of wedlock. This represented the first legitimate attempt in Russia to protect a child's life on the basis of fear of cruel punishment. The Law punished a murder of a legitimate child by his or her mother by a year in prison, while murder of a child born out of wedlock was punishable by death in order not to prevent a baby killing, but to prevent the very birth of out of wedlock children.

The new rules for care of children left without parents are associated with the name of Peter the First. They could be summarized as following (Y.D.Maximov, 1907):

- recognition of the government's duty to care for the needy, including children;

- recognition of the right of the government to establish mandatory rules of care and require following them;

- local authorities (city magistrates) became responsible for childcare as per government requirements. The duty to open schools was conferred upon the monasteries.

Thus, care for abandoned children was considered as one of the types of government activity under Peter the First. Peter the First required soldiers to execute his plans of Russia's renovation and so it became necessary to keep the children (future soldiers) alive. Decrees of 1714 and 1715 that would allow an abandoned child to live represented attempts to protect children's lives on the basis of preventing children being murdered. According to these decrees special houses of care were established where a child could have been brought secretly to prevent its murder.

We must note that society not only periodically attempted to pass laws protecting the right to live, but to execute this right as well by placing children in orphanages and houses for upbringing. The first experience of this kind occurred in the beginning of 18th century and should be credited to Job the Goodhonored who opened several orphanages in 1706 for abandoned children. The second well-known experience occurred in the 1720s and is associated with Peter the First who offered a more humane way of caring for abandoned children in special institutions similar to Job's orphanages.

The existence of these institutions made public the social aspect of the problem. Preservation of life of the one born out of wedlock is closely connected with secret admittance into an institution for care. The definition of secret admittance has a special sense. In the conditions of the day that dominated an official negative attitude to the facts of out of wedlock births a mother simultaneously wanted to keep secret the fact of a child's birth while trying to protect the life of a child.

That is why the admittance procedure into institutions opened by Peter the First and later by I.I.Betskoy was performed according to that established in the countries of Western Europe in 11th and 12th centuries and transferred into Russia. The procedure consisted of a mother or somebody else placing a child into a lot that would appear behind the wall of an institution by the use of a special mechanism. This allowed the keeping secret the name of the person bringing the child to the home. Later in order to keep at least some kind of a trace of relations alive between a mother and a child she would be given a registered certificate saying that her child was admitted into an institution from such a date. This allowed the poor mothers an opportunity to also know the fate of their child to a certain degree. However, this right was eliminated by several latter decrees.

Care for orphans was not complete; it was done through efforts of some public figures, charities and the church all playing a progressive role in creating the first forms of social aid. In spite of a variety of forms of institutions (orphanages, workhouses, farms) some researchers mention dreadful conditions for children everywhere. They had to experience hunger, poverty, abuse, assault and forced labor.

Children in the orphanages were coming from families of paupers; there were also children whose parents had died from hunger and diseases, as well as children born out of wedlock, whose parents had been trying to keep their "sin" secret.

The founders of orphanages had mainly honorable goals of saving children who otherwise would have either perished or would have become subject to illegal trade and various abuses. One of the good examples is Guinplain from Victor Gugoe's novel "The Man Who Laughs" (1869). The founder of the famous Paris orphanage Vincent de Boel (1638) proudly stated that during 10 years of this orphanage's existence 600 abandoned children had been saved (Y.Langmeyer, Z.Mateicek, p.62).

The results of activity of those charitable institutions became questionable at the same time. It was evident that most of the children died in these institutions and that the fate of those surviving was not that good. Dotty reports that out of 2000 children admitted into the orphanage in Venice in 1678 only 7 were alive 10 years later. The death rate in the orphanage in Florence fluctuated from 66% to 97% in the beginning of 17th century. Only every sixth child had a hope to live up to the age of 6 in the orphanage in London.

A child's life was directly dependent upon existence of the system of social care, which was developing rather slowly and even during its best years was unable to admit all abandoned children into its institutions. Even if they were admitted their survival depended upon medical care and feeding, which was especially true for babies. The lives of the majority of children in the houses for upbringing and orphanages were taken away by the absence of enough feeding women (wet nurses) and poor quality of artificial feeding. However, in spite of all of the above the very establishment of a system of social care for children deprived of parental care in the period between the 10th-18th centuries aimed at preservation and care was progressive in general.

4.1.2.   The Second Period of Development of System of Care for Orphans

The second period (18th-19th centuries) is characterized by the spreading of progressive ideas on the need for establishment of government systems caring for children with no parents. There were three directions in development of childcare institutions:

- charity assisted
- church assisted
- establishment of government-supported network of institutions

Catherine the Second laid a firm foundation for creating childcare institutions. In 1764 a child care house was opened in Moscow, and in 1770 in St.Petersburg (on I.P.Betskoy's initiative). There existed 126 child orphanages by 1900, not counting the church ones.

A definition of "born in unhappiness" was introduced in the latter third of the 18th century. It united two categories of children. One was those children born out of wedlock but abandoned by their parents under pressure from negative public opinion while the second were those legally born but deprived of parental care due to the extreme poverty of parents. I.L.Betskoy defined its content (the statement "born in unhappiness") in the following way, "I mean those innocent children who were abandoned or murdered by their dishonored and evil mothers and those abandoned by their legitimate parents due to extreme poverty". The criminal law of 1754-1768 "On those mothers and fathers who intend to kill their children" considered child murder as "a crime against life" punishable by whipping, hard labor for life, exile into monastery etc. depending on the social status of those found guilty.

Under the rule of Alexander the First in the conditions of general democratization the situation for babies born out of wedlock became better. It became possible to change their status by their parents' marrying each other. However, under the rule of Nicholas the First all requests on legalization of babies born prior to marriage remained unapproved. It was only at the end of 19th-beginning of the 20th century that legitimate and illegitimate children would obtain a kind of equal rights.

In 19th century punishments for child murder were differentiated in several directions. The boundary was laid between an abortion and child murder, between child murder and child abandonment and between murder of legitimate and illegitimate children. It was suggested to take into account the motives of shame, desperation, the emotional state of the mother and the mother's physical pains while giving birth that may have led to a cause for the decision on the baby's death by a parent.

Even in the beginning of 20th century society was not yet free from inhumane attitude towards a child. "The existing government is far from being inclined to consider abandoned babies as its rightful subjects deserving its care equally with the others". The local authorities were completely dissatisfied with the legal status of a child abandoned by mother. "Only when an illegitimate child would have a right to a mother and father as a legitimate one, only when the law starts to protect motherhood, the number of those in need of care would go down" (quotes by A.V.Gliko, p.21).

By the end of 19th century the range of problems that were influencing lives of illegitimate children has been researched more completely. With introduction of local self-government the view on ways and means of childcare has changed. According to local government physician A.V.Gliko the matter required "not just superfluous changes, but substantial reconstruction of the whole system...otherwise - sad results of a high death rate and a threat of the total dying out of the whole population in orphanages as a result from the existing system of care for abandoned children or children of unknown parents, which has now been transferred into the hands of local self-government".

The idea to create a special system of care for illegitimate children was strongly criticized. "It would not be wise to create special institutions for the children using the legitimacy of their birth as a factor. It is useless to suggest that illegitimate children...may have some special features to justify establishment of special institutions for them" (A.V.Gliko, p.180).

This was a period of transformation of patriarchal family into nuclear family and public recognition of roles in parenting. The problem of a child being deprived parental care is very serious in a nuclear family.

During the second period in development of the system of social childcare for children deprived of parental care the death rate of children within childcare institutions was also quite high.

The search for new forms of organization of orphanages in connection with new humanistic ideas in upbringing starts during this period. (J. J. Russo, I.G.Pestalozzi).

I.G.Pestalozzi put his ideas into practice by trying to establish an orphanage in a form of a large family and becoming a father and a friend for children. In 1799 Pestoluzzi opened an orphanage for 80 abandoned children ages 5 through 10 in the former monastery building in the city of Stanza. Both moral and physical conditions of the children were terrible. I.G.Pestoluzzi wrote in a letter to a friend, "I was among them by myself from morning till night...My hand was holding their hand, and my eyes were looking into their eyes. My tears were running along with their tears, and my smile accompanied their smile. They were out of the world, out of Stanza, they were with me, and I was with them. Their food was my food, their drink was my drink. However, I had nothing - no home, no friends, no servants, just them". (citation from Y.N.Medynskiy, p.69).

Fellenberg used I.G.Pestoluzzi's idea to establish a new type of an institution for children, which his follower Verly changed in such a way so as to introduce a system of placement of children into smaller groups. This system was later called a family-type system.

Thus, by the beginning of the 20th century the system of social care for children left without parental care comprised a wide network of institutions for children in Europe and North America, though their quantity could not satisfy the needs of society. Orphanages, workhouses and farms gave children shelter and some kind of care and taught them some primitive crafts at best.

These institutions lacked any system of education and upbringing; they had a low level of financial support, sanitary and personal hygiene, which caused high death rates among children. Government policy with respect to bereaved children has been relatively passive and a low degree of centralization stimulated abuses among those people responsible for caring for children.

In Russia the creation of a centralized system of childcare began in the second half of 18th century and this may be considered as a feature differentiating it from the Western analogues. A lot of great teachers and public figures took part in its establishment. Among them can be mentioned I.I.Betskoy, A.A.Barsov, F.I.Yankevich, N.I.Novikov, N.M.Karamzin, V.G.Belinskiy, A.N.Radishchev, A.N.Golitsyn, V.F.Odoyevskiy, D.I.Pisarev and others.

The system of care was actively developing and becoming better. Its basis consisted of humanitarian ideas that are still essential nowadays:

- moral upbringing as a patriot of the Fatherland;
- preference of general education at the expense of special education;
- taking into account of individuality and interests of children;
- esthetic upbringing;
- vocational training

There existed a wide network of municipal, church and private institutions for care of children deprived of parents along with the government one.

The institutions were segregated according to children's social status, there existed few institutions for children with low social status and the level of financial conditions was also different. The development of government orphanages and houses for upbringing was taking a way of making them bigger in size.

By the end of the 19th century it became obvious that military-type environment within institutions was causing harm to children's personalities. Children's death rate was quite high.

Prominent physicians, teachers and public figures of that time discussing the reasons for high death rates among children started to understand that they are not limited to terrible hygienic and epidemiological situation within institutions, but also represent the consequences of disparities in the psychological atmosphere within those institutions.

The advantages of family upbringing as compared to an institutional one started to get attention and mentioned.

One of the specifics of the Russian system of child care was that institutions did not only take care of children but were attempting to grow children up as worthy citizens ready to work for their Motherland. Children were receiving good vocational training, which was the reason for their good social adjustment to labor.

Thus, the Russian system of institutionalized care by the beginning of the 20th century was in fact a system of social and educational rehabilitation of children deprived of parental care and taking into account social, cultural and historical conditions in existence at that time.

4.1.3.   The Third Period of Development of System of Care for Orphans

The third period (20th century up until 1990s) is characterized by the governments' recognition of the necessity of social and educational protection of children deprived of parents and not based on their social status. The system of upbringing and social and educational rehabilitation is based in the knowledge obtained from the process of studying the features of personality development in a child suffering from social and psychological deprivation. This is in accordance with government prospects of development of the society as a whole.

In Russia the system of government protection of orphans as a complete mechanism did not exist prior to the overthrow of the monarchy (M.R.Zezina, 2000). It's creation began after February 1917 when the Department of Social Assistance was established with a directorate responsible for assisting children without parents and other needy children. In November 1917 its responsibilities were transferred to the People's Commissariat of Government Child Care that also had responsibilities of protecting motherhood and childhood and assistance to minors. (in April 1918 it was renamed into the People's Commissariat of Social Welfare).

The Council of Children's Protection was established in February 1919. It consisted of representatives of various People's Commissariats such as education (the chairman), social welfare, health, food supplies and labor.

Its responsibilities included provision of children with food, clothing, accommodations and their transportation into provinces, which were not suffering from hunger.

Since the fall of 1918 in many cities of Russia the public League for Children's salvation was functioning along with governmental bodies.

It did not distinguish between the children of White Guard and Red Guard supporters. Its branches would first refer children to a clinic where they would be treated for sickness.

Afterwards the children would be sent to a special vocational colony to be taught various crafts. The League assisted around 3500 children throughout the period of the Civil War.

The system of institutions for orphans was mainly established during the 1920s, during a period of fighting homelessness among children.

Various government bodies were responsible for various categories of children.

At first homeless children would be admitted into referral centers where it was decide where to direct them next.

They belonged to the People's Commissariat of education and its local branches.

Orphanages were eliminated in 1917.

Homes for abandoned babies were established for early age orphans and children's homes for preschoolers and children of school age.

Besides the referral centers a wide network of boarding institutions like sick children's homes, children's homes, labor colonies etc. were established in 1920s. They were a responsibility of correspondingly the people's commissariats for health, education and internal affairs. Upon elimination and exile of wealthy citizens the system of charity that represented the basis for pre-revolution system of social care for orphans became almost non-existent.

There existed two approaches to elimination of children's homelessness and future development of system of institutionalized upbringing among those responsible for childcare. Some of thought that a government institution would be a better trainer of a citizen of a communist society than parents that still possesses memories of the past. The others, including the People's Commissar for Education A.V.Lunacharskiy, considered children's homes not as the first stage of the future socialized upbringing in the communist system, but just as a laboratory of upbringing.

At the end of 1920s a realistic approach became predominant in this area. It is evidenced by the decrees of the RSFSR Central Executive Committee and Council of People's Commissars of March 8, 1926 "On Measures for Eliminating Children's Homelessness in the RSFSR" and of April 14, 1928 "On the Measures of Assistance to Children from the Poorest Families" where an idea of transition to total institutional upbringing of children within government institutions was abandoned.

The history of institutions for orphans in Russia evidences that caring for a child's life and health gradually yields to his or her **upbringing**, which is considered natural and understandable.

The new system of upbringing was in fact created and established by A.V.Lunacharskiy, V.M.Bonch-Bruyevich, N.K.Krupskaya, A.S.Makarenko, M.N.Pokrovskiy, P.P.Blonskiy, S.T.Shatskiy and others.

The following represents the main components of a new approach to upbringing:

- following the government policies in education and upbringing;

- collectivism of upbringing;

■ working with children under the slogan "All Children are the Children of State", which meant that the government was taking upon itself care of all children;

■ new approach to family as a "facet of society", "weakening of family influence" upon upbringing of the new generation.

Thus, the experience of Russian system of childcare was radically changed. N.K.Krupskaya wrote, "A working woman may not fail to value all the advantages of public upbringing. Her feeling of motherhood makes her wish her children to be brought up publicly, for communism and working people to win!" (1899// A Working Woman. Moscow, GIZ Publishing House, 1926, pp. 24-31).

Family upbringing was considered one of the remains of a bourgeois society. The accent was made upon collective upbringing and upbringing through a collective.

The pre-revolution Russia upbringing in accordance with a social status was changed into upbringing of all the new generation for solving new social goals established by the society, i.e. the idea of a free labor school. The ways of making school closer to real life were developed, the special role of labor in school education was emphasized, and the issue of real equality of rights of men and women was considered.

A.S. Makarenko's followers took part in establishment of various models of institutions for orphans and development of contents of their activities. A.S.Makarenko was an outstanding educator who enriched educational theory with new ideas, methods and techniques. He newly developed a theory of collective and family upbringing and successfully executed his ideas. He established special institutions for successful correction of young delinquents like A.M.Gorkiy's labor camp (1920-1927) and F.E.Dzerzhinskiy child labor commune (1927-1935).

The beginning of the 1930s was noted for a new wave of children's homelessness as a consequence of the destruction in the traditional peasants' way of life, the hunger of 1932-1933 and mass persecutions. The Decree of RSFSR Council of People's Commissars of January 29,1933 "On Measures for Containing Children's Homelessness and Liquidation of Street Vagrancy" and the decree of RSFSR Central Executive Committee and Council of People's Commissars of November 10,1934 "On Caring for Children of Those Persons under Arrest or Incarceration" were passed as the result.

1935 became a landmark year in the development of a system of social care for children. It was then that the decrees "On Elimination of Children's Homelessness and Vagrancy" and "On Measures Countering Children's Delinquency" were published.

The former officially declared that children's homelessness was officially eliminated in the USSR. Local authorities became fully responsible for timely placement of children left with no parental care into institutions. However, the number of children annually admitted into referral centers remained high. The second decree increased punishments for young delinquents. Commissions on criminal delinquents were eliminated and children could be tried and punished as adults from the age of 12. All institutions for criminal delinquents that were previously the responsibility of people's commissariats of education, justice and internal affairs all became the NKVD responsibility where a special department of labor colonies had been established and became a part of the GULAG system in 1939 (M.R.Zezina, 2000).

Thus, the system of social care for orphans established in the USSR by the beginning of World War II was aimed not at prevention of orphanhood, but primarily at elimination of its negative consequences. One could not expect anything else under the conditions when the increase in the number of orphans was a direct consequence of government policies of collectivization, exile of rich peasants, hunger and mass persecutions.

The new wave of orphanhood came during the years of World War II and post-war years. It is not associated just with losses at war. 1945 data evidences that only 20% of all children in RSFSR admitted into institutions were children whose parents died during the war or under occupation. The other reasons of orphanhood was again the hunger of 1946, hard economic conditions of the majority of the population and a new wave of mass persecutions that followed the decrees on increasing punishments for petty larceny.

The total number of post-war orphans was unprecedented. It amounted to 3 million children.

The new stage in children's institutional development started after the World War II. There were various categories of children placed within institutions. Real orphans and semi-orphans (lose of one parent), whose parents gave their lives during the war or children whose parents became subject to the mass persecutions after the war as well as children who had experienced the horrors of occupation and Nazi concentration camps.

There existed the following types of children's homes:

- pre-school - for children ages 3 to 7;

- for children of school ages 7 to 14;

- mixed (for both pre-schoolers and school age children;

- special - for those children whose parents gave their lives fighting Nazism

The search for lost parents and children for hopes in reuniting was taking a long time. This time was spent by the children having living parents but not yet able to be reunited being left within institutions where children of ages 3 to 14 were admitted. Upon reaching the age of 14 children were sent into vocational or railroad schools. Homeless adolescents ages 13 to 16 with minimal education were also sent there. A special group of children was represented by those with deviant behavior or long-term experience of vagrancy or who had experience of several escapes from a children's home or school. As a rule, those were sent into the MVD prisons for children.

The issues of orphan placement and upbringing was the responsibility of local authorities, as well as several central departments - education (children's homes), health (homes for abandoned babies and children's homes for handicapped), labor reserves(vocational schools) and internal affairs (referral centers and prisons). During the first post-war years the department on eliminating children's homelessness and vagrancy of the USSR NKVD/MVD became the leading coordinating body in those issues. In 1950 it was renamed into the department of children's prisons after the matters in the areas of homelessness and vagrancy became better.

Placement of children during the first post-war years, especially during the winter of 1946/1947 represented a very difficult task. The difficulties started from the work of children's placement commissions within local executive committees. They were doing a bad job, a lot of them showed no activity at all, while thousands of children without parents were wandering the streets. Sooner or later they were detained by the police and sent to referral centers and later to children's homes, vocational schools or prisons. There was a catastrophic lack of space in children's homes so children had to spend a long time in referral centers.

The conditions in institutions for children were extremely terrible. In a system of centralized distribution when the conditions of shortages of consumer goods and food supplies arise, children's homes were the last to get their share.

Children complained of cruelty, assaults, and attempts of rape by trainers. Information on abuses, assaults and torture of children rarely left the walls of children's homes and was often kept secret by local authorities. For instance, the principal of Rozhdestvenskiy children's home in Stavropol Territory over a long period of time would force 10-12 year old girls to become sexually intimate with him. It is doubtful that these crimes were rare in the conditions when many people that should not have been there at all, would become children's homes employees. Official documents never mentioned the fact of pedophilia. According to the court verdict the principal of Rozhdestvenskiy children's home was found guilty of terrorism and sentenced to 25 years imprisonment.

In the beginning of 1950s the numbers of children detained and sent to the referral centers went down. They mainly consisted of those runaways from children's homes that were adolescents of 14 years and over. The majority of children admitted into referral centers had living parents, or at least one of them. The children of the war years started becoming adults in 1950s, so the problem of their homelessness was going away by itself. The social sources of orphanhood started to become primary. They included impossibility or inability of parents to keep and bring up children due to poverty, sickness, handicaps or an immoral way of life. Out of 124,000 children admitted to referral centers in 1954 the majority left their families on their own free will - 43% due to lack of attention, 17.2% due to poverty and 14.2% due to their love for "travel".

Due to the fact that a majority of children had living parents or a relative, a decision was taken to reduce the number of children's homes and build more boarding schools. The regular boarding schools for orphans and children from disadvantaged families were most common. The boarding schools advantage was that they allowed children to keep closer ties with their families. Parents had to pay for their children's upkeep at the boarding schools while children's homes were completely government-financed. It was assumed that mixing the development of orphans growing up together with children having parents would have a positive impact on both categories.

The campaign on increasing the numbers of boarding schools began in 1956 after Nikita S. Khrushchev had called them "the schools of future" in his report to the 20th Congress of the CPSU. In September, 1956 The CPSU Central Committee and the USSR Council of Ministers approved a Decree "On Organizing Boarding Schools". The further decree by the Communist Party of 1959 established a program for development of boarding schools up to the year of 1965. The government's main position at the time was an idea of complete elimination of orphanhood through integration of remaining orphans with peers having families.

The majority of boarding school students were children from poor families. In 1964/65 they comprised 50% of all boarding school students around the country. 25% were the children of single mothers, 10% had handicapped parents and 15% of all students had no parents.

A lot of children's homes have been closed down along with the development of a network of boarding schools.

In the Russian Federation 206 children's homes were closed down in inner cities and 483 in various rural areas while 200 were reorganized into boarding schools during the years of 1959-1965. The first to be closed down were children's homes located in old buildings with no public utilities, such as central water supply, sewer removal and central heating.

In the 1960s and 1970s children's homes and boarding schools were experiencing difficulties due to lack of trainers and high number of students in a group, which would often comprise up to 30-35 children. It was very difficult to apply individualized approach within such groups.

It was also very difficult to find jobs for the graduates. Their age (mainly 14) was an obstacle to their finding a job. Later on the graduation age has been revised, and children have been allowed to remain in children's homes up to the ages of 16-18.

In 1970s the lives of children became more and more regulated through implementation of so called plans on upbringing. The existence of a common upbringing plan became a hindrance to development of children's personalities. There were a lot of measures having no educational value to influence children. The system of upbringing was becoming more formal, dogmatic and authoritarian.

However, the previously obtained experiences were so meaningful and traditions so strong that even during "stagnation" era children's homes did not become a closed zone, but developed and kept their best traditions. The examples could have been found within the children's homes of Altay Territory ("Educational Work within Boarding Schools.."), Belgorod, Vladimir, Perm and Rostov-on-Don Provinces where A.S.Makarenko's educational principles have been utilized. (V.S.Molozhavenko. The Heirs of the Brigade Commissar - from the Experience of the Nevel Children's Home of Pskov Province. Moscow. Pedagogika Publishing House, 1987, 136 pp.; S.Gavrilova. Labor as a Foundation of Upbringing (On Experiences of Trainers from Children's Home of the Town of Lakinsk of Vladimir Province//Narodnoye Obrazovaniye, 1987, #12, pp. 66-68).

The number of children in children's homes increased three-fold by the beginning of 1980s. (I.Chervakova. Home. Moscow, Molodaya Gvardiya Publishing, 1988, 160 pp.). The changes in social status of children could also be noticed. The so-called "social orphan hood" was on the increase, as well as the number of children with developmental problems. All of this was making it more difficult to conduct education and upbringing within children's homes while their closeness to society also did not help.

4.1.4. The Fourth Period of Development of System of Care for Orphans.

The fourth period - from the end of 1980s- represents the beginning of Perestroyka in our country. It is associated with changing approach in children's upbringing from government-centered to child-centered. This is when the main attention began to be paid not to collective upbringing of a citizen but to individualized development of a child's personality taking into account the demands of the society.

There are a lot of talented people among children's homes graduates of 1950-1980. It was easier for them to adjust to an outside life then than it is now for children's homes graduates. Unlike in 1920s-1980s when the majority of children in children's homes were orphans now the majority is comprised of children whose parents' parental rights have been taken away or whose parents are incarcerated etc. This is the so called "social orphans". Knowing they have parents who have abandoned them influences the children's mentality in quite a harmful way. Only a few of them can adjust to an outside life.

After the start of Perestroyka and glasnost the shameful state of affairs within children's boarding institutions became known to the public. Various charitable organizations and foundations were established with programs of assistance to orphan children. The policy of society towards orphan children began to change after 1987-1988 when the USSR Council of Ministers approved its decrees "On Measures Aimed at Radical Changes of Upbringing, Education and Financial Assistance to Orphans and Children Left without Parental Care" and "On Establishing of Family-Type Children's Homes".

The number of babies in the homes for abandoned babies care decreased from 21,300 to 17,800 or by 16%, the number of children in children's homes from 63,200 to 39,900, or by 39%, and the number of boarding school students from 35,700 to 25,600, or by 28% over the years of 1985-1991 in the Russian Federation.

However, it does not represent any progress if compared with general demographic indicators. The birth rate in Russia has decreased by 27% over the Perestroyka years of 1985-1991. Thus, a decrease in the general number of children was exceeding the rates of decrease in the numbers of institutionalized children.

The demographic situation in Russia by the beginning of 1990s was considered as the most disadvantageous in the period after World War II. In the subsequent years it became only worse.

By the end of Perestroyka period the number of children left without parental care began to increase due to the worsening of economic conditions in the country, an increase in ethnic conflicts and food shortages. In 1988 there were 48,000 children left without parental care while by 1991 their number was already 59,000. The number of those among them that were chronically ill due to hereditary pathologies (and whose parents were offered to leave the child within an institution) and those from disadvantaged families (parents drinking and leading immoral lifestyle) was also on the increase.

The system of social care for orphans established during the years of Communist power could cope with an increasing wave of orphanhood in the new conditions. However, the general weakening of government and authorities, as well as the system of Communist Party control and the decrease in general discipline made their impact of the increase more pronounced. The social and economic situation of our country after the fall of the USSR made it harder to resolve children's issues that still do not receive adequate attention and assistance from authorities.

Institutionalization of children without parents still remains the main form of care for them. Annually various institutions get about 1/3 of all children deprived of parental care.

The number of children's homes increased two-fold from 1992 through the end of 2000 (577 in 1992 and 1274 in 2000), while the number of special boarding schools for mentally and physically underdeveloped children increased from 153 to 203.

The Russian Federation Department of Labor and Social Development reports 158 boarding schools for handicapped children, 311 orphanages, 28 assistance centers for children left without parental care and 400 social rehabilitation centers under its control.

Annually the number of educational institutions for orphans increases (from 1429 in 1997 to 1538 in 1998). However, they are overpopulated by 10% to 40% in more than 40 provinces of the Russian Federation. Overpopulation is especially noticeable in special educational institutions for orphans with developmental problems.

Due to overcrowding and lack of proper medical care the rate of institutionalized children becoming sick is twice as much than that for regular children. Mental and psychological illnesses occupy the first place of all illnesses of institutionalized children (especially mental inadequacy and emotional immaturity.

The research of adjustment among institutionalized children shows lack of adjustment among 55% of all orphans. It can be observed in various changes in psycho-emotional areas, vegetative regulation, and development of deep nervous and psychological deviations along with an increase in negative emotions and decrease in functional abilities.

As compared to regular school students in the 1st through the 4th grades the degree of psychological underdevelopment of orphans is 5 to 7 times more.

Bad hereditary, biological and social factors are the reasons for various developmental problems of institutionalized orphans that create enormous difficulties for their adjustment in society, including school.

The research and practice show that children deprived of parental care have plenty of deviations in psychological development or emotional area and self-conscience development. They do not know how to communicate properly that causes domination of defensive behavior like inadequate loyalty or aggressiveness (including blaming others for their faults, inability and lack of desire to acknowledge one's own guilt etc.). Serious disabilities in self-regulation and self-control can be observed. Generally, they are unable to plan and control their own actions independently.

As a consequence, graduates of institutions continue to experience distrust to all other people in their adult independent life, they either become dependent upon others, or become ungrateful and extremely critical, expecting to be cheated by others. They often experience difficulties while trying to establish a family of their own.

Low level of self-conscience causes psychological infantilism and a desire to get everything from life without giving anything away. Insufficient independence, dependence on an opinion of a group, emotional problems and inability to withstand authority often push them into social risk groups.

Thus, deviations in social and psychological adjustment cause disharmony in relations between a personality and social environment. This can be observed in low socialization of institutions' graduates, their poor adjustment to real life, including life at school, as well as deviant behaviors.

The system of research aimed not only at diagnostics and labeling, but at finding various psychologically developing and correctional rehabilitation programs are required. Consideration of psychological and rehabilitative programs must be a condition of their education to prepare them in communication and preparation for integration into society with peers and parents. A transition into the environment of normally developing peers is an inalienable part of social adjustment and complex assistance to orphans having developmental problems.

4.2   The Need of Reforms in the System of Boarding Institutions.

At the current stage of social and economic changes in Russia the organizational structure of educational institutions for orphans requires development of new forms and content. Insufficient social and cultural communications make social deprivation deeper and decrease the degree of readiness of institutions' graduates for independent living. One must take into account that institutions have a high concentration of those adolescents who are lacking in their mental development, who have become victims of crime, who have experienced offenses against their dignity, as well as psychological and physical violence.

The Guidelines for educational establishments for orphans approved by the decree of the Government of the Russian Federation # 612 of June 26, 1996 are aimed at creating family-type conditions and organization of same-age and various-age training groups where the number of children would not exceed 10.

The process of institutional reform has started. The age for children's home eligibility has been changed in order to provide for full-value physical, mental and social development of children and now extends from 1.5 to 18 years of age. The conditions of living for children with still remaining relatives are being created, so that they can live in small groups of 10-12 children that facilitates their social adjustment. The process of downsizing the groups and institutions themselves is on its way. The age-adjusted groups are being eliminated and activities are organized within groups of children of different ages that are close to conditions of family upbringing. There are some positive trends in preparing graduates to independent living. The number of farms owned by children's homes and boarding schools has increased over the last three years. This trend can also be observed within institutions for orphans with limited health-related abilities.

However, the process of downsizing of institutions and making them more family like stopped in 1996. There were practically no more integrated children's homes, centers for vocational training and post-institutional adjustment established. The reasons for this are the cuts in government financing.

However, the faster transition of institutions for orphans to new economic and financial types of management, as compared with general educational establishments, allowed them to survive in difficult financial conditions and occupy a more advantageous place in the modern educational space in Russia. This made it possible for government policies aimed at stimulating the teachers and trainers of institutions in executing the tasks of **socialization** of orphans as their chief educational goal. Both educational and training programs, as well as increased mobility and freedom in selection of forms and contents of the process of upbringing became those means of socialization.

There are several types and forms of social and educational protection of orphans in modern Russia that are provided for by demands and opportunities in the society and educational necessities:

- children's home (for children of early age, pre-schoolers, school-age children, integrated);

- children's home combined with a school;

- boarding school for orphans;

- children's home for orphans requiring long-term illness treatment;

- special children's home for orphans with limited health-related abilities;

- family children's home;

- private children's home;

- orphanages and hostels;

- patron family;

- foster family;

- guardianship;

- acceptance into one's own family

The process in the upbringing of orphans proposes building up of multi-link and multi-functional systems in psychological, educational, medical and social support and protection for the rights of orphans.

In the analysis of experiences from various institutions it is shown that success is achieved through proper attention to the following as well: development of children's self-government, preparation of children for social self-defense, creation of situations for exercising a right of free choice and teachers' regulating the interaction between children of various ages.

The basis for children's socialization is their preparation for future labor. The content of labor education within institutions is changing towards individualization. Children in rural areas are taught some agricultural skills, while urban children receive various additional skills of individualized labor preparation.

The mechanisms of common activities in executing the creative potential of orphans in obtaining general and vocational education are then created. An opportunity in choosing a school for general and vocational training has changed significantly. Those schools are no longer tied up to a specific children's home or a boarding school. New types of post-boarding school adjustment have evolved. New types of institutions like hostels or centers for family upbringing or centers for post-boarding school adjustment and various private institutions (family-type, private children's homes) have been introduced.

Changes in the general situation of development in the system of education along with various economic and political factors have required reevaluation of several concepts regarding training and the education of orphans.

The factors mentioned above include a high percentage of children now remaining in government care. In spite of the sharp decline in birth rates in the Russian Federation the number of children in need of government support is increasing each year. It is important to mention that full orphans constitute only about 10% of all institutionalized children. The majority of the children are so-called "social orphans", i.e. children deprived of parental care due to poverty of their parents, military conflicts, immigration issues etc.

Financing of an enormous system of institutions for orphans is another separate problem. Upkeep of a child in an institution is more expensive when compared with other forms of placement, though one can observe some decline in expenses. It is obvious that none of the provincial governments completely abide by the Russian Federation Government decree #409 of June 20, 1992 "On Immediate Measures on Social Protection of Orphans". For several years in a row, institutions for orphans received financing only for two or three items (mainly, food and salaries). All of the above combine to make the impact of negative factors more acute.

Upbringing and education of orphans highlights another considerable difficult social and educational issue among this population. Due to their specific social status orphans are to a larger degree subject to a higher negative impact in certain social processes such as apathy, or the intentions to get everything from life without giving up anything or antisocial behaviors and addictions. In addition orphans often have to cope with such problems as the inability to live independently and establish a family of their own.

They experience a gap between their thoughts of life and actual reality. This shows up in their inability to function by themselves in modern situations. Their behaviors change along with their demands depending on the circumstances and this shows in their inability to work or to keep a job.

It is especially important not only to prepare the children for independent living by assisting them in choosing an occupation, but to help them form independent thinking. They need to be encouraged to show initiative and responsibility in search activity for work or entrepreneurship and the ability to find creative solutions for their problems.

The majority of institutions' graduates are unable to successfully adjust to life. Upon graduation they are unable to solve a lot of everyday problems without the support of adults (parents, relatives etc.)

Graduates of children's homes and boarding schools experience great difficulties from finding a job to finding appropriate housing. They are unable to communicate with adults or accommodate themselves after finding housing in preparing and adhering to their personal budget or to fight for their legal rights. Unfortunately, the government system of social support of this population is still lacking any organized system of assistance for orphans upon their graduation from an institution and up to them reaching the age of maturity.

As a result almost half of all children's homes graduates in several provinces of Russia belonged to a risk group (was a bum, a pre-trial detainee, committed various crimes, primarily crimes against property, i.e. robberies and muggings). It is obvious that the reasons for these clearly observed consequences in the lives of children's homes graduates are more comprehensive due to the processes occurring during their stay within institutions.

Thus, we may conclude that it has been established by now that a family is a source and necessary link for transferring social and historical experience to a child, primarily of an experience in emotional and business relationships between people. Loss of family is the most serious tragedy in a life of a child that leaves a deep mark in his or her fate, even in those instances when he or she quickly finds a different family. Institutionalization is compounded even with the changes of institutions and guardians for a child. As well, the late acceptance into a different family adds to the stages that traumatize a child's mentality and make it impossible to execute their potential abilities. This can radically change a child's fate destroying their system of relationships with an outside world for a long period of time.

5

THE FORMS OF FAMILY UPBRINGING OF ORPHANS AND CHILDREN LEFT WITHOUT PARENTAL CARE

5.1. Family Upbringing of Orphans as an Alternative to Institutionalization

5.1.1. The History of an Issue

The definition of adoption is as old as the history of humanity itself. In the Judeo-Christian tradition the definition of adoption finds its roots in the Bible story of Moses who was practically adopted by the pharaoh's daughter.

Family upbringing of illegitimate children is known from ancient times. The Bible tells us about children being brought up in the families unrelated to them.

In Russia family upbringing of orphans in unrelated families started during the period of establishment of a feudal state, since 988. An unwritten law existed then: "Do not observe Lent, do not pray, but take care of an orphan". A special tradition imitating a birth was introduced then at this time when an orphan would be adopted into an unrelated family. This birthing tradition would symbolize a duty on the family to treat him/her as one's own child. The financial status of orphans improved under the rule of Boris Godunov. That was not a bad time for orphans and families who had adopted them. In the 17th century, however, families started adopting orphans as laborers to work for food, and that made the lives of many of them unbearable. The first children's home was created in the 18th century by the decree of the bishop of Novgorod. The first legislative acts on patronate (then patronage) are associated with the name of Empress Catherine the Second (1762-1796) who decreed to adopt orphans into families due to high death rates at the children's homes at the time. This determined the need of transition to another form of children's placement - they were given for upbringing into peasants' families for a certain amount of pay. The definition of a patronate for the fallen was for a family to help a child to arise again into society, which included caring for a child's health, their education and development of an independent ability to work as a source of self-support in a future life. These requirements have not always been possible to be completely implemented in all the families adopting children. Patron families receive welfare payments of different sizes according to the age of the child placed with them. For example 5 rubles (essential assistance during those times) for a little child since the child would have been unable to provide any household help at all. Significantly less for older children would be given since they would be able to assist the household in duties, thus, earning money. The payments would gradually stop upon reaching an age of 14 by a child. Families of poor peasants have usually adopted the children where patronate have been a kind of a usual trade. To make easier the state of a child a system of supervision has been organized to oversee performance of patron parents. One of the professionals in protecting children's rights of the time N.V.Yablokov summarizing the practice of children's placement in families over many years came to the conclusion that family placement was the best way of child care.

The family placement has been a private initiative of some members of the Royal family and rich families of some businessmen. An upbringing of orphans in foster and patronage families had become widespread in Europe and the USA already since the mid-19th century.

Medical and charitable conferences in Moscow and St.Petersburg in the 1890s sharply criticized the then existing system of social assistance to illegitimate children. Physicians and practitioners of the system of social welfare concluded that a system of closed children's homes and orphanages was irrational and that its work had to be rated as unsatisfactory in its basics.

The main objection against the system of closed institutions was that it did not provide a child with the main thing needed - a mother. The criticism for lack of success of closed institutions of social assistance for babies came from the practical experience of such a system already in place. Methods of statistical analysis in the death rates of babies over the past 50-year period allowed the realization that the use of closed charity institutions for illegitimate children was not the answer. Observing babies in the conditions that deprived them from any communications with a mother figure, local practitioners made another conclusion. That closed supervision completely killed the energy of those being supervised and completely changed their moral outlook. In the physicians' opinion the system could be built more rationally if the law starts to protect a mother and a child and if the government, public institutions and private charities would facilitate upbringing of children for mothers, thus, eliminating the main reason for existence of children's homes (Z.G.Zhizhilenko citing Raschyotina, 2002).

The life of a child was directly associated, in the physicians' opinion, with the right of an illegitimate child to family upbringing. We find the first attempts to strengthen the connection between a mother and a child in activities of Empress Maria. However, it was only the local practitioners during the post-reform period that made this issue public. It is because of their activities on this issue that a public opinion had been formed. That the required strengthening of connections between mothers and children was largely depended upon government policy aimed at prevention of this and of not leaving out illegitimate children.

5.1.2.   Protection of Children's Rights.

Children's rights have not always been protected or even recognized. Society would always find ways to support and place children who have been unable to remain within families. However, these ways have not always been humane with respect to children. There have been widows' homes in the cities that would provide accommodation for poor children. The children were placed in workshops under an agreement with their master, as well as into poor farm families to be involved into slave-like labor. They have been placed and brought up in monasteries. Children have not always been protected from cruelty of their parents and trainers. For a long time a master of a house would act according to the principle "My home is my fortress", and children have been regarded as his personal property that could be disposed with at his leasure. **Children simply have had no rights.** Until the 1880's society had not been bothered by the issue of providing children with civil rights. The next story shows the development of the views in children's rights.

The story of Mary Ellen became one of the reasons for development of child protection laws in the USA. There are a lot of versions of this story and here is one of them. In 1875 in Albany one of the churchwomen was bringing food baskets to some of the rented houses. In one of the houses she seemingly heard cries, yelling and sounds of beating. Fortunately, this lady was brave enough to interfere. When she knocked at the door, a man answered. When questioned on what had been going on, he answered that this was his house and nobody could tell him how to treat his own child. However, the lady saw the crying child who appeared to be badly abused (Mary Ellen) and was so indignant that she began to seek help for the child. She went to the church, to the police, to the fire brigade and everywhere she was getting the same answer that nobody would be able to help. *After having become desperate she went to society for protection of animals and its representatives found some official reasons for interference after having them consider a child as the highest representative of all animals. This was true since there had been animal protection laws in the country, but no child protection laws.* The story finishes when Mary Ellen starts to live and grow up at the house of the lady that protected her.

This case caused recognition of a necessity to pass laws protecting children. When such laws were passed children would often be taken away from their parents and placed into orphanages or foster families. Some children placed into other families or orphanages under this system would be forgotten by the society. They would be treated with neglect or cruelty in some families. Under this system some families would be treated quite strictly giving them no chance for correcting themselves and bringing a child back.

In the 19th century Russia had at least three ways evolving in the development of mechanisms for child protection.

The first way of protection in the search for means of keeping children safe and alive is associated with the principle of physician Romanov from the city of Voronezh: "each child has a right to interact with his/her mother". According to this physician' thoughts it was necessary to get rid of laws and public morality that would put obstacles in the way to reunification of mother and child. For this reason the problem of protecting a child's life became closely connected with creating conditions where a mother giving her child into an orphanage would not lose connection with him/her. So the existing rules of keeping secret the children's admission into orphanages was criticized as repressive and tearing down the last connection that could evolve between a mother and a child.

An open admission that would guarantee feeding by their own mother to the children was considered as a condition providing the most rational form of care. This innovation provided an opportunity for a mother to feed her own child and also to feed another baby in case of such necessity. An insignificant payment to mothers feeding children allowed not only preserving, but in some cases also improving a family connection and relationship helping to diminish the number of cases of abandon children.

The second way of protection was that in the post-reform period the public conscience was considering anew the original practice of attracting peasants' families to the care and upbringing of babies. At issue and under discussion was the importance of a foster family for the moral and physical welfare of a child. The family-type of upbringing is considered as more rational since it is done subconsciously, every day and every minute, while a child living in an institution may not receive or feel this subconscious type of care. Situations when a baby would not survive in a closed type institution unless in the hands of a breast-feeder (wet nurse) would pose the question very early that it was better a child deprived of a mother should be placed into a foster family at least for the breast-feeding period.

Further practice had shown that it made no sense to admit children into orphanages even under favorable conditions of breast-feeding and upbringing since these institutions did not provide for the most important thing - spiritual healing of a child having lost his/her family. In this connection physicians and trainers directly participating in deciding the fate of a child had come to an opinion that family upbringing would be the only way and that decentralization of the system of patronage was needed in case of overcrowding of patronage-providing localities. Issues of supervision over patronage families, providing assistance to them and of adoption of children became closely connected with issues such as what families to place abandoned children into and at what age.

The third way of protection required the analysis in activities of closed type institutions and has shown that only the ideal upbringing inside such places will not cause moral and mental deficiencies in a child. The orphanage itself may become close to an ideal only if it is built as a family-type institution.

During the first years of the 20th century the methods providing success in this area and aimed at returning abandoned children to their mothers or their placement into foster families began to start developing.

The legal, social and medical aspects of the problem were considered in their unity by scholars and practitioners. Implementation of a right to life of an abandoned child at that time supposed a completely new approach to development of legal protection, social work and medical assistance that would jointly preserve a child's life.

The issue of protecting the right to life has become closely associated with the issue of child abuse and violence. In the last third of the 19th century the cases of children who experienced violence on the part of the masters whose workshops they had been placed in, on the part of their own parents and even strangers have come to be known by scholars and practicing lawyers. Consideration of this caseload assisted in active development of the definition of protection. Introduction of the definition of protection characterized the beginning of a new direction in charitable activities. These activities could now exist as a special form of practical assistance that could be widely defined.

An important step towards protection activities was made in Russia in 1892 when the Department of protection of children from cruel treatment was organized at the Society of care for the poor.

Protection has been understood as a series of activities by district providers of care associated with the establishment of orphanages or shelters extending to searching for families for children to be placed into and with providing weekend entertainment for children studying at vocational schools. Most importantly with making motions to the government to apply to children having committed crimes a punishment that would be more suitable for their age and with defending child's interests in a court of law.

The Law on Protecting a Family in the USA was passed in 1964. It was necessary to establish a legal foundation at that time to correct the situation regarding the difficult conditions of children isolated from their families and with taking away parental rights from families if needed. The Law on Protecting a Family was to balance the rights of children and families and provide conditions for placement of children into foster families. The law delegated authority to the states to make everything possible to preserve families and to place children into conditions with the least restrictions for their upbringing. The law supposes creation of all possible conditions for keeping children in touch with their families. Parents are provided with assistance in the case of their inability to perform their duties of parental upbringing until the emotional and physical conditions of a child would be no longer in danger. If a child is isolated from their family the law makes sure that they are placed into conditions that resemble ones normal family to a maximum possible degree. Placement of children into conditions associated with any limitations is justified only by their own interests. For instance, it is not allowed to place pre-schoolers into large dorm-type bedrooms or children's homes.

The US children are no longer kept in children's homes until the end of their upbringing. They are placed into patron families with a final goal of their return into their biological family. Any final taking away of parental rights must be justified. The law is applied in differentiated fashion. Only those children who suffered the most are isolated from their families. If before the trainers' responsibility was to provide food, clothing and accommodation for children, now they have to be able to treat children who have experienced abuse also.

Since the Law provides for obtaining a corresponding level of upbringing by children, each state has developed a program providing for some range of limitations. It is called a concept of complete upbringing. The main idea is to place a child into conditions that would be most suitable for his/her needs. Diagnostic centers are organized in such a fashion, so as to account for interests of each child isolated from a family. Each child is studied and tested in these centers in order to further decide how to place him/her. The most traumatized children are placed in boarding schools, while the less traumatized are placed into small groups within boarding schools and in patron families. Family assistance service provides support for later reunification of a child with a biological family. Not all children undergo this process. They are admitted into a referral center only if it is not overcrowded. Otherwise, they are sent directly into boarding schools or patron families. This system is not perfect, but its goal is to prevent frequent movements of children.

From children's homes to continuous family upbringing - such is the world trend (V.Chechet, 2001). The majority of countries have moved away from large institutions for children over the recent twenty years in favor of supporting children in their natural (family) living environment. This process started in Sweden after World War II.

The system of childcare in Sweden underwent two stages in its development in the second half of the 20th century:

1940s-1980s - closures of children's homes;

1990s - Recognition of a family as an institution of child care.

Children's homes closings were done by the organization called *Barnbun Sku* (Stockholm). It became an ideological center for development of the future system of social care for children in Sweden and other Scandinavian countries. Children were placed into families and were worked with in family environments instead of in children's homes.

We can distinguish the following features in the family-type children's institutions of foreign countries:

- the government children's institution of any type, however comfortable it might be represents only the temporary type of placement;

- orphans and children temporarily or permanently left without parental care are provided with former or new family environment in a mandatory fashion;

- a special government children's institution where children live and grow up starting from the age of 12 should approach to a maximum degree a family-type environment; each dorm houses about ten children in order for trainers to provide quality individual care, pay more attention to children and provide constant individualized care to each child;

- when searching for a new foster family a priority is given to those families already possessing a rich positive experience of upbringing of its own children (though even nowadays we may find some orphanages where unmarried women with no children of their own are employed, as was required by an Austrian educator German Gmainer, who was a creator of children's villages);

- biological parents are given an opportunity to visit their children in new foster families if these contacts are not harmful to life and upbringing of a child;

- children may return to their biological family if parents, who have previously stopped the process of upbringing of their children for various reasons (or who abused their children, belittled their dignity, used physical force in punishment) recognized their mistakes, acknowledged their guilt and started leading a regular way of life.

5.2.   The Condition of the System of Family Placement of Orphans and Children Left without Parental Care

The UN Convention on the Rights of a Child declares that "each child who temporarily or permanently is deprived of a family environment or who in his/her own best interests may not remain in this environment has a right to special protection and assistance provided by the government". According to this international act and the Russian legislation the following forms of child placement substituting his/her own families are established: adoption, guardianship and foster family (in its different varieties).

Domestic and foreign experience clearly evidence that efficiency of socialization and guarantees of favorable future are much higher for an orphan brought up in a family than for the one placed in an institution. The same experience provides irrefutable evidence that complete upbringing of an orphan within a family is tremendously cheaper for the government than institutionalization of any kind. At the very beginning of the system of communist power (over 80 years ago!) it was evident for politicians and professionals building that system that the idea of family upbringing was the one that should be taken as a foundation of system of assistance to orphans.

Children left without parental care are primarily placed with other families. 61% of all known orphans (71,000 children) were placed into other families in 2000 and only 29% (36,200 children) into institutions, while 10% (11,700 children) remained without being placed or in institutions for temporary placement.

In general, 72.8% of orphans and children left without parental care were brought up in families in 2000, including 482,500 children under a system of guardianship, while 180,000 children were brought up in institutions.

However, the local authorities that are responsible for protection of rights and interests of minors left without parental care are performing their duties unsatisfactorily.

The earlier existing mechanism of multi-agency cooperation of discovery of children requiring government assistance is now idle, and the number of homeless children is increasing as a consequence.

We are noting recent positive trends in decisions on children's adoptions. The share of children adopted and taken in trust by private families has also increased. There is no doubt that this trend continues (over the last three years the share of adopted children has increased three-fold in the City of Moscow), thus, the issue of adoption becomes more acute, especially in its psychological aspects.

In our country there exist the following reasons for adoption and guardianship - inability to have one's own child due to medical reasons, lack of desire to have one's own child due to social reasons, death or incurable disease of child's parents who are close relatives of a person adopting or taking a child in trust, taking away of parental rights of children's parents.

5.2.1. Adoption

Adoption is the most preferred type of placement of a child left without parental care.

Officially the legal system of adoption was recognized in the beginning of the 20th century to satisfy the needs of childless couples from the high society. Historically, poorer couples were frequently unable to get permission for adoption; however, some unofficial adoptions also occurred (Trisellotis J., 1970).

The main obstacles for development of adoptions were a strong prejudice against children born out of wedlock and very strong conviction that immorality, crime and bad character were hereditary.

Adoption is conducted in accordance with the Family Code of the Russian Federation. It is mandatory to abide by the Code rules. Otherwise, it is impossible to provide for stability of adoption and establish parental legal rights forever. It is extremely important for orphans since they do not have a second parent who would be able to neutralize an unsuccessful adoption. These children have no family where they could return.

The main condition of adoption is formulated in article 98, part 1 of the Family Code: "An adoption is allowed only for minors and only in their best interests". Considering that these interests are meant as proper upbringing, it is understandable that a child, especially an orphan child may not be entrusted just to anybody. That is why, according to article 99 of the Family Code "adoptions may be performed by the citizens of the age of majority, for the exception of those whose parental rights have been taken away, as well as those persons legally recognized as incompetent or having limited proficiency".

The decree of the Government of the Russian Federation #275 of March 20,2000 *On Approval of the Rules of Children's Adoption and Control over Conditions of their Living and Upbringing in the Families that Have Adopted them within the Territory of the Russian Federation and the Rules of Consular Service of Children that are Citizens of the Russian Federation by the Consular Establishments Abroad* provides for an orderly system of adoption.

The above legal documents establish rules of adoption of children; list the necessary actions to be performed personally by those wishing to adopt a child, as well as methods of supervision of conditions of living and upbringing of children in families that have adopted them. Now foreign citizens are allowed to adopt Russian children independent of the state of children's health, but only in those cases "when it has proven to be impossible to provide for adoption or guardianship of these children by Russian citizens or adoption by these children's relatives independent of their place of residence or citizenship".

The federal data bank on children left without parental care is being established to implement this principle. This data bank would contain information from corresponding provincial data banks, as well as documented information on all citizens wishing to adopt children in their families (Russian Federation Federal Law *On Establishment of the Government Data Bank on All Children Left without Parental Care* (passed by the State Duma on March 15, 2001)).

Adoption is considerably widespread. The Russian Federation Department of Education statistics accounts for all adoptions of minors, including those having one parent who wishes upon another marriage for his/her child to obtain a father and not just a stepfather. In other words, the total number of adopted children includes not only full orphans and children left without parental care, but also those whose good family becomes complete due to adoption. These children comprise a majority of all adopted.

There were 24,160 children adopted in 2000. Out of these number 17,870 (74% of the total) were adopted by Russian citizens and 6,290 (26% of the total) by foreign citizens. Major portion of Russian citizens who adopted children are their stepfathers and stepmothers (10,480 of all adoptions) the number of children adopted by other Russian citizens amounted to 7,390 in

2000. The comparison with 1995 statistics shows a decrease in the number of adoptions by both categories of citizens. Nonetheless the rate of decrease became smaller since 1997 and we may talk about stabilization of this process nowadays. The ratio of children adopted by their stepmothers and stepfathers compared to those adopted by other citizens remains practically constant over the recent years.

We also note an increase in the number of court decisions canceling adoptions. In 1997 303 adoptions were canceled, while the number was 401 in 2000. This evidences a need in more accurate selection of potential candidates to adopt, as well as a need in strengthening supervision of families with adopted children over performing their parental duties.

On September 7, 2000 the Russian Federation signed the Hague Convention of 1993 on protection of children's rights and cooperation in the process of international adoptions.

The total number of children adopted by foreign citizens amounted to 6,300 in 2000 which is only 1,100 children more than the number of adoptions by Russian citizens who are not children's stepmothers or stepfathers and comprises 46% of all adoptions by citizens that are not stepmothers or stepfathers. Analysis of age distribution of children adopted by Russian and foreign citizens show that Russian citizens mostly take for adoption children younger than one (64% of all children adopted by Russian citizens who are not stepmothers or stepfathers) while foreign citizens prefer to adopt children of older ages.

The majority (64%) of children over one year of age was adopted by foreign citizens. 236 handicapped children was adopted by people who are not their stepmothers or stepfathers in 2000, only 10 children out of this number were adopted by Russian citizens.

According to the data of foreign social services and special research, as a rule, the majority of families adopting children represent mixed families with one or more of its own or other adopted children.

The research conducted in England has shown that the majority of people taking children for adoption are in their 40s. This result agrees with the data obtained by Dando and Minty (1987) showing the average age of women taking children for adoption to be 44, and the average age of men taking children for adoption to be 47.5. The results also agree with the data obtained by Bebbington and Miles (1987) that shows 80% of all mothers taking children for adoption are between ages of 31 and 55.

As several researches shows (Fanshel, 1966; Kay, 1966; Dando and Minty, 1987) the key motivation for adoption is people's desire to be parents for a child and improvement of family life combined with self-identification with an unfortunate child stemming from personal experience.

Rachel Jenkins research (1965) of 97 people taking children for temporary adoption indicated 9 following categories of leading needs in temporary adoption:

1. alternative to permanent adoption;

2. substitute for one's own child;

3. obtaining a peer for one's own child;

4. pity for children in difficult situations;

5. repeat of previous experience of happy relationships;

6. compensation for lost or unsatisfactory relationships;

7. feelings of guilt;

8. a need for a mother to have somebody dependent on her;

9. Other undetermined reasons.

The comparison of motivations of mothers taking children for adoption in Great Britain and Romania showed the following. 96% of British mothers indicated their own inability to bear a child as a main motive for adoption, and only 6% mentioned altruism as an insignificant motive.

Though 78% of Romanian mothers also mentioned inability to bear a child as the main reason for adoption, many parents also named altruism as motivational factor: 18% as the main factor and 54% as the second one in their ranking. Also, though 28% of Romanian mothers named altruism as the main reason for adoption, many of them also mentioned inability to bear one's own child: 49% as the main reason and 6% as the second one in their ranking. Taking into account interaction between the reasons for adoption an evaluation of three groups has been performed:

1. altruism as the main motive (inability to bear a child as a secondary);

2. inability to bear a child as the main motive (altruism as the secondary one);

3. Altruism and inability to bear a child as reasons equal in their importance.

The last group received the highest evaluation.

One of the few domestic studies of people's motivations for adoption conducted in the children's home #19 in the City of Moscow showed the following distribution of the motives for adoption: self-fulfillment (favorite job) - 35%, assistance to children and other motives -35%, desire to have a child (inability to bear one's own or one's own have grown up) - 30%.

Unfortunately, an issue of adoption in Russia is currently encountering numerous organizational, social and psychological difficulties. First, there is no developed procedure of social and psychological selection of parents. Second, only a few people can afford to adopt and afford a child for financial reasons. Thus, we can see examples when parents are selected not according to their psychological values, but according to their financial status. Third, there are no stereotypes in the Russian mentality unlike in the Western one that would give people incentives for adoption.

Thus, we encounter a serious social and psychological problem of optimal choice of a family for a child from a number of candidates for adoption.

The important part of successful selection of candidates for adoption is in its turn adequate determination of their motivation for adoption.

Thus, the problem of adoption is extremely acute from social, ethical, humanitarian, psychological and educational points of view.

5.2.2.   Guardianship (Trusteeship)

Guardianship is the most common type of placement of children left without parental care into families and is the most humane form of placement in keeping ties between relatives.

Guardianship and adoption have in common establishment of favorable conditions for upbringing of a minor. At the same time, unlike adoption, guardianship does not cease legal connection of a child with his/her parents. This point significantly facilitates the use of this type of placement and makes it more available. However, certain rules also exist here. Guardianship is established for minors who were left without parental care as a result of parents' deaths, taking away their parental rights, sickness of parents and other reasons, as well as to protect personal and property rights of these children. However, this rule has more of a general nature. Article 122 of the Family Code outlines the rules for finding children needing guardianship and their temporary placement.

Financial conditions of children in trust are regulated by the decree of the Government of the Russian Federation #409 of June 20,1992 *On Immediate Measures on Social Protection of Orphans and Children Left without Parental Care*, as well as by the decree #374 of May 14, 2001 *On Immediate Measures on Improving Situation of Orphans and Children Left without Parental Care*. The children in trust enjoy the same privileges as the ones established for children in children's homes.

After a certain period of decline the number of children placed in trust increased in 2000. If 5,500 children were placed in trust in 1999, this number increased to 6,500 in 2000. Practically everywhere the main obstacle for development of this form of children's placement is untimely and incomplete payment of welfare monies for upkeep of children in trust. Only 56% of children trusts receive these payments.

There are cases when due to non-payment of welfare monies the trustees request child welfare authorities to revoke the decision of establishment of trusteeship since they are unable to bring up children at their own expense only. Moreover, guardians do not receive timely legal, social, psychological medical and educational assistance in bringing up children who have suffered serious emotional and psychological traumas.

Article 34 of the Civil Code of the Russian Federation establishes that a local government authority is a child welfare authority. Thus, the local governments are in fact child welfare authorities according to article 53 of the Constitution of the Russian Federation, article 56 of the Federal Law *On General Principles of Organization of Local Government in the Russian Federation* of August 28, 1995 and The Law of the Russian Federation *On Local Governments in the RSFSR* of July 6, 1993.

According to article 121, part 2 of the Family Code of the Russian Federation "All issues connected with provision of child welfare with respect to children left without parental care are organized and decided by the local authorities on the basis of a local charter, provincial laws, the Family and Civil Codes of the Russian Federation".

Presently 60 provinces in Russia have passed laws *On Organization of Child Welfare Work* where relevant departments of education are recognized as local child welfare authorities.

Some local governments who have not included issues of organization of child welfare work in their charters are passing separate resolutions on those issues, which regulate in detail all child welfare work.

In the majority of child welfare authorities it is one professional, who, as a rule, performs all responsibilities associated with providing for child welfare. Such situation allows only for performance of emergency work associated with representation of rights of minors in court, preparation of reports on the request of courts (which sometimes appear to be unprofessional due to the lack of necessary skills and knowledge) etc. Protection of rights and interests of children is done quite unsatisfactorily. The current legislation (Article 121 of the Family Code of the Russian Federation) gives a full opportunity to organize child welfare work now in a new fashion. The reforms here are quite possible through organization of professional services and institutions that would take upon themselves a part of child welfare authority's duties (excluding the legal ones) like professional assistance to families and children. Thus, the creation of such institutions of a new type is vital for proper performance of duties of a child welfare authority.

In the conditions when local governments represent child welfare authorities there is a need in creating a legislative basis to establish unified minimum government standards in social and legal servicing of children requiring government protection and organization of work of local governments in the area of child welfare. Thus, it is necessary to pass a federal law on government minimum social standards of organization of work of local governments in the area of child welfare.

The current system of work of child welfare authorities requires radical reorganization. The main attention should be paid to selecting potential parents and systematic work with them on creating more comfortable conditions of living of orphans within families.

Insufficient number of forms of children's placement into families does not allow implementation of an individual approach to each child considering his/her personal, cultural and ethnic background. There is a lack of scientific techniques for provision of the process of placement of children into families and establishment of guardianship, as well as a lack of system of continuing education of relevant professionals (social workers, psychologists, psychotherapists, and lawyers). There is no system for psychological and educational training of future parents and guardians preparing them for acceptance of orphans within their families and no system of social and psychological support of adopted and guardian families. There are no adequate medical and psychological requirements for candidates for adoption and guardianship.

5.2.3.   A Foster Family

Adoption and guardianship represent traditional forms of orphan placement into families. However, a need in providing for the interests of large numbers of orphans has always caused a search for new ways of protecting the interests of minors. Moreover, each individual case of loss of parental care between a parent and child, as a rule, does not represent one single fact but a whole variety of causal-consequential relationships. Each of these is different in their significance and in the degree of actual danger for a child. Each one of them is completely different from another and has its specific nature determining an orphan's fate. That is why it is not always possible to make each situation of losing parental care compatible with a particular ready placement form. Obviously a child's upbringing suffers and is at a loss from such incompatibility. It is always understood that people who have intentions in becoming the substitute for a child's parents do not only have humanitarian reasons in mind. Many have their own thoughts and ideas as how this should work out each time for their own opportunities not considering the child' needs. The forms of orphan placement were always influenced by national traditions, religious beliefs, historical experience and finally, by the nature of economic development in a country, its richness or poverty.

A family-type children's home is a radically new form of upbringing for orphans. It was suggested by the Vladimir I. Lenin All-Union Children's Foundation. The decree of the CPSU Central Committee and the USSR Council of Ministers of July 31, 1987 became the legal basis for such placement of children left without parental care.

In development of the above decree the USSR Council of Ministers passed another decree on April 17,1988 *On Creating Family-Type Children's Homes* in order to help "each child to regain a feeling of being sure in oneself and conviction that he/she is needed by the people, to develop positive qualities for participation in production and social life of the country".

In those years the goals of family-type children's homes were to have been achieved, first, by creating children's towns in one-apartment flats of a building having multiple-rooms for families to bringing up no less than 10 orphans and children left without parental care. Second, by having separate families living in multiple-room private apartments in regular houses, specialized houses or groups of such houses taking care of no less than 5 orphans. However, it became immediately obvious that it is not that easy to create children's towns. Their creation required not only projects, but also significant financial resources that should have been coming from investments by local governments and federal departments. The Russian Children's Foundation and its local branches were also supposed to directly participate in financing, building and equipping of these towns. The second type of a family children's home, which had not been called a foster family yet had less difficulties with its organization. In other words, each type had its own history of development.

Even the first steps on creating children's towns as special zones of happiness were causing doubts about their rationality first of all when surrounded by the whole sea of children's unhappiness and from an educational point of view. However, the future continuation of these towns was determined primarily by economic difficulties. Especially since they were suppose to be created in each region primarily using local financing, of which there was none. That is why this type of a children's home was never successfully created in Russia. What is established in the town of Sasovo in the Province of Ryazan' represents several cottages built on one territory with a multi-child family living in each of them and this is the second type of family children's homes.

It has been developing in seemingly disorderly fashion since establishment of family-type children's homes was determined by the desire of local people to be substitute parents for orphans and did not depend upon directives and orders from the government.

The Temporary Guidelines on Family-Type Children's Homes approved by the USSR State Committee on People's Education, the USSR State Committee on Labor and Social Issues, the USSR Department of Finance, the USSR Children's Foundation and the All-Union Central Council of Labor Unions was the first legal foundation for a way in the protection of orphans that had been previously unknown. This way of protection has already exceeded the framework of an experiment and now has become a realistic way in the upbringing and social protection of orphans and children left without parental care. The main principles of this type of placement have already been determined. It was subordinate to the local government; it depended not only upon local child welfare authorities, but of the Children's Foundation as well. The issues of selection of trainers and their salaries have also been resolved etc. By 2000 there officially were 61 family-type children's homes registered with 500 orphans being brought up there. Over the later years it was becoming clearer that these establishments do not in fact represent a special type of institution for orphans, but resemble more a foster family with its own rules that provides for family upbringing as a priority.

Foster family. A certain type of child uses the assistance of foster families. First of all, these are boarding school students having no relatives and who have lost absolutely every connection with their biological family. A foster family also becomes a home for handicapped children, who have no place in their biological family. A foster family may house children from multi-children families when it becomes impossible to separate siblings who know of each other, so it makes sense to place all of them into a new foster family together.

According to the Regulations on foster families it represents one of the types of family placement of orphans and children left without parental care with complete government financing for children and reimbursement for foster parents. This type of a family is organized by a decree of a local government on application from the relevant education department. After a decree is approved an agreement on conditions of upbringing and upkeep of children in a foster family is signed.

The preference is made for families or single citizens having experience in parenting and who already have adopted or taken children in trust and provided good care for them.

The contract nature is not the only feature of a foster family. There are several of them. However, they all agree with each other creating a family as a result. First of all, the foster family would be considered as such if a citizen would take no less than 5 orphans or children left without parental care for upbringing. This represents an incentive for placement of a larger number of minors. However, the total amount may not exceed ten children.

The other essential feature of a foster family is government financing for children and foster parents. The children enjoy full government financing of their needs and parents are paid for their job.

Thus the main features of a foster family are its contract nature, selection of parents and recognizing their labor on an equal footing with production jobs.

Parental legal relationships are not established after placement in foster families. A child in a foster family continues legal relations with his/her biological parents. He/she has the right to all child welfare payments that normally go to the biological parents (they are credited to his/her personal account at the savings bank). Placement of a child into a foster family does not destroy those relations with biological parents that are provided for by family legislation (child support payments, inheritance etc.).

Guardianship is closer in its definition to a foster family. This means that foster parents obtain rights for upbringing a foster child and responsibilities to protect his/her interests. A foster child has the right to receive all child welfare payments in the same fashion as a child in trust care. However, a trustee spends all the monies received to care for a child instead of crediting those to a child's account since he/she has no other sources of financing. Thus, a foster family child has certain financial advantages being fully provided for by the government.

The obstacle in development of foster families is an absence of provincial laws governing an issue of salaries of foster parents and privileges for such families. Moreover, several issues of a federal nature remain unresolved including labor and social guarantees for foster parents, in particular the issue of future social security retirement payments for them.

An active process of reorganization of family-type children's homes into foster families and establishment of new foster families began in 1998. Out of the 68 researched provinces of the Russian Federation all family-type children's homes were reorganized into foster families in 46 of them.

New foster families have been created during the process of reorganization of family-type children's homes. This occurred, for instance, in the Province of Samara where continuous work is done in resolving issues of social orphanhood since 1992.

A total of 1626 children were brought up in 1154 foster families in the Province of Samara as of January 1, 2001 (G.Gusarova, 2001).

Foster families established in the Province of Samara are stable with 40% of them in existence for more than one year and 30% existing for more than three years. There are 1026 complete and 128 incomplete families out of the total number of 1154 with 928 having children of their own while 226 families do not have their own biological children.

The growth in the number of foster families has an economic aspect besides humanitarian and social aspects. Foster parents are paid for childcare, however, these amounts are less than 3500 to 4000 rubles a month or more (depending on the type of an institution) spent on each child in a children's home by the government.

However, there exist local obstacles to transition of children into foster families in the majority of provinces of Russia. The heads of local governments refuse to establish special services needed for children's placement into families.

A family that decides to adopt or take care of an orphan in trust, experiences difficulties associated with limited amounts of available information for parents and in particular, with the specific type of development requirements of a child who has been institutionalized.

The need of special knowledge about the psychological problems of children and adolescents is explained not only by the extreme lack of information in this field for any non-professional (even including teachers themselves), but also by extremely high rates of psychological pathologies observed in social orphans.

Practically all children (90 to 100%) have those pathologies; this is explained by three factors (Iovchuk, Yavrozova, Shcherbakova, 2001):

1. genetic (inheriting pathologies of personalities or psychological diseases of biological parents);

2. organic (unfavorable pregnancy that was ongoing during a period of intensive emotional tensions, hard work, malnutrition, and most often misuse of alcohol, narcotic drugs, toxic substances; premature birth, fetus hypothrophy, problems when giving birth; serious illnesses in the age of breast-feeding);

3. Social (in one way or another all children placed into families have had an experience of orphanhood or experienced hardships of all sorts in hard family situations that influences the nature of their development).

As a result foster parents often think that they made their decision too fast, that the problems they are facing can not be overcome. They experience problems in contacts with foster children that cause feelings of irritation and disappointment. In rare cases they try to get rid of such a child, returning him or her to an institution where they came from. There are known cases when foster children are simply left in the department of psychological and nervous diseases of a children's hospital by the foster parents after their treatment has been over. These are extreme examples, but they do exist.

In order to assist a foster family in understanding their child's nature and becoming goal-oriented in trying to achieve an optimal effect for a child's positive socialization a family needs not only the basic knowledge of psychology, psychiatry, impairment treatment, drug addiction treatment etc., but a constant support from a team of professionals in various fields within a system of complex multi-disciplinary patronage.

Increase in medical, psychological and educational proficiency of parents is no less important.

In order to scientifically prove the efficiency of a **foster family** model as a substitute for professional family V.N.Oslon and A.B.Kholmogorova (2001) conducted a psychological research of 40 families of different status and different terms of children's placement.

The research completely proved the expressed positive dynamics of emotional, cognitive, social and personal development of all orphans after placement into foster families without any exception.

After being placed into a family a child builds relationships not just with an adult taking care of them but with a family as a whole, so they have begun to learn to deal with systematic process. A widespread mistake in the process of social and psychological guidance is putting placement of a child with a mother or foster parents as the first priority. That is primary concentration on child-parent relationships while ignoring the role of a family as a proven effective system with definite structure, allowing patterns of interaction with its history and ideology, values, traditions and rituals in positive development of a child' personality. A child needs to adjust to functioning in a family system as a whole otherwise risk poor overall development in character and being rejected by the family (and eventually society) later.

During the process of adjustment a family tries to change a child making them more compatible to family system requirements. However, the family structure also may not escape changes in its own turn despite the resistance to do so and must either undergo restructuring (on both structural level and development of a new repertoire of strategies of functioning) or reject the child.

During an integration process the child becomes part of a family system and then either becomes adjusted or remains an external element which means an absence of adjustment. Families have certain psychological conditions that may either facilitate a child's adjustment or push them out of a system. That is why V.N.Oslon and A.B.Kholmogorova (2001) accepted a system paradigm as a main methodological approach for selection and psychological guidance of a foster family. They consider two family systems in their study:

1. a system of a basic family where an orphan is placed;

2. A family system that evolves after an orphan is included in it and which radically changes a situation of a basic family.

The first period of adjustment lasts about two months in families that are psychologically prepared and according to various signs it may be called *orientation*. Families view behavior of their new member quite positively, they are inclined to see a foster child as quite normal in such behavioral areas as aggressiveness, anti-social behavior, fears, depression (a special scale was used to estimate parental opinion of a child's behavior). Parents usually specify attention deficit as a child's problem area.

A child after being placed into a family from a children's home environment experiences a clearly defined crisis and subconsciously begins to resist changes required of them by the new environment. Children that underwent a prior preparation before being placed into a family go through this stage more easily.

Children are tense inside, though they try to behave normally since they have a high motivation and desire for family living. A child who is unprepared for placement experiences serious crisis that can be observed in various deviant behaviors (most often anti-social acts). Lack of emotional adjustment can be observed in a form of depression.

Unprepared and unassisted families go through this stage during a term of almost a year and this causes extreme tensions in all members of a family. From this unprepared setting they usually perceive foster children as aggressors and hopelessly anti-social persons.

The second stage, which may be called *tensions stage* is also different for the families within a system of support and outside of it. Tensions rise to an extreme degree in families having no psychological guidance. The amount of applications for assistance increases significantly. Episodes of stealing usually begin to appear. We can also observe certain patterns here. If a child establishes good relationships within a family, episodes of stealing usually occur at home while if relations in a family are emotionally cold children commit larcenies at school.

However, even at this stage all indicators of a child's development in all families start significantly improving. Children make an intellectual jump already after the second month of placement. Their grades improve, their speech improves, especially its lexical and grammatical structure and vocabulary increases. A good example is an eight-year old girl that was diagnosed as an imbecile by a psychiatrist and unable to learn. A foster family had her admitted into a special school where she became second in class by the level of her grades.

Indicators of emotional welfare also increase and the depression level goes below average. By the eighth month after placement families usually undergo a certain crisis period that lasts one or two months. Parents radically increase their level of criticism of foster children. Children's negative opinions of families also increase almost two-fold. Families complain of becoming tired, that children irritate them etc. This state may be called a *crisis of restructuring* that is expressed in a certain level of rejection. In spite of the external rejection levels the children's emotional stability remain quite good. By the end of the first year stabilization occurs within families. Teachers evaluate dynamics of children's development quite high by all indicators. Families outside a system of psychological guidance experience a long-term tension stage that usually lasts from one year up to 18 months.

The level of tension within a family decreases after the first year, positive changes appear in relationships, and indicators of development of foster children continue to improve. The level of conflicts between foster children themselves remain quite high, they often view each other as competitors within a family system. Members of biological families start feeling more guilt before the members of foster families. Foster children subconsciously identify themselves with their biological families and desire to be accepted by them. There can be observed a certain state of calmness in families, so we can identify a *stage of calmness* (usually from 11th until 24th month after placement) when mutual attachments are established. By the end of the second year (plus-minus two or three months) this calmness ends up in unexpected outburst that is observed during research in an increasing level of dissatisfaction in practically all areas of family life. Foster children are being viewed as even more aggressive and anti-social. This stage can be called a *stage of disappointment or depression.*

Some families cease their existence as foster families at this stage and bring children back to a child's home. This crisis may also end up in deeper acknowledgment of problems and responsibilities associated with placement. The mother as the head of the family usually experiences this crisis and the realization of the problems in the hardest way.

After realization of the problems a period of their acceptance and acceptance of the new family identity comes. A family begins to function as a new system.

Thus, the authors distinguished the following periods in development of a family system during the first year after an orphan's placement:

1. orientation (mutual study - two months);

2. tensions (emotional discomfort prevails - from three to eight months);

3. rejection (negative attitude to foster children prevails - eighth through tenth month) or the first crisis of system restructuring

The following stages are distinguished during the next two to three years after placement:

1. calmness (realization of mutual attachment -11th -24th months);

2. depression (gradual realization of problems associated with placement - 24th-30th months) or second crisis of system restructuring;

3. acceptance of problems (acceptance of a new family identity and finishing the process of establishment of a new family system)

Thus, the dynamics of development of a foster family has its psychological rules, stages and crises. Foster families need science-based psychological assistance since psychological guidance significantly facilitates and improves the dynamics of mutual adjustment of an orphan and a foster family.

In spite of all efforts of government institutions and public organizations aimed at family placement of children left without parental care, society in general and its citizens are not yet ready (even under conditions of adequate financial compensation) to accept responsibilities of upbringing of children that are not their own, especially school-age children, in their families.

It is obvious that a combination of financial conditions and bad housing conditions in the majority of Russian families (along with emotional tiredness and difficulties of everyday living) remain as obstacles for the development of families who can bring up orphans. At the same time the problems of social orphanhood are successfully resolved in those provinces where trustees and foster families receive regular financial support. It is in those regions also that the mass-media regularly informs the population about good families with adopted children. This also brings awareness for the need in reorganization of children's homes and for the success in trustees and foster families in receiving psychological and legal support along with financial help.

An introduction of the role and occupation of a family psychologist is especially important in this context. His/her functions should include the following:

- continuous psychological support of a family;

- dynamic observation of psychological condition of family members;

- discovering problems in development, education, emotional and psychological health of children;

- discovery of psychological problems and educational difficulties of parents;

- assistance in overcoming crisis situations;

- assistance in decreasing of emotional tensions and conflicts in a family;

- consultations for parents on problems of upbringing and development of a child and family relationships;

- assistance in organization of family entertainment that has great importance for keeping family members close to each other (admission into arts and sports sections, organization of joint tours for parents and children, creation of conditions for joint vacations of parents and children etc.)

Everything that was said here about foster families requires to be noted that as a group they have a lot of legal signs inherent only to there structure. That legal structure serves only as an external expression of their educational essence to society as a whole in developing orphan care. Foster families do not represent something artificial therefore, but have proven their viability even though they may not be the largest influence on orphan care. However, they assist in resolving a task that is very important for the country - a task of placement of orphans who find themselves in trouble and is seemingly not needed by anyone.

Another form of family upbringing, that of creating patron families is in the process of development. This model allows for a positive resolution in the issue of an orphans' placement into families and also to create a mechanism for the temporary replacement of biological parents. The resolution is in the case where time is needed in dealing with charges of unlawful behavior and a necessity of social rehabilitation is needed before a child could be later returned into his/her biological family.

6

PATRONATE AS A NEW SYSTEM OF FAMILY UPBRINGING.

6.1.   The History of an Issue

The patronate upbringing is known since ancient times, though it started to spread in Europe and the USA only since the middle of the 19th century. Let us consider an example of patronate upbringing in the USA.

Dr. Robert Cook Buckner was a baptist pastor from Tennessee who was a founder of the Children's home (now Buckner Children's home). Dr. Buckner was also the editor of *Religious Digest*. He used his magazine, which was later renamed into *Baptism in Texas* to gain support for his dream of establishing a children's home. In 1877 at an annual convention of pastors it was decided to begin construction of a children's home as soon as a sum of $2,000 would be accumulated. Dr. Buckner was appointed as a receiver for the monies.

He started his activities literally within two days. He collected his first $27 by asking his house guests for donations.

By the summer of 1879 he already had $1,200 collected and decided to start preparing and seeking approval for the necessary paperwork in the state of Texas. During the fall of the same year after having obtained a personal loan of $800 at a local bank in addition to the monies collected he rented a small cottage in East Dallas. The first three children were placed there in December 1879 in care of L.H. Tillman and his wife.

In September 1880 Dr. Buckner bought 44 acres of land six miles east of Dallas. It is there where the Buckner Children's home is located nowadays. However, Dr. Buckner did not stop and continued to buy land and collect monies. By the end of the century the Buckner Children's home was the owner of 500 acres of land.

Dr. Buckner died on April 9, 1919, 40 years after the construction of his Children's home had begun. The Buckner Foundation and its various affiliates all over the state would not have been established without his ability to achieve his goals.

The Buckner Foundation nowadays is the largest private social welfare foundation in the country serving 15,000 people a year. The Buckner Foundation is a multi-profile charity working with children, families and the elderly, which is engaged in treatment, rehabilitation and upbringing.

The Buckner Foundation provides assistance to all needy independent of their race, religion, financial or social status.

Encountering various social problems in the state of Texas the Buckner Foundation uses modern techniques and means by constantly expanding and diversifying its programs of fighting various social diseases. The Buckner Foundation is involved in educating children in boarding schools, treatment of mentally ill adolescents, providing shelter, diagnostics, patronate upbringing, care for the elderly with their independent living, care for Alzheimer disease patients, control over child protection and acceptance of children into different families, pregnancy consultations, barrier-reduced housing, assistance to incomplete families, assistance to victims of domestic violence and homeless. It also has a summer camp and rehabilitation center.

Buckner Foundation's children and nursing homes are located in 13 cities within the state of Texas.

Presently all accumulated knowledge by the Foundation is also used to provide services of the same type in various other countries. Working in partnership with national and local government structures in other countries combined with efforts of other American foundations and churches gave an opportunity to get deeply involved into the culture of various countries and societies and make a difference for children there.

The Department of International assistance to orphans has existed since 1995 when the Buckner Foundation started its work in Russia and Romania at the invitation of the governments of these countries that became interested in the Buckner Foundation's experience in overcoming increasing amount of problems in the children's homes over there. Hundreds of thousands of children in those countries are living in institutions for orphans. These children have become innocent victims of social and political changes that are experienced throughout the world. In the changing moments in governments while the political systems are striving for stability and affecting the way so many live now inside the new borders, immeasurable numbers of children get lost within the system going deep down into poverty, hunger and desperation.

The Buckner Foundation today is making a serious impact upon the lives of children and families working with them in many countries all over the world. The Buckner Foundation has over a hundred years of experience in organizing foster families and preparing patron parents.

One of the main goals of the Buckner Foundation is assistance in development of programs that would decrease the numbers of institutionalized children and allow improvement of quality of child care in the institutions if children having no other alternative.

One of the first programs developed regarding this issue was the program of patronate upbringing. The program pursues the following goals:

- Providing an opportunity for assistance to a child as an alternative to institutionalization;

- Find a family for a child that would become a source of support and assistance in upbringing;

- Decrease the number of institutionalized children;

- Provide for continuity in planning of a child's future;

- Provide more individualized approach and attention to a child.

Over the last 6 years the Buckner Foundation is involved in the program of patronate upbringing in Russia.

According to an agreement with the Russian Federation Department of Education the Buckner Foundation along with Christian Solidarity around the World Foundation and governments of several Russian provinces (Moscow, Vladimir, Kaliningrad etc.) is working on establishing a regional model of patron family using foreign experiences and adjusting those to Russian reality.

The development of patronate upbringing started in various countries of the world in the 20th century, especially after the end of World War II. Throughout the first post-war decades the development of this form of upbringing allowed closure of large children's homes almost everywhere. Family upbringing appeared to be much cheaper for the states' budgets and more suitable to the needs of children.

Family-type homes (USA). The Federal laws "Assistance in Fostering" and "Act for Providing Child Care" (1980) took into account children's needs for stability and continuity. It allowed for the placement of children outside a family home for a term not exceeding 18 months. Upon this term's expiration a decision has to be made which family would undertake responsibility for a child's upbringing. If no rehabilitative progress is seen in a child's biological family, it would be recommended to place him or her with a patron family.

This decreased the terms of a child's stay in family-type homes. Biological parents gained wide support in order for their children to finally come back to their families. The children were placed not far from home to allow the biological parents to participate in the everyday life of their child more frequently and to a larger extent. The financing has been extended to place children whose placement back into their biological families appeared to be impossible into a more advantageous environment. As a result 75% of children were returned to their biological parents while the other 25% were placed into advantageous family environments.

Patronate in Great Britain. The Children Act was adopted in the UK in 1989. It included the following principles:

- It is only the biological family that is capable of providing a child with an opportunity for maximum development and welfare;

- Recognition of unconditional priority of biological parents for parental rights. The parents have the right to keep their parental rights even if their child is placed outside of home;

- The government authorities, foster parents and others providing child's upbringing outside of home have a legal responsibility to provide for a child's communications with biological parents or relatives;

- The government authorities have to work in cooperation with biological parents and establish such sort of cooperation;

- The biological parents have a right to participate in the process of making decisions on assisting a child since this kind of partnership is an effective way of achieving progress in the development of a child during his or her stay outside of a home;

- A family of relatives or friends has a priority during a process of a child's placement; if this becomes impossible a foster family is located for a child;

- If a child is brought up outside of home some active measures must be taken to bring him or her back into a biological family;

- The main responsibility of all authorities responsible for assistance to a child and family is making up a program of individualized measures that would provide for achievement of child's welfare and development;

■ A child's opinion must be taken into account when deciding upon all kinds of issues related to planning of his or her life.

A foster family is a family providing conditions for upkeep and care of a child, "who represents a responsibility of local authorities". According to The Children Act the family does not receive parental responsibility with respect to a child (it is shared by parents and local authorities), but receives responsibility "to act according with reasonable necessity to protect and provide care for a child".

Patronate in Sweden. There are certain institutions in Sweden where trainers with higher education (usually teachers and psychologists) create advantageous family conditions for children aged from several weeks to 12 years. Social support services send the children that have difficult relationships within their own families into these institutions. If the parents, who for different reasons neglected their children, insulted their dignity and abused them begin to realize their mistakes and feel remorseful about what was happening, then children can be returned to the family after 8 weeks. As for those remaining in the institutions, the staff creates for them the home-like environment – common dinners, TV watching, games, holidays etc. Each child has his own room and his friends and classmates may visit him. The children attend regular schools and kindergartens. If it's still impossible to establish normal relationships between parents and children, a child may be temporarily transferred in care of a new family, which signs an annual contract. The preference is given to the families having their own children. After a year the biological parents may get their children back. Moreover, they can visit their children throughout the year. (This is something new, before recently any contacts between biological parents and children were strictly limited.)

Patronate in Russia. The term 'patronage' appeared for the first time in 1936 and is directly connected with the Decree by the All-Russian Central Executive Committee and Russian Soviet Federative Socialist Republic Council of People's Commissars 'On transferring Children for Upbringing (Patronate) to Working Families'.

In 1942 37,490 children were in the patronate system. According to the official data 678,000 children in Russia had no parents at the end of WWII. 41% of them (278,000) were brought up in foster families.

In 1943 the patronate upbringing was for the first time included into the USSR legislation. It was then that the People's Commissariat of Education had adopted a Decree that set up the guidelines for this type of guardianship when the responsibility for a child is divided between the government, the patron family and biological parents. Unfortunately, the patronate was subsequently substituted for the system of guardianship.

The development of patronate system in Europe was gradual. The **first stage** of this development coincided with the post-war reforms. The goal was set to transfer children from institutions into the families as soon as possible. There was an opinion that only appropriate, i.e. little and healthy children may be placed into the families. Payments for childcare were very low since it was considered that the patrons take care of children because of love and not for money. Nobody was assisting these families. They were considered substitute families for the child's own and had to assume all parental responsibilities. The biological parents were almost completely removed from the child care process. During that period of time a lot of children were transferred into different families. However, due to lack of assistance and proper selection process the issue of incompatibility was arising, so the children had to be moved from one family to the next.

The second stage of the patronate development began when it became obvious that some prevention work with biological parents is needed, otherwise, the government assistance would turn into a conveyer for transferring children. The practice has shown that the number of children taken away from their biological parents may be decreased and the time for finding a patron family may be shortened if certain amount of work is conducted with biological parents. For this reason they would need more understanding and sympathy. The social patronate was also established within children's own families. New difficult tasks arose before the patron trainers – providing care for very difficult children that had to be taken away from those families that could not be helped in any way. Thus, there appeared a need to teach the patron trainers. The government social worker was a single person making decisions and bearing full responsibility for the fate of a child, biological parents and patron trainers, as it used to be during the previous stage.

The third stage is associated with the beginning of placement of handicapped children and adolescents with behavioral problems into the families. There existed an earlier opinion that the patron trainers are incapable of taking care of this types of children, though the orphanage personnel was considered to be capable of this. The practice of placement of this type of children into the families caused the need to develop new approaches to interaction with these trainers and providing assistance to them. The practice of signing written agreements and labor contracts has been introduced. For the first time the patron parents started receiving salaries as well as child care payments. Biological parents and adolescents were viewed as equal business partners.

The fourth stage refers to the stage when labor of patron trainers became professional. The relationships between social workers and patron trainers have become normal working relationships.

The fifth stage. Right until the end of 1970s the consequences of guardianship were not taken into account by the children protection services, i.e. what happens with those young people when the government officially stops taking care of them and they leave their placement families (usually at the age of 18 or earlier). In England 86% of children that had been taken away from the families with anti-social way of living and due to it would come back to their parents. As the result the majority of them would become either street people, or drug addicts, or criminals. In some countries the new requirement of remaining 'a relative' for young people after the age of 18 has been introduced for the patron trainers. The need to develop a payment system for this work (at least up to the age of 23) is now recognized in a lot of countries.

The sixth stage is using patron trainers to reestablish child's relationship with his biological family in order to preserve the family. In many countries the so called 'patron families in assistance to biological parents' exist as a logical continuation of evolution of the role of patronate system aimed at preservation of a child's own family. Nobody can deny the need for professional patron training at this stage.

The above-mentioned description of evolution of the system of patronate care in the world is worth knowing and will probably help to overcome existing stereotypes. It is not necessary to start from the very beginning, it is possible to use the experience already gained and develop the working system that would satisfy the interests of children and their families to a maximum degree.

6.2. The Development of System of Patronate Upbringing in Modern Conditions

In Y.Y.Chepurnykh's (2002) opinion, today when the number of children left without parental care is increasing annually and the number of institutionalized children is close to 250,000, an assumption that family is the best place for normal life and development of a child becomes very acute.

Russian and foreign legislation announced family placements of children requiring government care as a priority. Thus the main goals nowadays are the following:

- Placement of a child not in an institution, but in a foster family;

- Professional assistance and support to a family so that a child could remain with parents.

The patronate upbringing represents a new flexible form of a child's placement into a family and assistance to problem families that helps to resolve the main issue of **how to preserve a child for a family and a family for a child.**

In 1994 some Russian professionals formed a working group under sponsorship of Moscow Christian Solidarity Foundation - The Center for education and Research of Children welfare Issues. The goal of this group was development of the model for reforms of the system of guardianship and foster care in the Russian Federation on the basis of unconditional recognition of value of a family, primarily biological family for upbringing of a child.

Children's home #19 "Our Family" was established for this purpose in Moscow, which represents the first children's home in Russia for patronate upbringing.

Russian Federation Department of Education signed several agreements with provincial governments in Vladimir, Kaliningrad, Perm and other provinces to execute projects of patronate upbringing using assistance of American and British colleagues. An interesting experience was obtained as a result that led to new analysis and development of a new model of patronate upbringing with its main principles, methods and techniques.

6.2.1.   Main Provisions of the Russian Patronate Upbringing Model

Here are the main provisions of the new model (cited from M.F.Ternovskaya, A.Z.Dugayeva, N.P.Ivanova, V.I.Lopatina, 2000).

First, the number of children, whose legal protection and interests are represented by departments of guardianship and fostering, is increasing. Along with orphans they would now include family children or children in trust of some legal representative **that require government protection.** These are those children who reside with the families, but are not provided (or insufficiently provided or unable to achieve in given conditions) the level necessary for their normal living without assistance from local authorities.

The second element of the new model is introduction of a system of **social patronate over children (family)** that require government assistance. A family with a child requiring government protection gets a personal patron trainer to provide necessary assistance in upbringing of a child and rehabilitation of a family. This work may be performed through a specialized social patronate institution. This might either be a new established institution or an already existing institution for orphans (children's home, an orphanage or a boarding school) that would change the range of its activities.

As of now the legal basis for introduction of the system of social patronate child care in Russian Federation is Article 64 of the Family Code of the Russian Federation, which provides that "the parents shall not have the right to represent the interests of their children if the government child care body has established that there is a conflict of interests between parents and children. In case of existence of such conflict of interests the government child care body shall appoint a representative to protect the rights and interests of children". The Family Code of the Russian Federation does not provide any guidelines for appointment of such representative. However, it follows from the above cited Article that a representative does not substitute a parent whose parental rights have not been taken away. He shall perform the duties of a supervisor as to the child's rights being protected within a family. In some situations he or she also undertakes all necessary kinds of assistance to protect the rights and interests of a child under the conditions of all parties' mutual agreement.

The third element of the model is development of a **program on protecting rights of a child**. It represents a regulation of a local authority on fostering and guardianship that establishes the list of measures to provide for execution of legal rights and interests of a child requiring government protection, as well as the time frame of their execution and division of responsibilities while executing a program between all parties participating in the process of upbringing and care for a child. After a program is developed and approved by the Committee on protection of rights of children (consisting of representatives of various authorities directly working with a child and possessing all information needed) a regular control over its execution is established.

The fourth element of the model is **distribution of fostering and guardianship authority between various representatives** of local authority that would be responsible for performing the tasks of a program (in reality, this authority is a local department of education or department of social welfare or department on motherhood and children, which does not change the essence of the matter since all issues of fostering and guardianship are normally a responsibility of one or several professionals in protection of children's rights). All workload on fostering and guardianship may be distributed between these professional and other responsible services.

The fifth element of the model is an **establishment (or re-orientation) of an institution that would be representing patronate care.** This is an institution where children requiring government protection stay, receive training and get prepared for placement into families. Its functions also include search for, selection and training of patron parents, assistance in upbringing and rehabilitation of children living with biological and patron parents and still requiring government protection.

The principal of an institution calculates an average personnel salary as per each child in care and within the salary fund available. This gives an opportunity to hire and execute a labor contract with a trainer for each of the children in care of an institution.

A patron trainer accepts a child into a family, is responsible for a child's life and health, has to abide by the regulations of a child's home and decisions of its medical, psychological and educational council and takes care of a child under a supervision of the institution's professionals and under control of its special social service.

In order to solve the tasks mentioned above a specialized service consisting of social workers, psychologists and teachers is established within an institution.

The sixth element is **distribution of rights and duties on protection of legal interests of a child.**

It has traditionally been the case (also supported by the legislation in effect, including Article 123 of the Family Code of the Russian Federation) that legal interests of a child may be represented only by his or her parents, adopted parents, guardians, trustees, foster parents or by representatives of an institution if a child is in this institution's care. Until a child is placed into a family or an institution, representation of his or her legal rights is performed by the social welfare authority.

Placement of a child into a family or an institution means transfer of legal representation rights in regard of this child to this family or an institution. After such transfer the social welfare authority may only exercise superfluous interference into the conditions of living and upbringing of a child (for instance, by semi-annual check-ups of children in care). If children are placed into an institution this means the end of any supervision of social welfare authority over them.

This approach is unacceptable within the framework of a new model. A definition of distribution of rights and responsibilities on protection of rights and legal interests of children in need of government protection is introduced for efficient protection of such rights and interests, which means distribution of duties on legal representation of child's interests between an institution, biological parents (effective legal representatives of a child) and patron parents.

The decision on distribution of rights and responsibilities on protection of legal rights and interests of a child is made by the head of the local government acknowledging a child as the one requiring government protection or other legal regulations establishing legal status of a child as the one left without parental care.

The program on protecting children's rights establishes the actual boundaries of distribution of rights and duties in protecting legal rights and interests of a child between biological parents (effective legal representatives of a child), patron parents and an authorized institution.

The seventh element of the model is represented by the **Committee on protecting children's rights** ("The Committee"). The Committee is headed by a professional in the area of child protection. The main task of the Committee is approval of a program on protecting children's rights (prepared by the relevant service or an institution), making necessary changes and conditions in this program after analyzing the results of check-ups of living conditions, upbringing and development of a child in need of government protection by a relevant service. The Committee considers and reconsiders a program of children's rights protection with respect to each minor in need of government protection.

Professionals in protecting children's rights are the permanent members of the Committee. The other Committee members are invited for each individual case consideration if their participation is needed. They represent professionals from institutions of education, health care, social welfare, police, as well as from educational, health care, social welfare and police authorities, mostly those who have had direct contact with a child and are capable of providing relevant information about him or her an participate in making a decision relating to this child.

The eighth element of the system is **control** of a relevant authority **over the state of development of a child in need of government protection.**

The difference of this type of control from traditional check-ups of children in care is in controlling the progress of implementation of a program on children's rights protection and not just a routine check-up living conditions and upbringing. This type of control includes checking the health of a child, his or her mental development, self-conscience, relations within a family, child's appearance and hygiene, his or her emotional and behavioral development and skills of taking care of oneself.

Here is the list of major terminology of the new model of family childcare.

Patronate is providing the necessary assistance to the children that need government protection, which is done in the forms of patronate childcare or social patronate.

Social patronate is assistance provided to a child living in his own family by the government child care body since the need for such assistance has been established.

Patronate childcare is care for a child needing government protection in a family of a patron trainer.

Thus, the modern definition of patronate childcare may look the following way:

Patronate child care is providing of the necessary assistance in care and protection of rights for a child living with his own family, a form of family living for a child with mandatory redistribution of responsibilities for protection of his or her rights and legal interests between parents (legal representatives of a child), government child care body or an institution providing the patronate care.

The main sense of patronate child care lies in an agreement on partner relationships and close interaction of patronate child care and a child with the government child care body that has referred a child for patronate care. The patron trainer does not receive all parental rights; as part of these rights goes to the government body that referred a child to a patron trainer.

The goal of the patronate childcare is providing for the childcare within families of those children that need government protection.

The status of the patronate family can be characterized by the following: a child remains as an orphanage client and is provided for with food and clothing according to the orphanage's rations while at the same time he or she is transferred into a family according to a contract. The orphanage retains the right to legal representation of a child and its psychologist, social worker and other teachers and medical workers continue to perform their duties in respect to a child, participate in his or her upbringing and protection of his or her rights.

The orphanage retains its rights as a legal guardian of a child while the patron trainers become responsible for his or her life and health. The trainer and the institution sign a contract specifying the areas of responsibility for protection of a child's rights.

The patronate childcare is different from the other forms of transferring children to the families; in particular it differs from foster care and guardianship.

Foster care and guardianship mean complete transfer of responsibilities in children's rights protection and legal representation of his or her interests. The foster care transfer of responsibilities is limitless in time, and guardianship lasts until the age of 18. The transfer is done only for the children whose legal status is clear. The guardianship can be established also for the children without clear legal status; however, no childcare payments are made.

The foster family receives all legal rights to a child in accordance with the contract that establishes the terms and conditions of child care payments. Only those children whose legal status is clear may be transferred to foster families.

The trainer of the home group of children cared for by institutions of social rehabilitation and orphanages of the Department of labor and social development, does not receive all the rights to a child and the term that he or she gets a child for is limited by the term of a child's care at the orphanage (half a year as a rule). The law also does not provide for clear division of responsibilities between such a trainer and an institution.

As compared to the above mentioned forms of family placement the patronate care is the most flexible form since

- This form is applicable for placement of the children with and without established legal status;

- The term of patronate care is established taking into account the exact needs of a child and varies widely;

- There is a strict division of responsibilities of the parties – an institution (a service), a patron and a biological parent in the case of social patronate over a family as a whole – with respect to protection of a child's rights.

One of the distinctive features of patronate is that the people who care for a child are considered to be working. They receive a salary and social guarantees. In fact this is a 24-hour job on adapting to life in society of those children who have experienced violence, are lacking in their development, can not service themselves and do not know the rules of life in the society. It is difficult to live with and care for such a child. One needs to possess a lot of patience, skills, and experience and, of course, love.

6.2.2.   The Types of Patronate Upbringing

Patronate care is available to different categories of children needing government protection. The priority is given to restoring a child's care in his biological family if there is an opportunity of bringing him or her back there. Then in preparation, a child is transferred to a patronate family for a short period of time. If after such a period a child's biological family is capable of his or her upbringing, a child is returned into his or her family. If this opportunity does not exist a child's placement into the patronate family is for the long-term. In those cases when there is no hope for restoration of the biological family and the parental rights of the biological family are taken away, a child may be adopted by a patronate family.

There are several types of patronate care based on the experience of foreign foster families and actual needs of children who need governmental protection.

There are the following types of patronate care based on its term:

- Emergency care for a period from one day to one month;

- Short-term care for a period from one to six months;

- Long-term care for a period of over six months;

- Periodic care for a couple of days, for the weekends, during the vacation time.

There are the following types of patronate care based on its goals:

- Emergency care for small children as an alternative to children's homes;

- Placement into a patronate family with the purpose of future adoption;

- Placement of handicapped children into a patronate family;

- Placement of orphans or schoolchildren with behavioral problems, i.e. those children for whom a patronate family is the only way to spend their lives in family environment;

- Placement of adolescents with the goal of transition for after-orphanage adjustment and preparation to independent life.

Whatever type of care would dominate depends on the social situation in the region, i.e. on the type of malfunctioning families and opportunities for care to such families, as well as on the demands and abilities of those families that desire to become patronate families. The primary form of patronate care is long term care or care with the purpose of future adoption. The main reason for this is the absence of institutions that would detect malfunctioning families at the early stages of the malfunction's development, as well as the services that would get involved into the process of rehabilitation of those families. The existing services are providing care only for the children that were taken out of the families already completely broken down. The rehabilitation of these families is practically unreal, and the children have no opportunity to return to their biological parents. For this reason these children are placed into patronate families until their age of maturity.

Due to the fact that adoption and fostering are more common and understandable types of care in our society, the majority of candidate parents are willing to take a child into their families for a long-term, meaning "forever". The majority views an idea of short-term placement quite negatively, especially if it means a child's return into his or her biological family.

There is also a practice of placement of adolescents and handicapped children. The process of finding patron families is not easy in these cases. In case of handicapped children the family that is ready to accept such a child is found first, after that the family is researched and prepared and only then a child is legally placed into the family. To illustrate a connection of different types of patronate placement with social and psychological image of candidates to be patron families we give the main principles that those willing to become patron parents put down into their applications.

The reasons for becoming a patron parent.
Religious. I want to become a patron mother since providing charity is a duty of each Christian. If I am going to provide care for poor children who nobody needs I will enter heaven with a star (crown) upon my head.

Peer for own children. I have two adolescent sons, my daughter is eight, and she always wanted to have a sister. I would like to become a patron mother of a girl of a similar age, so that they could play together.

To have one's own company. Our children have grown up, and now when my husband is retired, he's got plenty of free time, which he would like to spend with someone. We would like to take care of an 8-9 year old boy; so that my husband could take him out to football games or to do some work together in the garage.

As a substitute for a child who has passed away. Our daughter Linda would be three this month. She died in an accident last fall. She was a beautiful child, and nobody could be compared to her. However, we feel a need to love somebody and would be willing to help another child, a girl aged from one to three.

A substitute for a handicapped child. Our son is six. He attends a special school since he can't talk and do what the children of his own age can. We thought that if we take a child of his age under patronate, our child would observe how the normal children behave.

A substitute for grown up children. Our house became empty after the youngest of my five children had graduated from high school. All our children had been good, everybody had loved them and they had been excellent students with no problems. We would like to take care of someone else again now.

Adoption. We don't have children, and it is practically impossible. Since we want to have a child very much we see patronate care as the best choice. We can't wait until we'll be able to adopt somebody.

Helping other family. There are a lot of articles in the media about suffering children and broken down families. I would like to know if there is any support in place for those families. I would like somehow to help a family and society. Someone must take care of those children. Why not me?

To make a family bigger. We always wanted to have a big family; however, we can't afford to have more than two children of our own when the cost of living constantly goes up these days. The patronate care gives us an opportunity to make our family bigger without any additional financial burden.

Financial reasons. Our children are little and I can't work outside my house. We think that patronate care is a good way to help orphan children and provide an additional family income.

Protection. I think I'll never understand those people who abuse their own children. I would like to become a patron parent because somebody's got to help the poor children.

6.2.3.   Psychological Preparation of a Child to Family Placement

Children left without parental care experience a double trauma. On one hand, it was the negative life experience and bad attitude from biological parents; on the other hand, it is the very fact of being deprived of a family. As a result children experience delayed development and problems with behavioral adjustment, as well as destruction of deep social and emotional connections and the very ability to further establish those connections.

Thus, the job of a psychologist is to evaluate and provide for compensation from the consequences of these traumatic experiences of a child. There consists four consequential stages for this:

1) preliminary stage;

2) preparation to placement into a family;

3) placement into a patron family;

4) working with a child placed into a patron family

1.   Preliminary stage.

It includes getting to know a child and evaluation of social and medical information in determination of the problem areas.

Observation of a child's behavior in various situations (communications with known and unknown adults and peers, analysis of playing and productive activities, testing) - all of these allow to indicate individual psychological features of a child. Also it allows for defining the nature of his or her problems. Subsequent evaluation of child's needs and tasks of a corrective program allow making a conclusion on the possibility of pursuing this particular case. (Refusal to pursue a case is possible if serious psychological or social problems are discovered, i.e. child's attachment to criminal environment.) Social rehabilitation would be required then first. However, cases of refusal are quite rare, and normally all information gathered serves to develop a preliminary program of assisting a child and choice of those responsible (leading social worker and psychologist).

2.   Preparation to placement into a family.

At this stage a child is placed into a **rehabilitation group** - a family-type group that includes two permanent trainers of a children's home (a husband and a wife living with children) and 10 to 12 children.

Children may have personal problems of all kinds upon admission into a family-type group:

- social (behavioral problems);

- psychological (emotional and mental problems);

- physical (delays in development, psychosomatic problems)

Idealization of one's biological family while missing it leads to self-accusations, distrust to new trainers and outbursts of aggression or lack of communication. Transferring of past traumatic experiences into this new environment seems to provoke bad attitude and all of this is characteristic of children during the period of adjustment in a children's home.

Rehabilitative factors in children's home conditions:

- **atmosphere of care and continuity established by children's home trainers;**

- **specialized therapeutic and social assistance:**

- assistance in understanding of time continuity (past-present-future) in order to preserve positive experiences and reevaluate negative ones;

- assistance in resolving emotional reaction problems aimed at self-acceptance;

- correction of problem of bad grades at school and lack of certain kinds of knowledge;

- assistance in obtaining skills of reflection and self-control etc

- **program on protecting rights and interests of a child** (main problems and needs, social and legal issues);

- **contacts with biological family** - whether they are applicable and possible

The main goal in preparing a child to life in a patron family is to create some convictions in a child regarding his or her past, the reasons for being moved and future prospects. It is also very important to help a child understand that what happened is not at all their fault.

3.   Placement into a patron family.

Potential patron parents are selected and prepared. Specific needs of a child (his or her background) as well as expectations and opportunities of potential patron parents are considered in the process of selection. Placement of a child is done in accordance with an individual program that is jointly developed by all participants of the project. This program may be corrected in the process of its implementation, but its main idea is in its gradual nature allowing for time to get acquainted and used to each other.

These are the usual consequential steps:

- acquaintance of potential trainers with the children's backgrounds, who in professional opinion are internally ready to be placed into a substitute family (criteria - level of adjustment, decrease of emotional stress and desire of a child)

- discussion and approval of an option and immediate plans;

- personal acquaintance with a child, short-term common activities: walks, visits of theater or a movie theater etc.;

- child's visits to a family over the weekend;

- living in a potential patron family during school vacation time;

- placement into a family for three months under a signed agreement;

- permanent agreement with trainers on placement of a particular child into this family

Psychologists keep in constant touch with a potential patron family and the child throughout the whole process of acquaintance.

At first both a child and potential trainers desire to speed up the process of placement, they experience a preliminary effect of mutual attachment (based on a need in love and expectations), idealization and a kind of euphoria. It is important for professionals not to get caught by this mood and strictly adhere to all consequential steps since a break-up in relationships at the stage of getting acquainted is less stressful for a child than his or her return from a new family would be.

4.   Working with a child placed into a patron family.

The experience of psychologists of children's home #19 in the City of Moscow shows that the process of adjustment of a child to a new family lasts approximately a year and may be conditionally divided into three stages.

The first stage may be called **Idealized expectations** for both a child and patron parents. Each side is full of hope and tries to get liked or accepted by the other. The difficulties of real relations destroy an ideal image in approximately one month and the first crisis may occur. A child is still attached to an old family while there is still no attachment to a new one, adjustment to new demands and regulations require considerable effort, which results in conflicts that represent a part of normal gradual process of adjustment of family and child to each other. In consideration of this psychologists and social workers keep active contacts with a patron family leveling the stress down and providing support for both adults and a child.

The next stage may be called **Fitting in** and represents an adjustment. It includes getting used to the boundaries of what is allowed, getting used to mutual needs and rules of behavior, individual features and habits. The main achievement of this stage that lasts a little bit less than a year is development of **mutual trust and subjective feeling of permanent nature of relationships** from both sides, which begin to realize themselves as a single entity. Many people start getting an understanding that a patron family represents a special type of a family that is different from a biological one, but no less real. Thus, some kind of **Equilibrium** is achieved, which represents a third stage of relationship in a patron family. During this stage a family becomes relatively independent and requires less assistance from professionals. During the first months psychologist contacts a family each week, later on - each month, then, after one year , a semi-annual appointment is usually enough (in case of need patron parents call professionals on their own).

Professional duties of a psychologist of the children's placement service:

- Consultations for social workers in the training groups,
- Organization of training,
- Evaluation of applications from future patron parents,
- Consultations for future and existing patron parents,
- Family consulting for the families of patron parents,
- Participation in discussions when a family for an individual child is selected,
- Training for the existing patron parents,
- Training for the children's homes personnel,
- Participation in conferences, seminars and other activities,
- Techniques development

6.3. Principles and Techniques of Organization of Patronate Care

6.3.1. A Patron Family

Patronate care gives families a unique opportunity to have a child who needs to be in a family environment in their home. Pre-schoolers requiring placement outside of their own family are usually placed in a patron family except for those cases when family environment can make matters worse for them. School age children may also be placed into a patron family if they are capable to establish close relationships needed for family living and if their behaviors do not require any types of limitations.

Who may obtain assistance?

Patronate care may be provided for any child who is in need of living separately from his or her own family since the time of birth and either until 18 years of age or the age of graduating from high school. Candidates must satisfy the requirements of being able to establish close relationships needed for family living and being able to cooperate with members of patron family. The decision to place a child into a patron family is based upon necessity only and is not associated with race, ethnicity, religious or political views or economic status of a child. The following children may not be placed into a patron family:

- those requiring psychiatric assistance;

- with uncontrollable behaviors;

- those representing a threat to themselves and others;

- those addicted to psychoactive substances

The Choice of a Patron Family

The chief determining factor in the choice of a patron family is the needs of a child. Based on information regarding a child a family is chosen that corresponds to his or her needs the most. The correspondence of a family to the needs of a child is determined based on the following:

- To place together children originating from the same family, or if it is not possible to provide for their relationships through mutual visits and common activities;

- To place a child into a patron family that resides close to his or her biological family if the biological parents' have not lost parental rights under the law;

- To place a child into a patron family that corresponds to his or her needs the most;

- Not to place two children requiring professional care into one family, if this family has at least two minor children of its own, except when other reasons exist for such placement, for instance, joint placement of brothers and sisters.

Principles of Selection of Patron Families

Preliminary selection is conducted over the phone and by interviewing. In order to be considered as a candidate a family must have the following qualifications:

- Be interested in working with children selected by the service.

- Be interested in providing temporary care for these children.

- The patron parents must be legally married for no less than three years.

- The candidates must not be younger than 23.

- The candidates must have a university or a vocational school degree.

- The candidates must respect religious views of a child and be ready to participate in various religious activities of children.

If a candidate qualifies with respect to the above he or she is offered an information package that contains the following information:

- An application form where the information needed has to be filled in

- A copy of the 'Principles of the program of patronate care'. The list of required documents: results of tuberculosis testing, confirmation of vaccination of family pets, results of the fire and sanitary inspections, floor plan of a house, police records of candidates. The other documents that may be required during the process of application review: birth certificate, marriage certificate, conscription papers etc.

An Application Review Process

An application for patronate care review process begins after it is submitted to a children's home.

A potential patron family has to be willing to undergo a special training course for patron families. Throughout participation in the course and visits to a family and interviews with its members an assessment of a family is done and it is decided whether it has the qualifications necessary for patronate care. The patronate care study materials make possible an understanding between a family and the service. The training course includes role-playing and discussions of actual situations that can arise in a life of a patron family. The candidates are given an opportunity to express their opinion and feelings on all the issues discussed. The families are offered to evaluate their abilities and their need for support when working in the following fields:

- Child's protection and care.

- Development assistance to a child, paying attention to any lack of development.

- Providing for continuation of a child's relations with his biological family.

- Establishment of close ties with children that must remain the same over the lifetime.

- Interactions with other participants of patronate care.

To be approved as a patron family the family itself and the children's home must make sure that the candidate family satisfies the above demands.

This is also established through preliminary training and through communications with other candidates. This all helps a family to correctly evaluate its abilities. During training the service representative also has an opportunity to evaluate whether candidates have the following qualities:

- Responsibility and emotional stability, good character and reputation. (Children's home representative makes an assessment of these qualities through an estimate of candidate's life achievements, their relations with others and references information. If there are reports that the candidate family has ever been suspect in using violence or neglecting children, if any of the family has a criminal record or is currently a defendant in a criminal case their application will not be further considered).

- Physical health and energy to be able to take care of a child. (Children's home representative makes an assessment of these qualities based on the current health condition, negative results of tuberculosis testing and the style of everyday life of a family).

- Ability to form and sustain normal relationships with other people. (These qualities are evaluated based on information about spousal relations, relations with children, other relatives, as well as with friends and acquaintances).

- Communicability and ability to solve problems. (These qualities are assessed based on the candidate's behavior during the training course). Any additional information may be obtained from candidates regarding the methods they use in problem solving, as well as about their experiences, views and perception of the process of care provision, their childhood memories, relationships with parents, including case of violence and neglect and ways of resolving those issues.

- Necessary financial resources to bear additional expenses of having one more child in their family. The patron family must have sufficient income of its own. It can't count on the support provided for patronate care or government assistance. (Children's home representative assesses financial ability of candidates based on income information provided and while discussing the future expenses associated with a child's placement into a family).

The criteria of selection of patron parents should not be formal, excluding the presence of criminal records and transferable diseases, since each child presents a special case and needs a family that would be suitable only for him or her. For instance, an adolescent girl who has suffered from sexual violence may not be placed into a family where there is a man; she needs a single-woman family. Some cases require mature women who may act like grandmothers.

6.3.2.   Principles of Children's Placement in Care

Parents or guardians in respect of those children who may successfully function in a family-type or similar environment submit an application for patronate care. A child must be ready to establish close ties that are needed for living within another family.

The patronate care program provides for planned and emergency placement of children. Emergency placement is required when a) a child is in danger or b) is left without parental care and any other means of subsistence and supervision. In all other cases the process of planned placement works. It includes an assessment of future living conditions of a child and a development of a plan for assistance and care within the time framework that satisfies the minimal requirements.

Except for the cases of emergency placement children are placed into patron families only after an application is filled out by parents or legal guardians and after all the required paperwork, including physical and vaccination reports, birth certificate, school grade card, a copy of the court order establishing guardianship and a copy of psychiatric, medical, educational and psychological evaluation results (if they exist), is supplied. *A written psychiatric and psychological report is required during the process of placement of children in need of special care.*

The reports must be dated no more than six months prior to children's placement and must contain a diagnosis and future prognosis for a child.

Preparation of parents by the patronate service (children's home)

After a family is approved for patronate placement of a child an agency's representative starts working with the family on a plan for preparation. The time needed for the preparation process varies depending on the needs of patron parents and a child.

Placement of children into families

It is essential that parents or a legal guardian prepare a child before his or her placement into a family. Information given to a child must be accurate and truthful. A child must understand why he or she needs to be isolated from his or her parents, where they are going to be and for how long it will be required for them to reside separately, how often they would see each other and what must happen before their family is reunited. In case the patronate placement is temporary he or she must be informed on when his or her fate will be determined finally.

An agency representative assists in preparing a child for placement into a family by providing him or her with information on patron parents, as well as on methods and principles for his or her care. In case of an emergency placement at least one visit to a family is required. It is preferable to have at least two visits. The first-time meeting should be held on a neutral ground for child and patron parents just to get acquainted. The second meeting should be held at the house where a child would be living, so that he or she can obtain some information regarding the family and its rules of living.

Individual Assistance Plan

An individual assistance plan or a plan of work with each child is composed to provide assistance in patronate care. It includes the following items:

- Physical development and health.

- Family relations.

- Education.

- Social development.

- Emotional, psychological and spiritual development.

- Behavior.

- Skills of independent living that are age appropriate.

- Entertainment.

Financial Reimbursement for Patron Parents

Patron parents receive financial reimbursement for the needs of a child they are taking care of. This reimbursement may not be considered as an additional source of income for patron parents.

A patron family is going to receive money in rubles that is an equivalent of US$100 for one child and an equivalency of US$50 for each additional child placed into a family. The payments cease if a child is taken out of a patron family.

Taking a Child out of a Patron Family

Patronate care is needed to develop a feeling of self-respect and improve a child's opinion about themselves. One of the main goals of care for older children is development of skills for independent adult living. That is why interaction with children is conducted in many directions to achieve successful preparation towards independent living. Unfortunately, sometimes it becomes necessary to take a child out of a patron family in the following situations:

- A child becomes dangerous for him- or herself and others,

- A child needs drug addiction treatment,

- A child needs a level of care and upbringing that exceeds abilities of a patron family,

- A child escapes from a patron family.

Family Support Services

A representative working with a child is responsible for planning and implementing a support plan for family and child. Subsequently, ongoing contacts between a child, patron parents and a representative are mandatory. If there is a need in additional contacts in order to resolve arising problems and providing support etc., they can be arranged over the telephone.

The frequency of visits and telephone contacts is determined by the needs of a child. The scheduling of visits is determined by an agreement that is signed during the time of placement of a child into a patron family.

Communications with the children's home representative can be established 24 hours a day over the weekdays and weekends if an emergency situation arises. The children's home principal provides to the patron parents the contact phone numbers and the phone number of a person on duty.

The children's home conducts weekly inspections. The patron family has to adhere to all regulations for patron family that are currently in existence. A copy of regional regulations is provided to parents for study during the preliminary period. According to these regulations a patron family has to provide the children's home personnel with all information regarding serious incidents and medical information. Besides the planned visits a patron family may be visited without prior notification. The patron parents must provide a child with constant care in accordance with the guidelines. The program of patronate care supports the creation of normal conditions for a child within the family, school and church environments. We believe that the children who are availed to a wide range of responsibilities will be better prepared for adult life from the point of view of health, abilities and responsibilities.

Contact with Biological Families

Contacts with families are encouraged except for the cases when the parental rights are taken away from biological parents or the contacts would disadvantage a child. An agency's representative coordinates parental visits and their contacts with children. The representative reviews the visitation plan monthly. The patron parents will bring a child to the place of meeting and take him or her back. Exceptions from this rule have to be arranged and approved by an agency's representative.

Contacts over the Telephone and by Mail

Children are allowed to send and receive messages (including e-mail messages) at any time except when care plan provisions are to the opposite. The child, the parents and agency's representative agrees upon all limitations. Children also have access to phone conversations with parents. A child's family rather than agency or patron parent pays the major portion of long-distance phone bill.

Contacts with Brothers and Sisters

If children originating from the same biological family may not be placed together into the same patron family an agency has to offer opportunities for regular contacts and phone conversations between the children. Such factors as distance, expenses and various limitations provide for developing of a special plan for each family. The strategy developed has to be mentioned in the individual support and care plan for a child.

6.3.3.   Education and Health Care in a Patron Family

Children from patron families attend school. They have the same rights and privileges as all other students, i.e. they can take part in all school activities, apply for vocational training, participation in extracurricular activities etc. They can use all types of special educational programs, take part in testing and be subject to research. The patron parents should keep in touch with schoolteachers to control the process of their children education and their specific needs determined by the program of upbringing.

The patron parents participate in all activities associated with children's education (admission and expulsion, parents' meetings etc.) The program of patronate care and patron parents work together in accordance to the methods and principles of a school district's work. An agency's representative acts as a liaison between school and parents to provide for efficient working relations and solution of all problems associated with education.

Attitude towards religion

It is necessary to take into account in the placement process that religious views of a family be compatible with needs and interests of a child. We believe that spiritual development and knowledge of God are essential for development of any child. Children should be encouraged to participate in church activities and other spiritual programs.

Medical and dental help

By the time of a child's placement into a patron family his or her parents or guardian should submit an application for medical and dental help for this child. Conditions of payment for medical help should be enumerated in a written permission to place a child into a patron family and signed by his or her parents or guardians.

If an institutionalized child is placed into a patron family a signed application of the principal of this institution is required to provide medical help for this child. The patron parents may use services of their family physician if a child is not already under care of a different physician. It is also necessary to agree upon a choice of a physician and a dentist with the program's agent responsible for this child. The frequency of visits to a physician and physicals depends on the child's health and is determined by a physician who has to make relevant recommendations.

The results of physicals, physician's prescriptions and recommendations, the need for and frequency of subsequent physicals must be placed in a child's personal file. Patron parents have to inform the agency on the conditions of child's health. For the exception of emergencies it is mandatory to submit a list of physician's prescriptions to the agency before acting on them. It is mandatory to ask a physician to document all types of treatment and frequency of subsequent physicals.

Moreover, the agency has to be provided with copies of all bills for medical care either for payment or for reimbursement to patron parents.

Keeping and using medications

- The patron parents have to supply a child with all medications needed, if he or she is not a participant of a program of an aided medication supply.

- All medications must be taken in accordance with instructions on their labels.

- Each prescribed medication must be kept in its own packaging having a label with child's name, the date of prescription, instructions for use and physician's name.

- All medications must be kept where they are inaccessible for children, i.e. in lockers or locked drawers etc.

- Medication must be thrown away if it expires or if a child leaves a patron family.

- Medications that are to be kept in a refrigerator must be kept there in a special compartment, separate from food.

- All medications given to a child must be prescribed by a physician. A child's personal file must contain the name of a medication, the dosage for each of them and the prescribing physician's name.

- Efficiency of medication influencing behavior and psychoactive medication, as well as the need in their further taking by a child must be assesses by a physician at least once every three months. If a child does not feel well after using a medication, or if a physician feels it to be necessary these evaluations must be conducted more often. Under no conditions medications of this kind should be used to achieve an adequate behavior of a child, even if other methods do not bring desired results.

6.3.4. The Skills of Everyday Social Communication in a Patron Family

The patronate care program is aimed at creating the most favorable conditions for a child's living within a family. Since a child's biological age does not always correspond to his or her maturity level and ability for social adjustment, the children who have demonstrated sufficient maturity and responsibility and cause a feeling of trust in them may receive some additional privileges in a form of activities commensurate with their age. These activities do not represent a required part of a child's life in a patron family, but are permitted exclusively as a privilege.

Sexual behavior commensurate with a child's age

The program of patronate care encourages and supports abstinence from philosophical, religious and educational points of view. Thus, the agency does not approve of distributing condoms, anti-abortion pills or other medication, so not to give children a reason to believe that premarital sex may take place. We believe that children in patron families should adhere to sexual abstinence. If a physician prescribes anti-abortion pills they should be treated like any other medication and used according to prescription instructions.

Use of cosmetics

Adolescent girls are usually interested in cosmetics. Any use of it must be moderate and commensurate with norms acceptable for children of a particular age. Boys should not be allowed to use cosmetics.

Piercing

Girls placed into patron families are allowed to wear earrings if their ears were pierced before that. Local authority may consider an issue of wearing earrings by boys as well. It is necessary to consider local requirements and public reaction and make decisions taking into account a child's interests. Children wanting to pierce their ears must have written permission of their parents or guardians. Piercing of any other body parts is prohibited for children placed in patron families.

Entertainment and leasure

Children placed in patron families participate in regular family entertainment along with other family members. The patron parents should account for the types of entertainment in the program of child's care and report of their effect on child's health and the degree of control during such activities. Outside entertainment include sports, visiting movie theaters, shopping, skating etc. Child's participation in entertainment activities requires certain degree of control on the part of adults unless his or her behavior does not cause any reason for doubt.

High school students are usually interested in the opposite sex and like to organize school parties. To participate in these parties a child must have achieved an age of 16 and have demonstrated an ability to independently make right decisions. Children wishing to participate in a party must inquire with the agency's representative if they are allowed to do this as a privilege. Permission to participate must be written down in a child's personal file.

Watching movies and videos

Selection of movies for watching is done with permission of patron parents.

Clothing and personal belongings

When a child is placed into a patron family he or she possesses minimal clothing. If this not so, an agency's representative responsible for this child must be warned. A representative will inform parents about the need to supply a child with clothing and make sure that this is done. Representatives of the patronate care program must ensure that children must not be deprived of the necessary supply of clothing because parents would not want to buy it for them.

Taking into account the fact those children would need new clothes during their stay with patron families a special reimbursement program for patron parents exist to compensate their expenses. They receive monies to buy clothes for children from a local budget.

Representatives of the program believe that a child's appearance and his or her self-esteem are closely connected. A person's appearance is very significant, so the choice of clothing should always be proper. Any type of clothing or hairstyle that would evidence an association with any organization or that would be perceived negatively at school, in church or in a patron family must be banned. Hair must be clean and styled in a good manner. During their stay with a patron family children are not permitted to shave their hair off or color it.

Clothing must be clean and not attracting attention. It is prohibited to wear short skirts, a bathing suit top without a blouse or a shirt (except on a beach), blouses or skirts with deep cut-outs, shirts not reaching the belt level or underwear with nothing on top of it. Clothes must not have pictures or words advertizing alcohol, tobacco, narcotic drugs, containing swear words, gang-related signs, racial slogans or other signs that may cause anger of patron parents.

Children may wear sports clothing that complies with requirements of relevant sports in their free time.

Children may bring some of their personal belongings into a patron family, for instance, toys, books, radio, player, bicycle etc. Children are not permitted to bring any furniture, TVs, pets, cars, motorcycles, firearms, knives, tobacco, narcotic drugs, indecent or pornographic materials. They are also prohibited from having posters, pins, tapes, disks etc. advertizing alcohol, tobacco, narcotic drugs, containing swear words, gang-related signs, racial slogans or other signs that may cause anger of patron parents. Neither an agency, nor patron parents are responsible for loss or breakage of personal belongings. Expensive things must be left at home until a child reaches an age when he or she would learn how to appreciate and keep his or her belongings safe. Children should be taught not to sell, lend or borrow clothing or personal belongings.

General Principles for Conducting Searches

It is important for the personnel and patron parents to respect a child's right to privacy. However, the situations may arise when this right may become secondary with respect to child's own security and security of other people and living premises. These situations usually arise with the risk of possession by a child of various dangerous and illegal items that may not be kept in the house and are not allowed to be in a child's possession. Besides those some situations may arise when it would be necessary for patron parents or a personnel representative to search a child's room, his or her belongings or him or her personally. The search process should be well thought of. It is not wise to compile a list of child's belongings or to make him or her unpacks them in the presence of patron parents or personnel. According to the methods and principles of the program the search of belongings should consist of asking a child to show the contents of his or her pockets without more serious measures that are used during searches. Since the search procedure represents an intrusion into a child's privacy it is important to undertake it with the only goal of providing his or her personal security and security of other people. In no case should the patron parents use the search procedure to intimidate or embarrass a child.

The Search Procedure

If the patron parents have reasons to believe that some dangerous or illegal objects are hidden in the house or are in a possession of a child, they need to be confiscated through the search procedure. A representative of children's home administration or an administrator on duty from the children's home is asked for permission to conduct a search. The fact of a search and its results with a list of confiscated illegal items must be mentioned in a child's personal file. A written report must be made if any illegal items are found. It is not necessary, but recommended to conduct a room search in the presence of both patron parents to provide for the safety of belongings and to prevent any accusations addressed to patron parents.

It would be rational for patron parents to allow a child to be present during the search of his or her room and personal belongings unless in their opinion it would jeopardize his or her daily routine.

The children's home principal or an agency's representative must be notified if any illegal items (such as narcotic drugs, illegal weapons etc.) are found. The principal must inform the police and confiscate those items, as well as undertake certain measures with respect to a child. If the authorities refuse to receive illegal or dangerous items they must be completely destroyed or taken out of the house while making sure that they would not be brought back there. The children's home principal writes off or destroys dangerous items and those items that do not have any significant value to be placed in safekeeping, so that they could be later returned to child's parents or guardians. Neither the principal, nor the patron parents, nor an agency's representative should be held liable for any compensation for written off or destroyed items of the above nature. All confiscated items must be mentioned in the confiscation report together with their disposal results – destroyed, placed into temporary safekeeping, and returned to parents or guardians.

Personal Search of a Child

In addition to the above principles of searches the parents must acknowledge the personal privacy rights of a child within all possible limits in a situation that may arise. Two adults belonging to the same sex conduct the personal search. An agency's representative must also be present during this procedure. The patron parents must explain the reasons of the search and how it will be conducted to a child beforehand. The patron parents should seek the child's cooperation during the process of undressing unless they believe that this cooperation would represent an obstacle to the search or may represent a risk for the others. Only clothing that represent an obstacle for visual search must be taken off.

Children's Complaint Procedures

Any child placed into a patron family has the right to make a complaint if he or she considers that his or her rights were infringed upon. A child may ask the personnel representatives not personally interested in a case to help in making a complaint.

A written response to the complaint is sent to a child by the supervisor of an agent or program with respect to whom the complaint has been made. If a child is not satisfied with the response he or she may make a written appeal the next day after receiving the response. An appeal is made to the children's home principal or to a representative of a responsible agency.

6.3.5.   The Rights and Responsibilities of Participants of Patronate Care Process

The patronate care has to provide advantageous conditions for normal development of children. Establishment of these conditions supposes cooperation between a child, a family and responsible authority.

The Rights and Duties of a Family

The patronate care is based on a conviction about priority and inviolability of a family. A family is an ideal form for complete physical, emotional, spiritual and social development of its members. It forms the relationships that are important through the lifetime. Though all families strive to achieve this ideal many of them experience difficulties in communicating with each other.

- -Members of the family have the right and duty to reside together, if no problems arise that would become obstacles to the needs satisfaction of each family member.

- Members of the family have the right and duty to communicate with each other.

- The family has a right to privacy and keeping family secrets.

- The family has a right to receive assistance from society.

The Rights and Duties of Parents

- Parents have the right and duty to provide care and upbringing for their children.

- Parents have the right and duty to make major decisions with respect to life of their children

- Parents have the right and duty to do everything possible in the interests of their children.

- Parents have the right of access to their children, the right and duty to sustain relationships with them.

The Rights and Duties of Children

- Children have the right to be in a humane and secure environment that is free from violence, neglect and exploitation. A child who knows about or suspects violence with respect to him- or herself or other children has to inform personnel, a teacher or any representative of authority about that.

- Children have the right to due upbringing, care, supervision and advice and a duty to accept and use these activities properly. Children have the right and duty to sustain relations with parents, relatives and other adults who have something to do with their fate.

- Children have the right to communicate with their brothers and sisters if those are placed into a different family or into an institution.

- Children have the right to privacy of their correspondence, to an opportunity to send and receive messages and to make telephone calls.

- Children have the right to express an informed consent or to refuse treatment or taking medications, if the procedures do not constitute a part of the main program of care, or if their rights are not limited by law or the court's decision in this respect.

- Children have the right to know about the consequences of their taking certain medications or their refusal to take them in the cases mentioned above.

- Children have the right and duty to participate in appropriate educational programs.

- Children have the right to be educated in the areas of health care, hygiene and sexual relations.

- Children have the right and duty to make decisions with respect to their religious beliefs and upbringing.

- Children have the right and duty to participate in decision-making when it influences their lives and future.

- Children have the right to participate in development and discussion of the plans for their care and obtain information regarding personnel qualifications and about those personally taking care of them.

- Children have the right to free communication within the limits established by the plan of individual care, if any limitations for their communications are documented in their personal file.

- Children have the right to express their opinion regarding their care and upbringing and may present their thoughts to the responsible personnel representative. An authority representative in each district appoints an agent who would receive complaints regarding each program or establishment. Children who submitted a written complaint must receive timely written response.

- Children have the right to obtain information regarding involuntary actions, including when they can be applied, who makes a decision to apply them and what actions are needed to get rid of the limitations.

- Children have the right to privileges and freedoms that are appropriate to their age and maturity level.

- Children have the right to personal clothing that is age and size appropriate, as well as the right of clothing choice to a certain degree.

- Children have the right to receive all necessary personal hygiene accessories and to learn personal hygiene skills.

- Children have the right to keep the monies earned or received as gift that have to be counted separately from the monies allotted by the agency to a patron family for child's care.

- Children have the right not to use personal money to pay for accommodation or food if this is not provided for in the support plan and with a written approval of their parents or guardians, as well as the placement agency.

- Children have the right to bring their personal belongings into a patron family, to have other personal belongings and to have a secure place for keeping those.

- Children have the right to non-dissemination of information about themselves. An access to this information is limited for their parents or guardians, if a child is a minor, as well as for the authorized personnel employed by the Program of patronate care, except for the cases involving violations of law.

- Children have the right to know the contents of their personal file, however, the employees of the Program do not have an official right to disclose information or provide children with data supplied by the third parties, for example, psychological reports.

- Children have the right to inviolability of their person and personal property.

The Rights of Children Must Include an Access to such Opportunities as:

- Normal personality development - sports, music, visits to various clubs etc.

- Social relations.

- Vocational training and gaining experience of business relationships.

■ Activities necessary for cultural development

The children's home and patron parents sign an agreement, which establishes in writing goals and conditions of patron care, duties of the children's home, schedule for visiting a family by a service representative and information on financial reimbursement of child care expenses.

The Rights and Duties of a Children's Home as an Authorized Agency of a System of Patronate Care

- To determine the ways and directions of their assistance and care.

- To establish if its activities satisfy the needs of individuals asking for assistance or receiving it.

- To participate in joint planning with the assisted families and other social organizations involved in working with families.

- To evaluate the needs of families, parents and children from the professional point of view and to present this information to families.

- To provide assistance within the framework of a policy conducted by a children's home in accordance with the official requirements existing in the region and taking into account the existing standards in the area of child's care.

What does children's home expect of parents and children being assisted?

Duties of parents

As people directly in care of a child patron parents bear responsibility for his or her life in a patron family. The patron parents have to do the following to provide the necessary care for children that would encourage their proper development, growth and upbringing:

- Keep their home and the surroundings according to the rules, methods and principles of the program of patronate care.

- Provide for 24-hour care and control of a child according to the requirements of the guidelines noted above.

- Participate in the process of planning of a child's placement into the family, his or her current affairs and the process of ending patronate care.

- Provide for medical and dental treatment of a child.

- Participate in annual training seminars to be aware of current requirements to patron parents.

- Follow the guidelines on childcare determined by the program of patronate care.

- Provide a child with transportation to school, physician's office and various activities etc.

- Provide the children's home principal with necessary reporting from time to time.

- Accept children for patronate care only through a children's home.

- Not to accept into a family dependents of 18 years of age and older if they are not related to patron family or children in its care.

- Not to let a child go anywhere with other people without the children's home principal's consent.

- Respect the rights of a child as determined by methods and principles of the program of patronate care.

- Respect the rights of child's parents and other family members as determined by methods and principles of patronate care.

- Obtain children's home principal's explanations in case of any misunderstanding or irregularities in the program of care.

- Inform a children's home principal of all cases of violence or abuse in respect to a child. If the principal is absent this information should be referred to his or her authorized representative.

- Provide care for a child in case of short-term absence for personal or business reasons. Never to leave a child with persons younger than 21.

- If absent for 5 hours or more and with a children's home principal's consent leave a child in care of friends, family members, other patron parents or any persons older than 21.

- Fulfill financial responsibilities with respect to childcare.

- Attend appointments and conferences on patronate care.

Duties of children:

- Cooperate with patron parents and agency's personnel.

- Obey the rules, regulations and methods of agency's work.

- Accept responsibility for one's own actions.

- Attend school, clubs and other planned activities.

- Tell interested persons of one's needs and get advice from them.

- Participate in planning of one's own future.

- Pose questions if the policies of a child's home and guidance services are not understood.

6.3.6.   Behavior Control in a Patron Family

Discipline

Many parents believe that discipline includes punishment only, although it would be more correct to view discipline as a part of the whole process of upbringing. One can figure out the state of a child based on his or her behaviors. That is why parents have to understand them correctly and react adequately without first punishing, or being rude or violent. Patron parents must show children that their inadequate behavior would always have certain consequences. The patronate care program has been developed to provide children with living in regular home conditions. In spite, however, of greater freedom that children enjoy in a family as compared to an institution their behavior must not go beyond reasonable limits and has to be fairly and attentively controlled by parents. When disciplining a child one has to take into consideration this child's personal needs, abilities, age, personality and general level of development.

When making a choice of disciplinary measures it is important to remember that many children get into a patron family from a cruel environment. Loss of some privileges, temporary isolation, change of activity, as well as encouraging good behavior may serve as examples of disciplinary measures. Use of such measures as loss of privileges, turning off the TV, refusing entertainment as a consequence of a child's bad behavior is possible only during that period of time that is necessary for a child to realize and correct his or her behavior. If temporary isolation is used as a disciplinary measure one must use the following formula to determine the length of isolation for preschoolers and children of primary school age - multiply a child's age by one minute. If bad behavior continues this should be repeated. However, when evaluating which disciplinary measure to use it is important to remember that their only goal is to improve child's behavior.

If it is necessary to temporarily isolate an adolescent it is suggested that patron parents choose the length of such isolation on their own. When children are isolated in their room for long periods of time the patron parents should periodically check their behavior and security. If children deliberately break things or steel them the best choice would be to change a patron family. If property is stolen it must be returned. A representative of the program must help parents in resolving this issue.

Physical punishment or threats of one are ABSOLUTELY UNACCEPTABLE. Since the majority of children in care have experienced violence in the past all efforts must be made to avoid cruelty in punishment. Under no conditions is it acceptable to beat, punch, slap, shake or drag a child. Patron parents must realize the necessity of a punishment to be equal to a degree of disobedience. Physical punishments may not be used in any form, including making a child stand on his or her knees, do physical exercises or accept an unnatural pose. It is prohibited to punish a child by having him or her change appearance by wearing certain type of clothing or haircut. Foods, including light foods, such as chips and chocolates should not be used either as encouragement of good behavior, or punishment for a bad one. It is prohibited to make a child perform some useless jobs like carrying stones from one pile into another, as well as cleaning a toilet. It is unacceptable to punish a child by giving medication to him or her. One of the features of children in patronate care is low self-esteem. They have experienced violence and abuse in the past and are used to see only bad in their lives. By emphasizing their abilities and good qualities one can help them realize their importance and increase self-esteem. Consequently, patron parents must try to encourage good behavior and various achievements of children in their care by expressing their approval and praise on plenty of occasions. Patron parents' disciplinary measures should be coordinated with agency's principles and may not be abusive either physically or morally. Only adult members of a patron family are allowed to criticize a child. Punishment may not be rude, cruel, unusual, belittling or offensive. One may not punish a child by prohibiting visits to other families or receiving mail. Patron parents may not threaten a child by telling him or her that they would get rid of a child if he or she would be exhibiting bad behavior. It is vital to explain a child a reason for a punishment or loss of privileges. If a child is not permitted to leave a house for more than 24 hours parents must mention this fact in his or her personal file. The main thing for the parents is to make a child understand that they want to teach him or her to respect their authority, be obedient and control his or her behavior. All these issues must be discussed between parents and service representatives. If any problems in application of disciplinary measures should arise it is important to contact a service representative responsible for this child.

Limitation of physical activity

Sometimes it might be necessary to limit physical activity of a child to avoid trauma for him- or herself or the others. It is necessary to follow the same methods of limitations used in children's home. Patron parents must be trained in these methods and demonstrate their proficiency before they would be given a right to apply them.

Limitation of physical activity may be applied only when all other security measures would have given no result. Each case must be reflected in a child's personal file in accordance with existing regulations. The full report must be placed into a personal file. When parents do not allow a little child to commit something threatening his or her life or health like playing on the road, touching a hot stove or stop his or her anger outbursts, this is considered as timely intervention and not as limitation of physical activity.

Control of a child's threatening behavior

Patron parents should regard any suicidal thoughts or threats to other people expressed by a child very seriously. Parents must convince a child that human life is valuable and unique. It is important to understand whether he or she really wants to harm him- or herself or the others and take all necessary security measures to prevent it up until the end of a critical period. Each case of aggressive or suicidal fantasies of a child must be properly reflected in his or her personal file by way of making a report. If a probability of a child harming him- or herself or the others is established it is necessary to make an immediate contact with the program's representative responsible for this child and request an opinion on a risk of suicide. If a representative or his or her supervisor is inaccessible parents should immediately contact a psychiatrist for evaluation of a possibility and a degree of risk of a suicide. At any time patron parents may demand consultation of a program's representative who is responsible for a child or an agency' representative for evaluation of the degree of risk from a child's behavior.

If a child is absent without leave

If patron parents find that a child is absent without leave they have to ask other children where, in their opinion, an absent child might be. The search must begin from those places where a child might possibly be. If a child is not found, the following measures must be taken:

- if a child is under thirteen the fact must be immediately reported to law enforcement and to the service representative

- if a child is thirteen or over a principal or a person on duty in a children's home must be informed immediately If a child is absent for more than three hours during daytime parents must report this fact to law enforcement. (If patron parents believe that a child might be in danger such a report may be made in a lesser period of time since the discovery of child's absence). If a child disappeared during nighttime and patron parents have a reason to believe that he or she left a house in order to escape the law enforcement must be informed immediately. After this it is necessary to warn a children's home principal and an agency' representative.

7

MODELS OF PATRONATE CARE

By 2002 twenty provinces of the Russian Federation got involved into the experiment of establishment of the models of patronate care. Kaliningrad, Perm, Novgorod and Altay provincial legislatures and Moscow City legislature have passed laws regulating patronate care. Similar laws have already passed through first or second readings in legislatures of four more provinces. In other provinces the experiment is done by way of reorganizing children's homes or directly by child care authorities and is subject to executive decrees of local and provincial governments.

In 2002 the Federal Department of Education included establishment of patronate care into the Federal program on orphan children. It may be currently said that the stage of experimental reorganization of orphanages into patronate system agencies is successfully completed. In the majority of 20 provinces mentioned the guidelines regulating the system of patronate care have been developed along with methods of work of relevant services.

The new principle of patronate care is transfer of authority on childcare to relevant services engaged in issues of children's rights protection, i.e. to institutions of education, social welfare and health care. During this process relevant services are established or reorganized to provide patronate care, prepare children in need of government protection for placement into a family, search for, select and train potential patron parents, assist in caring for and rehabilitation of children living with their biological parents, but still needing government protection, as well as those already placed in patron families.

Complex guidance of patron families includes diagnostics of a child's condition at various stages in life, looking for ways of overcoming problems and difficulties, as well as for efficient ways of development and socialization, development and regular reviews of the Program on protecting child's rights and organization of continuous support and assistance to a child in resolving his or her problems. The model under review has its economic advantages. Foreign experience shows that living costs for children in a patron family are 10 times less than those for institutionalized children.

One of the basic conditions for success of these models is proper education of personnel for the jobs of authorized representatives of relevant patronate care services.

7.1. The Model of Patronate Care Agency in the City of Moscow

(Children's Home #19 as an Authorized Agency of Patronate Care)

Children's home #19 in the City of Moscow became the first children's home in Russia providing patronate care. Its experience has shown that almost all children requiring permanent family placement sent to this children's home are actually placed into families. During the five years of work 160 children have been in care of this children's home, out of whom 104 children have been placed into patron families, around 30 children have been returned to their biological parents and only 3 children have been transferred to different institutions.

This was an experiment that allowed establishing a model of an agency providing patronate care and work out the main working techniques of:

- social and rehabilitation guidance services for a child and a family during a child's placement into a patron family;

- child placement services;

- methods of social patronate and child care planning

The goal of a children's home is providing for the right of a child to live and grow up in a family by placing a child into a patron family or, if possible, his or her return into a biological family, as well as assisting those families in difficult life situations, which they are unable to overcome on their own in order to perform the necessary changes and keep a child within a family (social patronate). The tasks of the children's home include execution of scientific concepts of an educational institution for children requiring government protection that performs certain duties of government placement agency in respect to children's placement into families, provides social patronate over families and protects children's rights, as well as determination of an optimal structure of the institution, execution of social and rehabilitative methods in the work of its various structures, preparation of personnel possessing relevant qualifications and working out a system of institution's management.

In-house groups for children:

1. Admission

2. Rehabilitative group

3. Family placement preparation group (into social family)

These groups are kind of patron families that are located within the children's home. Children live there together with social mothers (social parents). Admissions social mother does not reside in the children's home. Each group, as a rule, has 8 to 16 children of different ages. During a child's stay in the admissions group he or she goes through a physical, receives primary medical and emergency psychological help, all required paperwork for further placement of a child is prepared, a child receives necessary hygienic care, his or her identity is verified, as well as where his or her parents or persons substituting them reside. The issue of further placement of a child is also decided upon here. Further complete study of a child's personality is undertaken in order to develop an individualized program of child's care. In case further placement of a child is deemed necessary preparation for his or her placement into a family also starts here.

Social and legal services are comprised of:

1. **Children's social services** department performs evaluation and monitoring of children in in-house groups and families of patron parents, acts as a liaison of patron families with other departments, is responsible for protection of legal rights and interests of children, assists in collection of necessary data for determination of children's legal status, places of residence of his or her parents (legal representatives), his or her place of study, place where a child normally receives medical care, prepares a draft program on protecting child's rights and participates in annual revisions of this program in cooperation with an authorized representative of a child care authority.

2. **Social patronate service** organizes preventive assistance to families in difficult life situations, which they are unable to overcome on their own and where there may exist a threat to a child's life , health or normal development, works with biological families of children

admitted to the children's home to research possibilities of returning a child, supervises the work of patron trainers in biological families, prepares a draft program on protecting child's rights and participates in annual revisions of this program in cooperation with an authorized representative of a child care authority, performs evaluation and monitoring of children in social patronate, acts as a liaison of these children and their families with other departments of the children's home and is responsible for protection of legal rights and interests of these children.

3. **Legal counseling service** performs tasks associated with protecting legal interests of children and provides consultation for families in difficult life situations.

Family placement department (for patronate care):

This department informs the public about system of patronate care, searches, selects and trains citizens wishing to accept a child for care into their family or become patron trainers for children living with their biological families, provides any necessary assistance for them and consultations for patron trainers and families from the risk group.

Rehabilitative service performs individualized rehabilitative services for children, develops programs for individualized development of a child and implements programs on individual professional orientation. Children's medical and psychological services are parts of this service. An establishment of diagnostic class for home education preparing for education at a regular school is also possible.

Rehabilitative service provides the following services for each of the children:

- provides complete medical, psychological and educational diagnostics;

- forecasts the process of a child's development and determines methods and types of rehabilitative and correctional work;

- develops an individualized program of child's development;

- implements programs of rehabilitation;

- monitors child's development;

- participates in making a decision on selecting a compatible family for each child from the number of families chosen and trained by the service on organization of family upbringing and participates in approval of an individualized program of child's development;

■ provides consultations for trainers;

■ provides consultations for disadvantaged families within the community

The children's home #19 in consortium with the Center for education and research of issues of children's welfare and under the guidance of the Russian Federation Department of Education has developed and performed experimental implementation of **the guideline documents on patronate care**, such as:

■ The draft Federal Law of the Russian Federation *On Minimal Social Standards of Organization of Activities of Local Governments in Implementing a System of Care in respect of Children* (as well as amendments to be made into a Family Code of the Russian Federation along the lines of this draft).

■ The draft of an analogous provincial legislation.

■ The draft Guidelines on patronate care.

■ Written recommendations on why passing the Federal Law of the Russian Federation *On Minimal Social Standards of Organization of Activities of Local Governments in Implementing a System of Care in Respect of Children* is needed.

■ A package of worksheets *Care for Children* for child care authorities on planning child care, monitoring efficiency of activities aimed at protecting children's rights, evaluation of conditions of a child in care of an authority.

■ Program for continuous education of social workers enabling them to perform duties on family placement of children and social patronate in the authorized child welfare agencies.

■ Training programs for patron trainers and foster parents.

■ Work organization model for local government authorities in child welfare

7.2.   Model of Patronate Care in the Province of Vladimir

Kameshkovskiy children's home in the Province of Vladimir was opened in August 1994. Initially it housed 30 children, 23 of whom were young delinquents. Every one of them had a lot of life experience not measured in years, but in actions of their own and those adults surrounding them. Independent of their age they had to take care of their basic needs in food, accommodation and clothing. More often than not they would resolve these issues by way of stealing, fraud and asking for money on the streets. Each day children would lose a portion of feelings of security and trust. As a result of such life children would form wrong impressions on family functions and human morality.

Social adjustment may be efficient only within a family. For this reason the trainers of Kameshkovskiy children's home made a decision to establish a system of patronate care in May 1998.

Children's home conditions of growing up develop certain personality features in children:

- strict regulation of life, limitations of personal choice cause suppression of independence, initiative, which makes personality self-regulation and development of internal self-control more difficult;

- children's contacts with wider social environment are limited due to relative isolation of a children's home from any outside life; The result is development of distrust and fear of the outside world in children and a position of an observer;

- conditions of collective growing up necessarily develop a conscience of a children's home "we" in children and children start dividing the world into "us" and "them" and they are ready to take advantage of "them"

It is no secret that a great number of former institutionalized children have been unable to establish regular families. The main reason for this is the absence of any positive experience. For this reason the main goal of a children's home has always been teaching children skills needed for independent living. However, even the conditions found in the most respectable children's home' does not allow for creation of a model of a regular family with all its variety of relationships and duties for each of its members that a child needs.

Having studied foreign experience of placement of children deprived of parental care into patron families and methods and principles of patron care the children's home staff in cooperation with the local school district and under the guidance of the provincial department of education has prepared a legal foundation for an experiment in patronate care.

As a way of informing the local population the children's home published an article on patronate care in the local paper in May 1998. A lot of people responded to this article and applied to the children's home to become patron parents for a child. Psychologists performed a selection process. Out of the 22 families that had applied, 10 were selected.

The main selection criteria were:

- interest of potential trainers in working with orphans,

- prior experience with children of the same age,

- preference was given to complete families,

- stability of family relations,

- good housing conditions,

- full-time employment,

- age limitations from 24 through 45,

- physical health of potential trainers,

- stable income

Representatives of the following occupations became patron trainers - teachers, physicians, and a judge, a chief of traffic police, an accountant, a factory manger, a librarian, a former military officer and some workers.

Upon introduction of the system of patronate care the structure of a children's home was reorganized. Children's home activities are now performed through a variety of services. One of those is a patronate care service. The children's home principal is the chief of this service.

According to the main guidelines of its activities the following people are members of the service - vice-principal on education and upbringing, social worker, physician, children's home psychologists.

The service is engaged in following activities:

- search for, selection and training of patronate trainers;

- selection of children to be placed into patron families;

- complex diagnostics, rehabilitation and social adjustment of a child in the course of preparing him/her to living in a patron family;

- correctional and developmental assistance to children placed in patron families;

- implementation of an individual plan of child's development;

- protection of personal and property rights and interests of children;

- control over performance of their duties by patron parents

Upon selection potential patron parents undergo a training course. The service of patronate care in cooperation with Nadezhda Foundation has developed a training program for potential patron parents that include discussion of issues and problems that may arise in substitute families and ways of their resolution.

Along with training of potential patron parents selection of children to be placed into patron families is undergoing. Then begins the period between them for bonding. The wishes of both patron parents and children are taken into consideration during the placement process.

Agreements are signed with patron parents, which determine rights and duties of both parties - the children's home staff and patron parents. 10 children from the children's home were placed into patron families on the basis of these agreements and the decree of the head of Kameshkovskiy district government #283 of September 2, 1998 *On Organization of Patronate Care for Children on the Basis of Kameshkovskiy District Children's Home.*

A special commission established by the order of the children's home principal controls adjustment and development of children in patron families. This commission is a coordinating body of the service of patronate upbringing. Individual plans for development of children placed in patron families are approved and reviewed at the meetings of this commission. The members of the patronate care service consider the main goal to be development of social proficiency in children that would allow them to adequately function in the society.

The patron family encourages development of a system of certain values in children; it encourages their choice of future occupation and personality development, establishment of emotional contacts with other people and development of skills for everyday living, social and leasure activities. The patron parents have a wide range of goals, whose achievement should result in the high level of preparedness of a child to independent living and activities. They include social preparedness, skills of collective working, skills of everyday living, skills of organizing independent living, readiness for taking a job (skills of servicing oneself, orientation in a world of occupations, occupational self-determination etc.), moral and psychological preparedness (adequate self-evaluation, adequate strength of willpower) and physical preparedness (skills of healthy way of life, absence of bad habits etc.).

Patron parents act in close interaction with the guidance team according to individual plans for children's development, which include such directions of activities as health, emotional and psychological needs, behavior, education, extracurricular activities, and contacts with biological families and teaching skills of independent living.

While living and growing up in a patron family a child is also under care of professionals of the patronate care service, i.e. he/she always has an opportunity to receive timely assistance of professionals. The following departments are a part of the guidance service:

1. Social and legal (staff, social worker):

- legal responsibility for life and health of a child, protection of his/her rights and organization of living,
- coordination of work of all departments,
- selection and training of patron families,
- regular inspections of children in patron families,
- work with biological family,
- interaction with schools and other organizations,
- monitoring of the results of children's occupational choices

2. Rehabilitative (physicians and nurses, social worker, teachers, speech therapist, trainers, librarian):

- diagnostics, rehabilitation, correctional work, education,
- individual consultations for children and patron parents,
- monitoring of general condition of a child (physical and psychological condition, emotional problems, social adjustment, self-esteem, and school adjustment)

3. Psychological (independent psychologists, children's home psychologist):

- diagnostics, correctional and developmental assistance,
- monitoring child's development,
- continuing training,
- child's guidance in a patron family

On September 1, 2000 20 more children ages 12 through 18 were placed into patron families. Socialization problems are most acute for children of this age. At this stage of development socialization goals are first of all associated with appearance and development of "feeling of being an adult", development of psychological and sexual identity. This supposes wider sphere of independence, acknowledgment by adults of the fact of a child turning into an adult, assignment to him/her of the rights and duties characteristic of adults. However, the conditions of growing up in a children's home limit the sphere of exhibiting a child's independence by default and "children's status" is more convenient for children's home trainers, as a rule.

The program of experiment includes undergoing of a child through three stages - organization, adjustment and corrective development.

The second stage, the stage of adjustment is already in the past. This stage may be called the most difficult one since it has to include resolution of the most psychological and social problems (psychological communication barrier, acceptance by children and adults of their roles of patron parents and the ones being cared for respectively and all the duties associated with those roles).

Currently the third stage of corrective development is on the way. The commission on methodology after having analyzed the first two years of the experiment has recommended acquaintance of orphans with theoretical systematic knowledge along with practical and ethical skills that they obtain in families. This is vital for complete and harmonious development of a personality. Special educational courses have been organized for children from the patron families at the children's home. These courses include economics among us, an adolescent and the law, communication, development of learning skills, club for future young women etc.

The patron parents organized their own support club. The goal of the club is providing psychological support to patron parents and children, exchange of experience and summarizing experiences.

The following positive results were noted in children placed into patron families after three years of existence of patronate care service in Kameshkovskiy children's home:

- improvement in general health condition of children: sharp decline of percentage of those having a flu;
- age adequate physical development of all children;
- self-evaluation of the majority of children became adequate, many children began to freely express their true emotions, they obtained

skills of emotional containment, the outbursts of anger and hysteria disappeared;

- clear successes in education: 8 children finished the school year with As and Bs only, 13 children started receiving higher grades and one girl graduated from school with honors;
- a feeling of isolation characteristic for orphans is gradually going away;
- 85% of children have mentioned having friends outside of the children's home;
- 80% of children build their relations with friends upon mutual understanding. While observing negative traits of their friends, children also notice their positive traits;
- 75% of children in patron families have developed a feeling of trust to other people, to members of patron family;
- children's range of interests also increased (30% are involved in sports, 40% are studying in a school for arts)

At the end of each school year written interviews of children in patron families are conducted. Analysis of their results indicates that

- all children in patron families recognize it as useful, having a priority, psychologically comfortable;

- 86% of all patron family graduates believe that a patron family will represent for them an almost perfect example of family life organization;

- 76% of children have significantly changed their beliefs on distribution of roles within a family. This is important since the majority of institutionalized children base their experience of family life organization on an anti-social way of life.

- 68.4% of children from patron families improved their learning skills, all children have gained new skills of independent living, and their aesthetic level and general behavioral culture have significantly improved as well.

All patron trainers have concluded that a patron family is the most effective way of social adjustment for institutionalized children, full and complete development of their personalities and the most favorable way of upbringing from the point of view of psychological protection and socialization of children deprived of parental care.

7.3.   A Family Center for Post-Institution Adjustment as a Model of Patronate Care

The new social environment of a person after his/her leaving a children's home is significantly different from the one that a child was used to. The living conditions change radically and a graduate of an institution usually experiences psychological stress.

An institution's graduate has to build and organize his/her living environment in anew fashion since there is no connection between an institutional life and independent living of orphans. That is why a graduate of an institution needs support in the beginning of his/her independent living and assistance in overcoming various problems and difficulties of social adjustment. Different models of post-institution adjustment have been established and exist for this purpose. They include social hostels, boarding schools with a specialized department for its graduates, centers for post-institution adjustment, adjustment centers at the workplaces.

A new model of post-institution adjustment called a family center has been established in the Province of Vladimir in cooperation with the Buckner Foundation as part of the experiment on patronate care (...).

The family center may be considered as a connecting link, a buffer between a life in an institution and independent living. It represents an interested middleman in the process of adjustment of an institution graduate to life within a society.

During post-institution adjustment a graduate has to undergo psychological restructuring to live in an environment radically different from the one in a children's home. A graduate has to change from

- external regulation of life to self-regulation, to the necessity to make choices and bear personal responsibility for them;

- passively accepting government care and a habit to rely upon assistance of others to self-assistance and caring for him/herself through his/her own labor;

- living among «one's own», often in an atmosphere of mutual disliking and self-defense by means of using violence to creative communication style and legal forms of self-defense;

- unconditional forced obedience to the trainer to abiding by law, learning his/her civil rights and personal responsibility.

A lot of graduates are unable to cope with this transition. Quite often graduates who are not used to self-support and self-organization choose a way requiring the least of efforts (larcenies, asking money off of others). Graduates are unable to adjust to social environment, they close up and do not attempt to take into account opinions of other people. It is difficult for them to find a job and stay with the job, as well as to create a family.

This transition would be successful and painless if it is done under educational guidance and if a graduate finds him/herself in a psychologically comfortable environment during this period that would provide stability, protection and security. The family centers are established keeping this goals in mind. The basis of a family center activity as a form of patronate care is the idea of sharing responsibility for a child between a children's home and family center's trainers. The children's home staff takes upon responsibility for resolution of social problems, providing for a need in education and medical help of a family center's clients. The trainers of a family center take upon responsibility for life, development and upbringing of children.

Family center's trainers are family couples working according to labor contract.

The goal of a family center is assistance to institution's graduates in post-institution adjustment and their preparation to independent living. The main tasks of a family center are associated with the main directions of its activity.

First, a center solves an issue of creating social and educational environment psychologically comfortable for graduates, as well as provides them with social and legal support. The specifics of this environment lie in family-type conditions of living and execution of a program of social adjustment for each of the graduates.

Second, the center provides for individual complex guidance of the process of post-institution adjustment for each graduate. This guidance is provided by the team members, i.e. children's home staff, social workers, physicians, psychologists and family center's trainers. Third, the center provides diagnostics and correction of the process of post-institution adjustment.

A family center represents a structural part of a children's home.

One may find the following common features of a family center and a children's home:

- first of all, the persons subject to training.

- second, the main goal of both is to create for the children conditions for development, upbringing, education, assistance in a choice of occupation, preparation for independent life and labor.

- third, both institutions are trustees for children and a children's home principal is a legal representative for a child.

- fourth, accommodation and education of children in both is fully paid for by the government.

- fifth, a trainer's job is a professional labor.

One may also find the following differences between a family center and a children's home (see Table 10).

Table 10
The main differences between a family center and a children's home (according to I.A.Bobylyova, 2002)

Family center	Children's home
A form of family upbringing of orphans and children deprived of parental care	A form of public upbringing of orphans and children deprived of parental care
Distribution of responsibilities between a children's home and patron trainers	Children's home bears full responsibility for a child
Residents already have a general high school degree and are working on their vocational training	Residents are in the process of obtaining their high school degrees
The length of stay has a range from several months to four years and is determined by the degree of a resident's social adjustment and readiness for independent living	The length of stay depends upon the time of admission into an institution, placement into the other form of upbringing and obtaining general high school education
Residents live in conditions close to those of their independent living	Residents live in conditions that are quite afar from independent living conditions
Family couples are the trainers in a family center	Children's home trainers for the most part are not related to each other
Family center trainers are men and women on an equal basis	Women dominate among the trainers in a children's home

There are two family centers in the Province of Vladimir - one for young men and the other for young women. The family center for young men occupies two (one- and two-bedroom) apartments in one of the two-storied houses in the town of Andreevskoye.

The apartments are combined into one big five-bedroom apartment with all necessary living conditions. The four young men are living by two in two of the bedrooms, while three young men occupy the third one. Each couple of patron trainers is living in a separate bedroom. During the family center's existence the patron trainers and young men have built a vegetable warehouse and a place for keeping cattle. There is also a garden with fruits and vegetables growing there around the house.

There may not live more than eight residents simultaneously at the family center. Two family couples live and work there - one of them (the main trainers) spend five days at the family center, while the second couple (substitute trainers) spends two days there.

All residents of the family center are graduates of institutions for orphans and children deprived of parental care. They had significant difficulties in social adjustment, as well as various health problems. All of them feared their future and were lacking many skills and qualities required for success in independent living. These are the children that were causing the most anxiety of children's home trainers. Their reference letters from children's homes and oral characteristics given to them by children's homes trainers speak loudly about it. «He just would not survive», «He is unable to live on his own», «We are afraid for her future», «His behavior causes anxiety» etc.

It has been established in the result of pre-admission diagnostics that all of young men had high levels of anxiety, problems communicating; they did not have any goals in life and had a low level of self-control development.

The family center for young women is located in the city of Lakinsk due to high level of development of highway and railroad infrastructure there, which significantly increase the range of vocational educational establishments available where the girls could be admitted. The family center is located in a specially built on the children's home grounds two-storied wooden house. The ground floor is occupied by the kitchen and dining room and the trainers' bedroom. The first floor has three bedrooms occupied by two young women each. There is a large basement in the house with study and relaxation rooms, as well as various closets.

Upon admission to the family center young women had low level of life and occupational self-orientation and low self-evaluation. The difference in living conditions in the children's home and the family center is enormous for them. That is why it is important for them to have caring , but demanding people around.

Taking into account all of the above, it has been very important to select and provide proper training for patronate trainers of the family center. This people would become major players in social adjustment of family center residents. Thanks to their efforts residents would get an experience they were lacking and which would mainly determine success of their first independent steps. This is an experience of family living, resolving everyday problems, an experience of social contacts. This is a personal experience of living through new means of interaction with others and experience of a new feeling of an outside world. This is a new, positive, emotionally rich experience. The patron trainers provide protection, stability, security and continuity of life, as well as the same demands to all of the residents. It is important for these people to be ready to joint discussion of problems, to be able to accept help and be open to cooperation with other trainers and psychologists.

The system of selection and training of family centers' trainers consists of the following levels:

- diagnostics that supposes studies of personal, motivational and professional readiness of candidates;

- training aimed at creation of psychological and educational culture of trainers;

- practical that involves professional consulting of trainers in the process of their work at the family center.

The system of work with future patron parents included the following types of activities:

- informational meeting.

- individual interview.

- selection for training.

- training.

- collection of all required paperwork by candidates.

- decision-making. Conclusion.

A full report on an ability of a candidate to become a patron trainer is made on the basis of the above. Personal qualities of a candidate, his/her health, an ability to perform duties of a patron trainer of a family center, an ability to cooperate with children's home professionals and other patron trainers of a family center, readiness to provide children with contacts with their biological parents and other relatives if this would be in their best interests - all of these is taken into account.

One of the conditions of successful social adjustment is organization of living. Family center represents a specific form of organization of living of its residents. Its specifics are in making conditions of everyday living of residents as close to independent family ones as possible and in having an individual social adjustment program to be developed and implemented for each of the residents.

A model of multi-children family is taken as a basis for organization of living. This family does not live in isolation, but among other regular families. This facilitates the process of social integration of children's homes graduates.

Living in a family center is based on complete self-servicing. Each resident feels that he/she lives in one big family where each member has his/her range of responsibilities that are necessary and regular. Life and health of other residents depends on how each one performs his/her duties, so one may not neglect these duties even if it is required to overcome one's own self, which is what happens with every resident until performing his/her duty does not become automatic. There are duties for men, duties for women and common duties for everybody. Each family member is surrounded by care and attention as in every normal family. There is no such thing as public property in a family center. Residents have their own belongings, their own place within the space of a house, their own events and human relationships and respect for their property from the others.

Thus, each resident of a family center finds him/herself in situations where he/she obtains an experience important for independent living (it is not a role-play) and while obtaining it each resident forms a model of independent living.

Content of living in a family center corresponds to vitally important areas of life for each resident (health, rights and responsibilities, leisure, self-servicing, occupation choosing, communication, family relations).

Everyday life and arising problems are discussed at family meetings where joint decisions are made. A family center has its rules that are approved by residents and patron trainers. They help put family requirements in order. The rules are less restrictive in a family center for young women.

Contents of living in a family center are based on a sum of principles - possession of information, psychological support, dialogue in communication and interactions, combination of freedom and responsibilities.

The process of adjustment to family center living may conditionally be divided into three periods:

1. **Period of initial adjustment.** It lasts about one month. This is a period of transition to new conditions. This period results in agreement of a resident to further stay at a family center, acceptance of its rules and requirements, development of attitude aimed at further interaction and communication with other members of a family center.

2. **Period of regress.** This is a period of difficulties when an adult and an adolescent have to overcome distrust to each other. This is a period when both have to overcome themselves, get mutually adjusted and find some common points. This period lasts from several months to a year. On average it takes 6 to 8 months.

3. **Period of progress.** This is a period when the process of adjustment prevails over the process of problems in adjustment. This a period when a resident becomes more and more independent until he/she is capable of starting life on his/her own. At a family center it lasts

from one to three years and is determined by individual personality traits of each resident.

After a resident has spent a month at a family center the team members discuss and approve an individual development plan for him/her. This plan includes individualized measures aimed at providing welfare and development of a resident. This plan is in effect through the whole period of a resident's stay at a family center. This individual plan is executed through various actions aimed at health care, resolution of emotional and psychological problems, behavioral problems, development of family relations, providing social and legal protection, obtaining education, learning how to communicate, organization of leisure time and learning skills of independent living through common efforts of an adolescent and a trainer.

Execution of a plan provides for individual trajectory of social adjustment of each resident. The process of post-institution adjustment at a family center is accompanied by complex guidance of a resident, which includes medical, social, legal, psychological and educational guidance and is performed by a team of psychologists, social workers, physicians, children's home staff and family center trainers. The contents of complex guidance are specific to an individual plan of each resident.

An individual development plan of a resident is a working plan for 3, 6 or 9 months dependent on the level of adjustment of each resident. The working plan describes goals, problems, needs, strong points of a resident, his/her progress (i.e. successes, moving forward), and criteria for evaluation of results and ways of achieving planned goals in each area of life of a family center resident.

The process of adjustment in the conditions of a family center is individualized. This individuality is explained by various psychologies of each resident, differences in experience, levels of physical health and physical development and shows itself in the rate of adjustment.

Residents of a family center have an opportunity to undergo the process of post-institution adjustment at an individual rate, which determines the length of their stay at a family center.

Thus, the diagnostics results allow us to speak about efficiency of a family center as a model of post-institution adjustment of graduates of institutions for orphans and children deprived of parental care.

8

LEGAL REGULATIONS IN RESPECT OF SOCIAL PROTECTION OF CHILDREN, THEIR EDUCATION AND CARE

8.1. The Rights of Children Left without Parental Care and their Guarantees.

Over the last ten years numerous changes occurred in our country and our society that lead to improvement of the situation with the problem of «social orphanhood». This was reflected in legislative documents passed over these years .

The Russian government is taking emergency measures aimed at social protection of orphans and children left without parental care. The existing system of government upbringing and education of orphans is undergoing a series of reforms. The Russian Federation Government decree #409 of July 20, 1992 *On Emergency measures Aimed at Social Protection of Orphans and Children Left without Parental Care,* as well as the decree #374 of May 14, 2001 *«On Immediate Measures on Improving Situation of Orphans and Children Left without Parental Care* are currently in effect.

In accordance with those expenses for upkeep if institutionalized children have been increased, the monies are also expended on children in trust and in foster care, as well as in children's homes of family type. The decrees also introduced a position of a professional in protecting children's rights into the staffs of local governments.

The important task in the current conditions is formulation of a new social policy aimed at prevention of social orphanhood, children's homelessness and establishment of system for social rehabilitation of children and adolescents in crisis situations.

Establishment of a radically new model of the government system of social prevention is characterized by necessity to guarantee a child an actual right to dignified existence within a social environment. It is this position that is reflected in the Decree of the President of the Russian federation #1338 of September 6, 1993 *On Prevention of Homelessness and Delinquency of Minors and Protection of their Rights* that created specialized services for minors requiring social rehabilitation within a system of social welfare authorities.

The Law *On Main Guarantees of Children's Rights in the Russian Federation* defined social rehabilitation of a child as «measures aimed at reestablishment of social connections an functions lost by a child, improving his/her living environment and increasing the level of care for children» (Article 15, part 2 of the Federal Law #124-ФЗ of July 24,1998).

The Federal Law #120-ФЗ of June 24, 1999 *On the Basics of the System of Prevention of Homelessness and Delinquency among Minors* has a vital significance for development of the system of prevention of homelessness. This Law set up the following goals:

- prevention of homelessness, delinquency and anti-social activities of minors, discovery and elimination of reasons and conditions for that;

- providing protection of rights and legal interests of minors;

- social and educational rehabilitation of minors in socially dangerous situations;

- discovery and prevention of all cases of getting minors involved in criminal and anti-social activities.

The Law names the following major principles on prevention of children's homelessness and delinquency:

- the rule of law, democracy, humane treatment of minors, support and interaction with families;

- individual approach to punishment of minors and observance of information confidentiality;

- government support of activities of local administrations and public organizations aimed at prevention of children's homelessness and delinquency;

■   responsibility of officials and common citizens for violations of rights
and legal interests of children.

The Law substantially changed levels of responsibility for prevention of
children's homelessness. Vagrant children are now subject to be placed into
specialized institutions of social protection and not into detention centers for
young delinquents.

In accordance with the above-mentioned Federal laws social welfare
authorities are now establishing centers for social rehabilitation of children
and adolescents and centers of assistance to children left without parental
care in order to prevent social orphanhood and children's homelessness.

The rules for legal regulation of these institutions have been established.
The Government of the Russian Federation approved in its decree #1092
of September 13, 1996 The Guidelines *On Specialized Institutions for
Minors Requiring Social Rehabilitation* that put an order the activities of
social rehabilitation centers for minors, social orphanages for children and
adolescents, centers for assistance to children left without parental care etc.

Specialized institutions for prevention of children's homelessness
for children requiring social rehabilitation assist in overcoming difficult
situations in families and provide temporary shelter for children until the
most acceptable form of their future living is figured out in cooperation with
child welfare authorities.

These institutions are established through a decision of local government
after thorough analysis of problems with adjustment of adolescents, levels of
social orphanhood and situation within the risk group families. Establishment
of these institutions allows solving several problems of immediate social and
legal assistance to children, adolescents and families in difficult life situations.
The timely prevention work with families in the risk group within the range
of institution's proficiency allows to keep children within their biological
families in a number of cases.

The activities of specialized social rehabilitation centers for minors are
aimed primarily at rehabilitation of a child's biological family. If this proves
not possible the measures are taken on organization of transferring children
into other families for adoption, guardianship or into family groups for
upbringing established on the basis of an institution.

The program of measures aimed at prevention of social orphanhood and
improvement of situation of children left without parental care up to the year
2005 was passed in 2000. The program underlines measures on resolving
such issues as legislation improvement, providing support to families in
upbringing and education of children, social protection of orphans children
left without parental care. An introduction of insurance policy for social

education of children from socially unprotected families, orphans and children left without parental care is suggested for the first time. This would provide more guarantees for these children to obtain education.

The Russian Department of Labor has passed a decree #9 of February 6, 1995 *On Approval of Recommendations on Establishing Job Quotas for Persons Especially Needing Social Protection.* It provides for primary job allocation for orphans leaving places of incarceration and graduating from special schools.

The legislative activity in the Russian Federation pays considerable attention to resolving problems of social and legal protection of children in the conditions of socio-economic reforms in the country during the period of transition to the market economy.

Russia has a good Law *On Employment of Population in the Russian Federation.* It supposes establishing job quotas for people needing social protection, tax advantages for companies offering jobs to minors that have to be established by executive branches of provincial governments and local governments. However, inspections conducted by local district attorney's offices show that cases of providing such tax advantages are rare and companies are not interested in providing jobs to adolescents.

The priority of children's interests is confirmed in *The Guidelines of Government Family Policy* approved by the decree of the President of the Russian Federation #712 of May 15, 1996.

This document provides that the main goal of government social policy is execution of children's rights for full-valued physical, intellectual, moral and social development. The following directions of the government social policy are distinguished as priorities:

- strengthening of legal protection of children;
- support for families as natural place of living for children;
- provisions for security motherhood and protection of children's health;
- improvements in providing food for children;
- provision of upbringing, education and development of children;
- support for the children in especially difficult circumstances.

The UN Convention on the Rights of Children is the main legal document protecting children from cruel treatment and establishing thirty eight rights, including several rights associated with the process of obtaining education.

The UN Convention on the Rights of Children gives the definition of «cruel treatment» and determines measures of protection against it (Article 19), as well as establishes the following:

- provisions for healthy development of a child to a maximum possible degree (Article 6);

- protection from deliberate or illegal intervention into the private life of a child, abuses of his/her dignity and integrity (Article 16);

- provisions of measures for prevention of diseases and malnutrition (Article 24);

- recognition of the right of each child for the level of living necessary for physical, intellectual, spiritual, moral and social development (Article 27);

- protection of children from sexual harassment (Article 34);

- protection of children from other types of cruel treatment (Article 37);

- measures of assistance to children who have become victims of cruel treatment (Article 39).

The Criminal Code of the Russian Federation defines physical and sexual violence against minors as a crime (Article 106-136) and has a special chapter devoted to crimes against families and minors (Articles 150-157).

The Russian Federation Law *On Education* reemphasizes the right of all children studying in any educational institutions for «respect of their human dignity» (Article 5) and provides for civil punishment of teachers for any physical and psychological «violence over a person of a student» (Article 56).

The Russian Federation Law *On Protecting Children's Rights* says in Article 14 that «cruel treatment of children and physical and psychological abuse of children are prohibited».

The new family Code of the Russian Federation came into effect on March 1, 1996. Approval of the new Family Code is associated primarily with radical changes in political, social and economic life of the country that directly affect such important institutions of society as marriage and family. Regulation of family relationships is now in line with the Constitution of the Russian Federation, other federal laws and, first of all, with the new Civil Code of the Russian Federation. The new Family Code regulations reflect international legal acts in the area of human rights that have been ratified by the Russian Federation, as well as positive experience of reforms in family legislation abroad. The Code took into account the practice of using current legislation, critique of some of its points made in the process of its preparation and proposals made during this process by various legislative and executive branches of provincial governments of the Russian Federation, practitioners and scholars.

The chief points of the Russian family legislation that include voluntary marriages, marriage as a union of two people, equality of spousal rights in a family, priority of family upbringing of children, provisions for priority protection of their rights and interests, as well as the rights and interests of handicapped family members remained unchanged.

The Code touches upon all aspects of family relations, including personal property and non-property rights, relations between various members of a family, relations in respect to children left without parental care and relations with participation of foreigners.

On e of the main trends of the new Code is intention to view a child as an independent legal entity and not as a subject dependent of parental authority. The corresponding regulations of the Code are based on the main principle that a child's legal status within a family is determined from the point of view of a child's interests (and not of the rights and duties of parents) and includes the following rights of a child:

- to live and grow up in a family;

- to know his/her parents (to the most possible degree);

- to be cared for by his/her parents (or by other responsible persons in their absence);

- to have his/her interests protected, his/her personality fully developed and his /her human dignity respected (Article 54);

- to communicate with both parents and other relatives (Article 55);

- to protection of his/her rights and legal interests (including the right to apply for their protection on his/her own to child welfare authorities and to the courts upon achieving an age of 14) (Article 56);

- to express his/her opinion on all issues related to his/her life (Article 57);

- to have a first and a last name (Article 58);

- to receive monies adequate for living and have property rights to his/her personal belongings (Article 60).

For the first time the Code defines the basics of legal protection of children against domestic violence. It has been established in this connection that methods of upbringing should exclude neglectful, cruel, rude or belittling methods, abuse and exploitation of children (Article 65). Regulations relating to taking away parental rights are strengthened (Articles 69-72). Return of parental rights for parents of a child who has achieved 10 years of age is allowed only with his/her consent (Article 72). The possibilities of limiting parental rights through a court's decision have been further developed (Articles 73-76). It is also allowed to take a child away from parents without a court's decision in cases of direct and immediate danger to his/her life or health in a family (Article 77).

The Code regulates in detail the rights and responsibilities of parents with respect to education and upbringing of a child and protection of his/her rights and legal interests (Articles 61-69).

An approval of the new Family Code brought a necessity of passing several new documents regarding orphans and children left without parental care.

Among those we have to mention the Federal Law *On Additional Guarantees of Social Protection of Orphans and Children Left without Parental Care,* the Decree of the Government of the Russian Federation *On Approval of Guidelines for an Educational Institution for Children Requiring Psychological, Educational, Medical and Social Assistance* and several other documents. These documents provided for priority of adoption compared to all other forms of social care for orphans.

One of the big legislative measures was approval of the Federal Law #159-ФЗ of December 12, 1996 *On Additional Guarantees of Social Protection of Orphans and Children Left without Parental Care,* which determined essential additional privileges and advantages in the areas of education, health care, property rights, housing rights and the right for labor.

The decree of the Government of the Russian Federation #919 *On Organization of Centralized Accounting of Children Left without Parental Care* is aimed at creating conditions for children's placement into families. The Federal Law #44-ФЗ of April 16, 2001 *On the Government Data Bank of Children Left without Parental Care* establishes the rules for using the government data bank on children left without parental care.

An institution of foster family has been legally defined. The decree of the Government of the Russian Federation #829 of July 17, 1996 *On Foster Families* is now being executed. It defines the rules of establishment of a foster family, conditions of children's placement into these families, the rights and responsibilities of foster parents, children's rights guarantees and financial assistance to foster families. The draft agreement between child welfare authority and a foster family that serves as a legal basis of establishment of a foster family has developed and enclosed to this decree.

In 2000 changes were made to the Family Code of the Russian Federation to include family-type children's homes into the number of possible forms of placement of orphans. The decree of the Government of the Russian Federation #195 of March 19, 2001 *On Family-Type Children's Homes* has established the Rules for organization of family-type children's homes.

The family-type children's home is organized on a basis of a family if spouses have had mutually agreed to take no less than 5 and no more than 10 children for family upbringing. A decision of provincial or a local government is required for its establishment.

The Federal Law #12-ФЗ of January 13, 1996 made radical amendments into the Russian Federation Law *On Education* of 1992 in particular with respect to orphans. It was established that orphans and children left without parental care have a priority right to be admitted into the state and municipal educational institutions after receiving passing grades during entrance examinations (Article 16, part 3).

A lot of legal acts on various forms of supporting welfare of children and families with minor children have been passed. For instance the Federal Law *On Welfare Payments to Citizens with Children* has been amended to increase the amounts of monthly welfare payments for children to single mothers (Federal Law #162-ФЗ of December 30, 1996).

The legislation increasing levels of parental responsibility for children has been also passed. For instance, the Russian Federation Civil Code's Article 1075 (in the 2nd part of the Code effective March 1, 1996) the court may require of a parent whose parental rights have taken away to be responsible for any harm to his/her minor children within a 3-year period after these parental rights were taken away if a child's behavior that caused this harm was a consequence of improper execution of parental duties.

The following are the main directions of legislative activity in the provinces of the Russian Federation:

■   protection of families, mothers and children;

■   social support of children with special problems;

■   social protection of children's rights;

■   employment of minors.

The National Doctrine of education in the Russian Federation passed by the All-Russian Conference of teachers (January 14-15, 2001) and approved by the Government of the Russian Federation determines the goals of education and upbringing and the ways for their achievement up to the year of 2025. One of the priority tasks of the government in educational area is establishment and implementation of conditions for obtaining general and vocational education by orphans and children left without parental care.

In spite of numerous acts passed over the recent years and their multi-character nature the problem of improving legal mechanisms aimed at protecting rights of families and orphans, as well as legal mechanisms of their execution remains acute.

The legislative acts aimed at determining of rights of orphans and children left without parental care for government social protection and increase in social welfare payments are needed.

The Family Code has not completely resolved an issue of family placement of children left without parental care. The problem of parental violence and violence of institution's trainers remains.

The new legislation providing for new principles and mechanisms of providing families with social assistance , including child welfare payments is needed.

The old regulations that are inadequate for difficult socio-economic conditions in the country and that are unable to prevent their negative impact upon children and families still remain in the legislation of the Russian Federation, which leads to increase in the numbers of social orphans.

The legislation has not established full measure of responsibility of adults for violating child's rights on inviolability of his/her person, for abuses of his/her honor and dignity. The cases of child abuse are on the increase. Incorrect methods of upbringing and psychological and physical violence can be observed in both families and educational institutions.

There is no legal responsibility of adults for making children commit crimes and introduction to criminal environment.

The acts completely devoted to children and families, as well as those containing separate regulations of attitude to children within families and in society in general should be passed.

There are no legal documents in existence relating to

- legal guarantees of minors brought up in foster and patron families;
- establishment of system of government social services for families and children;
- establishment of job quotas for orphans, tax advantages and reimbursements for businesses hiring orphans;
- establishment of a juvenile justice system, special family courts;

■   protection of rights of children during divorces and procedures for placement of children left without parental care into other families etc.

8.2.   Legal Regulations Establishing Rights, Duties and Responsibilities of Parents for Children's Education and Upbringing

Over the recent years legislation on issues of protection of children's rights has been changed substantially. This includes passing of a Family Code of the Russian Federation (passed December 8, 1995, made effective March 1, 1996, #223-ФЗ), Federal Law *On Additional Guarantees of Social Protection of Orphans and Children Left without Parental Care* (passed December 4, 1996, made effective partially December 27, 1996 and in full January 1, 1998, #158-ФЗ), Federal Law *On Education* (passed July 10, 1992, the new version passed January 13, 1996, made effective January 23, 1996, #12-ФЗ)), the Housing and Civil Process Codes have been amended, special regulations have been introduced into new Civil and Criminal Codes, a lot of regulations on implementing new laws have been also passed. We have to note the legislature's attention to the issues of children's rights protection. The new Russian legislation has been developed in consideration of international legal regulations, including Convention on the Rights of a Child (passed November 20, 1989, ratified September 15, 1990), which is also a positive sign.

Nowadays the rights, duties and responsibilities of parents or legal representatives of children are regulated by the Declaration of the Rights of a Child, Convention on the Rights of a Child, Family Code of the Russian Federation, the Russian Federation Law *On Education* and the Guidelines on an Educational Institution that takes into account the provisions of the General Declaration on Human Rights.

According to the legal regulations of the above acts parents (or legal representatives) have the following rights in accordance with

■   Article 50, part 7 of the Russian Federation Law *On Education* (RFLE) on free first primary, general, high school and primary vocational education within the standards determined by the government;

■   Article 63, part 1 of the Russian Federation Family Code (FC) the priority for upbringing of their own children before any other persons;

■   Article 52, part 3 of the RFLE to provide primary and general education to a child in a family.

Article 52, part 1 of the RFLE gives parents an opportunity to choose between:

- forms of education (in an educational institution, in a family, combination of various forms of education);

- educational institutions;

- types of protection of legal rights and interests of a child;

- additional (including private) educational services (extracurricular education, education in special courses, disciplines, more complete learning of certain subjects etc.) outside the framework of corresponding educational programs and existing government educational standards

In case a child is failing in two or more subjects parents have a choice according to Article 17, part 4 of the RFLE to continue his/her education as

1. repeat education (in the same grade);

2. compensating education class with less number of students;

3. family-type education.

Article 15, part 7 of the RFLE gives parents an opportunity to get acquainted with rules and contents of educational process, with student's grades, charter of incorporation of an educational establishment and other local regulations of an establishment.

Article 19, part 6 of the RFLE determines relations between adolescent and local educational authorities. It provides that upon reaching an age of 15 and with local educational authority's consent a child may leave an educational establishment to obtain general education later.

Article 50, part 10 of the RFLE contains regulations pertaining to transferring children into other educational institutions. Children may be sent into special (correctional) educational institutions with local educational authority's consent and upon a report from psychological, educational and medical commissions.

Article 19, part 7 of the RFLE enumerates those having a right to receive government child welfare payments. Those include:

1. children in low-income families;

2. single mothers (fathers) and families with many children;

3. handicapped children;

4. children of drafted fathers;

5. minor children when their parents are undetermined

Article 19, part 8 of the RFLE regulates an issue of additional welfare payments. Parents may receive additional payments if their child is brought up and educated within a family for

- professional consulting of teachers and professionals from educational institutions regarding education and upbringing of a child;

- consultations at the government psychological clinic;

- organization of children's leasure time at school and institutions of additional education;

- information of teachers' qualifications;

- protection of personal rights in government institutions and courts (including respectful attitude towards themselves and their children from all employees of an educational institution);

- participating in managing an educational institution

Parents have the right to

1. elect and be elected into the educational institution's council and other authorities;

2. participate in development and approval of charter of an educational institution and other local regulations;

3. attract additional financial resources for financing educational institution's activities within a framework of its charter;

4. resolve conflict situations with children at an educational institution.

Parents (or legal representatives) of students are required according to *article 18, part 1 of the RFLE* to teach a child the basics of physical, moral and intellectual development in his/her early childhood; according to *article 52, part 2 of the RFLE* they have to abide by the charter of an educational institution and other regulations of same, including an agreement between an educational institution and parents (or legal representatives) of students. They have to make sure that their children obtain general education on time and before reaching an age of 18 according to *article 63, part 1 of the FC*. According to *article 17, part 5 of the FC* the parents have to:

1. provide physicals for their children in order to correctly determine the type of an educational institution and the form of education;

2. inform children of their rights and responsibilities and the norms of behavior in public places;

3. provide children with belongings needed for studies at school;

4. receive information from an educational institution regarding children's education, especially in cases of conditional transition of a child to the next grade due to academic debts;

5. inform an educational institution about the reasons for child's absences in class (including health reasons);

6. take measures to find employment for a child or his/her admission into a different educational institution in case of his/her expulsion for illegal acts or serious and numerous violations of educational institution's charter.

Article 40, part 7 of the FC regulates parental when receiving government welfare payments. Parents or legal representatives of children have the right to use child welfare payments money to pay for:

1. child's stay at the boarding school;

2. purchases of belongings necessary for a child to attend school

Parents may not force a child to accept employment or to be a beggar if it harms the process of obtaining general education by a child. Parents must create favorable conditions at home for a child to perform homework and obtaining of general education by him/her. With this purpose in mind they have to:

1. determine a place for a child to do homework;

2. provide a child with any possible assistance in learning;

3. organize reasonable day schedule for a student, including weekends, holidays and vacation days;

4. Not to harm children's psychological and physical health and their moral development.

Article 65 of the FC prohibits neglectful, cruel, rude, belittling treatment of children by parents, abusing or exploiting children.

According to *article 69 of the FC* parents have no right to:

- refuse without a good cause to take a child back home from medical, educational, social protection or other similar institutions;

- force or encourage use of tobacco, alcohol, narcotic or toxic substances by children;

- deliberately abuse life or health of their children or spouses;

- refuse to provide financial assistance to their children (including refusal to make child support payments);

- force or encourage unlawful acts on part of their children and involve them in criminal activities;

- misuse their parental rights

Article 52, part 44 defines responsibility of parents (legal representatives) of students in the following way - «parents (legal representatives) of students are responsible for their upbringing, obtaining of general education by them and elimination of academic debts during the following school year».

Thus, parents (legal representatives) of students are administratively, civilly and criminally liable if they do not adhere to the articles mentioned above. However, lack of proper control or the complete ignoring of abiding by the existing law and the absence of punishment for those parents who are violating the rights, duties and responsibilities of educating and upbringing of their children, has created an increase in the numbers of problem children, social orphans, homeless children drug addicts and substance misuse.

The legislation in effect has mostly a declarative nature. Having proclaimed a wide range of children's rights the legislation has not provided for mechanisms of their execution in practice. The problems lie not in the absence of needed legislation, but in the system of organization of practical work by law enforcement and legal authorities (courts, district attorney's offices, probation offices, police, child welfare authorities etc.).

This problem may, however, be partially resolved by passing new legislative acts and amending the existing ones. We suggest in this connection:

1. to amend article 50 of the RFLE with the provision on establishment of multi-agency centers for social analysis located at the provincial educational authorities that would account for the number and the state of education of school age children.

2. amend article 65 of the FC by including there the right of the court while processing disputes on children's upbringing to apply administrative punishments to parent or parents if in the process of case consideration it becomes obvious that a dispute has not

been resolved prior to the court's interference due to the parent's or parents' fault.

3. to amend article 63 of the FC in the following fashion:

a) the title of the article to be «Rights, duties and **responsibilities** of parents in child's education and upbringing»,

b) to amend part 1 of the article in the following way: «Parents have responsibility for development, upbringing and **education** of their children. They must take care of their children's health, physical, psychological, spiritual and moral development».

The decision on limiting parental responsibility may be taken with their consent either directly by local governments (in case of violating conditions of upbringing or education) or by the courts (in case of child abuse or reasonable threat of violence over a child or neglect of his/her interests). If a decision is taken to limit parental responsibilities, the local government takes upon itself the part of responsibilities, in which parents have been limited.

Consequently, the definition of joint responsibility may be introduced into article 63 (for instance by a stepfather and both biological parents or by biological parents and local government) with clear definition of who would be responsible for what.

4. to increase criminal liability for neglect by parents or legal representatives of their duties on children's education and upbringing. To introduce (or bring back) administrative liability by parents or legal representatives for these types of offenses.

Currently the following types of liability are in existence:
Article 69 of the FC provides for taking away parental rights;
Article 156 of the Criminal Code of the Russian Federation provides liability for neglect in performing duties of minors' upbringing: «Neglect in performing duties of minors' upbringing by parent or other person having these responsibilities, as well as by teacher or other employee of an educational, medical or other institution that has to perform supervision over minors and if these acts are associated with cruel treatment of minors is punishable by a fine of fifty to one hundred minimal salaries or in the amount of monthly salary or other income of a guilty person or by probation for a term not exceeding three years or by imprisonment for a term up to two years with no right to be employed in certain occupations or perform certain activities for a term of three years thereafter or without such restriction».

The earlier Russian Soviet Federative Socialist Republic Code on Administrative Offenses contained *article 164* that provided for administrative liability for neglect by parents or legal representatives of their duties in child upbringing and education. The current Russian Federation Code on Administrative Offenses has no similar provision.

The above proposals on changing and amending Russian legislation in no way decrease the importance of ethical and moral principles in increasing parental responsibility in children's upbringing and education. Substitution of family upbringing by a public one has practically destroyed small communities as the basis of ages-old way of human living and natural means of transition of human experience. It is vital to increase the status of a family, to strengthen it and to promote the cult of a family in mass media.

It is necessary to establish liability of certain authorities and institutions, as well as parents, legal representatives and institutions substituting them for minors' obtaining general education until the statistics of all children and adolescents deprived of care and not attending educational institutions would be introduced.

The decisive measures are needed in fighting for children, their happy childhood and stable future for the country. They must include introduction of liability of education and local government officials for not implementing the Law on Education that establishes mandatory general education for all, creation of government data base of all vagrant children and those teenagers that do not study or work anywhere and control over disadvantaged families.

A single coordinating authority on working and controlling youthful vagrants and delinquents is needed. Until recently this came into responsibility of the police. However, after the Federal Law *On the Basics of System for Prevention of Homelessness and Delinquency among Minors* came into effect the resolution of the problem of homelessness was transferred to temporary detention centers for young delinquents. The multi-agency approach is needed in the work of social protection departments and local governments' executive branches in order to establish in the country a complete system for prevention of social orphanhood, homelessness among children and delinquency among minors.

At the earlier stages of the development of the system of care for orphans and children left without parental care the efforts of the society and the government were aimed primarily at overcoming by educational and economic means of any social hardship that would create multiple situations of potential risk of disharmonic development for each particular child.

Current state of affairs requires some provisions for coordinated performance of the following activities:

- social protection of families and preservation of children within families;
- establishment of upbringing and development conditions for each orphan that would be as close as possible as those that children are enjoying while being reared within families;
- providing quality education, upbringing, psychological and educational guidance for orphans and children left without parental care within establishments for education/

It is the solution of these problems that constitutes the goal of the government program for the social protection of orphans currently on the agenda in Russia.

PRACTICAL THOUGHTS ON ADOPTION RESEARCH AND ITS USE

By

Gordon D. Lewis

INTRODUCTION

To keep in line with the intent of this book to be informative and educational these concluding pages will present information from an adoptive agencies perspective. This information is just that, information and not given as conclusive research. The conclusions drawn by the writer are based on the everyday practice of completing adoptions as shown in this concluding material. However, the present guidelines governing Intercountry adoptions today in part are built from past components of adoption research. A brief look back over some of that history in adoption research will help in understanding the continued influence on policy observed in present adoption practice. The combining overview of the past history with present day practice as shown herein can assist in supporting and applying any conclusions that may be arrived at.

CANADIAN EXAMPLE

Research presents opportunity. This concluding material will be used to show how research has influenced the formation of the Intercountry adoptive policies in Canada. Ontario will be used as a more obvious example in demonstrating this influence of research and policy on that Provinces governing of Intercountry adoptions. Ontario represents an excellent study subject for this showing how influences of both practise and theory when applied can produce a well structured and successful Intercountry adoption process. Ontario allows for a more practical observation on the present direction Intercountry adoptions are being influenced by the ground work from research for two other reasons. One is density of population; the largest in Canada, the other is the diversity in the population living there. Ontario has always accounted for most Intercountry placements to Canada from among the provinces and as such has a more diverse program encompassing both relative and non-relative adoptions. Canada presents an interesting country for a review of why so many Intercountry adoptions are completed by this population. The overall population of Canada is around thirty two million people. On average the number of adoptions into Canada each year from foreign nations is rather low when compared to nations such as the United States. However the ratio of adoptions for Canada per capita would be considered high when comparing the populations of each country. The question here is why are there so many applications to adopt foreign children from such a small population of people in Canada?

In 2006 Statistics Canada noted that the birth rate in Canada was about 1.5 children per family. This is a low rate and not one to sustain the future population needs for growth of the country. Several reasons for the low birth ratio are high divorce rate (50% of all marriages end in divorce), high infertility and couples opting for fewer children or waiting longer into a relationship to have a child. All the reasons above have created the need for adopting a child. Add to that the numbers who desire to adopt internationally as a humanitarian decision and those immigrants who are adopting relative children from abroad and it is understandable why adoptions are rather high in respect to the overall population.

It is in this background that adoptions and regulations governing them in the Province of Ontario Canada will be examined.

INTERNATIONAL INFLUENCE

Russia will receive special notice based on that countries historical application of Post Adoptive Reports (PAR'), which has become a more universal requirement for most Intercountry adoptions patterned after the Russian model. The PAR' offer an enormous wealth of information for researchers in the field of adoption. How this information was and is being used will be examined as it applies to both Ontario and Russia.

Early researchers have gained recognition for presenting material to influence and shape policy determining the governing of Intercountry adoptions. A brief look back to that material influence and those who wrote it and it's affect in Intercountry adoptions is needed in comparing with today's materials. Logically then, a continued look at how present opportunity for research could be used to assist further safe and best practice principles in adoption now and for the future should be noted.

As Intercountry adoptions to Canada have grown from the tens to the hundreds and now into the thousands per year it would be assumed that the research has kept pace. This may or may not be true based on how the information is used from the research and how broad the subject base was for that research. Intecountry adoptions have become far more global and diverse for provinces such as Ontario were the population is representative of almost every possible cultural and ethnic group. As well the move from non relative to more relative adoptions has sped up this diverse change in the international adoption environment and added many complexities not there before. The question to be asked, "Is the research likely to keep pace with the changing environment and diversities of the Intercountry adoptions being fulfilled today in Ontario and else where"?

That question will be answered accurately only through the passage of time but it should be noted that governments tend to react more quickly from political will and far more slowly to the circumstances supported in the findings of researchers. That does not mean the flow of good research should stop nor has it. The rapidly changing environment of Intercountry adoptions has created policy makers to address issues in Intercountry adoption on proper priorities. In Ontario that has been proven by the following;

1. First a sharp decline in adoption break down has been recorded.

2. Second child safety in placement from international settings has achieved a credible success despite the ever-increasing numbers and complexities in adoptions.

3. With those observation it can be said that research of professionals in the field of child placement did have impact and was on pace within Ontario.

The same cannot be said regarding other foreign jurisdictions that are now still developing their international adoption laws. In some settings the governing of adoptions are based on very subjective media or political spin rather than real research of the issues creating the negative perceptions. As the negative perceptions are continued they create the stifling or lethargic governing regulations that tend to hinder rather than help children find security in adoptive families domestically or foreign. Many laws are passed sighting child protection when in reality they do more to keep needy children from there right to family. This usually is due to the government's ability to pass the laws but there inability to actually enforce them. Meanwhile the enormous increase numbers of children without family's demands immediate action by governments.

Adding even a greater burden on all societies is the fact that the children in foster care homes or institutions are growing older and research clearly shows that older children face far more obstacles in fitting into families and society. This in turn creates the need for solutions, which may or may not have been given proper verification through research. It is a vicious circle with the innocent children of all nations caught up in the wake of a truly global problem. Research and law has and still can work in harmony together to establish international adoption practices and principles that work in the best interest of all the worlds' children.

The reality confronted by those attempting to maintain current research in this field is frustrated due to the complexities of confidentiality, legalities and governance but it is encouraging to see the attempt is there despite the difficulties.

Legalities and Governance

Each nation has its own law for adoptions both those sending their children out to a foreign destination and those who are receiving the children in from a foreign destination. A bridge of international law* also governs the transport of children between countries as it pertains to adoption. (*see Hague Convention or Intercountry Adoption Act) Within each country there are federal, regional and district governing laws or policies. Some of these dating back over many years' even generations and are not adaptable to the current events that have created the need for children from within their borders to be placed beyond them. This effect also creates a dysfunction in research specific to that region, district, province, country or culture.

The point is that the exchange in research was not as universal or useful to governments in the early development years particularly prior to 1997. The reality was that development of family law was the neccasary priority that first had to be implemented and then would lead to the structure for domestic and foreign adoption laws later. In some cases, the implementation of adoption laws focused internally excluding that country from being able to ever adopt externally without again restructuring there family law.

Research of foreign adoptions obviously was not likely to be an influencer in those early legal developments. However today, adoptive research in both practices and theory could greatly assist countries who now realize that Intercountry adoption is a valid option for there orphan children.

Research was more specific particularly in the formative stages of international adoptions accommodating more local rather than international adoption philosophies that are becoming more obvious today in Eastern European countries. What led to this for example was that some countries had no real foreign adoption policy or others had a non-uniform practice. This early type of unbalanced approach allowed adoptions to foreigners to be completed by regional political leaders such as mayors or governors until legal structures could be made uniform and brought into effect through the justice systems and court rulings. Obvious wide spread abuse could rule the former type of adoptive proceedings and today in response to those early abuses strict and stringent legal procedure has come into play. As well international law formed another protective covering over the movement of children from one international setting to another. This is known as the Hague Convention or Hague Treaty. (The Hague). The Hague brought the first defined discussions on international adoptions and developed ideals that led to the Intercountry Adoption Act. Once international law such as The Hague came into place adoption research would take on a more respected global awareness and this book is evidence of that approach. Today, because of the early work in establishing uniform structure in law the opportunity is afforded for global compliance in legal governing of adoption proceedings. Most nations now require agencies to be licensed in both the receiving and sending country before working on any child placements. The great reward for families living in every country and for the orphan children is that Intercountry adoption has forced governments to review their family law. This in turn has led to more justice for birth mothers and their children released for adoption into a global setting. Although these are only some of the positive steps regarding the universal regulations for adoptions there still are many hurdles yet to overcome in this area.

Confidentiality

It should be noted that the research findings in Russia and contained in this book falls in line with the research findings of American , Canadian and other researchers on the issues of orphan psychology. However, a key point also is that the Pshchology of Orphans supports the need of parents, or family, in the life of every child for utmost development. Based on Russian research of its own orphan population, it also notes that every child needs to have a strong support and structure system in there life as well.

Russia has always been capable in collecting information. In the case of Intercountry adoption of Russian children there was an early mandate that could have allowed for greater understanding and far less concern in how the placement of children into the homes of foreign families had turned out.

One of the main pioneer additives of the Russian adoption program that needs to be noted is the demand for Post Adoptive Reports (PAR') implemented in 1996. This is of note based on the fact that no demand for such reports has been ordered as part of any international regulatory body to date governing the movement of children by adoption orders. Even though The Hague and the Intercountry Adoption Act (IAA) is used as the major protectorates of children by the United Nations. In reality Russia was ahead of most nations in realizing the importance of follow up reports due mostly to their own internal research on orphan development. The opportunity for credible and ongoing research of at least the Russian adoptions was presented through the early demand of that government for PAR'. This material was available in Russia and Ontario as well as every other receiving country taking in Russian orphans. The lack in this potential material being used to further the positive realities of placements in every adoptive case was the confidentiality aspects.

Even today it is very difficult to have any assurance that the PAR' and the sensitive material they contain would be carefully used by researchers and not expose the identities of adopted children or families needlessly. As well circumstances that have required government interventions in adoptive cases are carefully guarded. Because of this concern the PAR' are still not used to there fullest potential. As well, PAR' could have been used in comparing one Intercountry program with another in developing the best practices, principles and policies for all participants.

Valuable information correcting many of the negative perceptions or other key issues of adoptions are still locked away inside the PAR' on children from many countries such as Russia. That information could be used in a positive manner by all governing bodies to remove many obstacles for children of all ages to find a permanent home and family.

ADOPTION HISTORY AND RESEARCH

Research is prepared in many different formats such as clinical, scientific, and theoretical or as in this setting practical information is drawn from the statistics of actual caseloads. The history of Mission of TEARS (Ontario) allows for a very wide variety of research from case files, not only regarding Russian orphans placed but also other countries in Eastern Europe and beyond. The statistics are based on a wide age range in the children placed as well as multiple child placements into one family. The statistics also cover both relative and non-relative adoption cases, which fall in line with the demand from the diverse population, centered in Ontario.

Before the statistics of Mission of TEARS (Ontario) placements are discussed, there needs to be some review of the history in adoption research within Canada which may have led to particular governance of some of the adoption regulations that are unique to Ontario. As well these provincial policies reflect the changes in Mission of TEARS (Ontario) caseloads, which are noted in the statistics given.

The Ames Report (*1)

The most wide spread and used research creating the backdrop for Intercountry adoption in Ontario was the Ames Report. Based on research documented on Romanian Adoptions and the development of those children that took place in the early 1990's the report examined why the Romanian children seemed to have such difficult adjustments periods and what conclusions could be brought forward to safe guard future Intercountry adoptions from breaking down.

The Ames Report was required reading for all adoptive parents in Ontario until recently were it is no longer a requirement but is still a leading recommended reading for all perspective parents.

In concluding the Ames Report covered seven main recommendations with another eight subsidiary ones. Among the conclusions was for parental training of the inherent risk of institutionalization and other dysfunctional behaviors occurring in adoptive children. Not only training but also services to assist families needed to be set in place for both pre and post adoption. Recommendation for the referral structure and training should cover all professionals and agencies that assist parents in adoption including government sectors. The Ames Report observed that children who spend there formative and developmental years in an orphanage do have more trouble in bonding to family setting, structure and routine. The Ames Report advised that whenever possible the youngest children possible should be the first proposal for adoptive parents.

Post Ames research has defined and summarized the formative years of an institutionalized child' life in this basic ratio that for every three months spent in an institution by an orphan they loose one month in overall neurological and physical development.

A follow up report was done in the late 1990' on the Romanian (*2) children and updated some of the findings even though the original Ames Report was still the required reading by all adoptive applicants at that time.

It should be kept in mind that at the time of the Ames Report, adoptions into Canada overall were very limited and remained so until the very late 1990'. Also, Romania was the main Eastern European country being chosen in adoption by Canadian families.

In the 2002 fall edition of the Journal of the Adoptive Council of Ontario it was noted that the Romanian children from the Ames Report had been followed for ten years in post adoptive research with each individual seen three times. Conclusions of the researcher' showed that the results have been very consistent across the three assessment times. The older adoptive children did show more significant difficulties and delays in development when compared to parallel groups of either early-adopted children from the same area or Canadian born children.

The environment for international adoptions into Canada was starting to mature during this time. Russia was developing their adoptive program at that time but still slowly and Romania had not yet experienced the permanent closure of Intercountry

Adoption that was to come. As an example of the numbers of adoptions by one agency limited to Eastern Europe for the time frame being discussed refer to Chart # 1.

The adoptions in this Chart # 1 are before the influence of the Ontario government regulating agencies in Intercountry adoptions. This time for adoptions was also before some of the early research found in the Ames report and other similar reports by Dr. Dana Johnson (*3) influenced future adoption policy. Ontario was basing there policy on actual case experiences of older children or sibling settings from international adoptions that had to have interventions. (Refer to list of reading materials designed to assist adoptive parent research)*4) The Ontario policy in part was to limit the age of an adoptive child (preference not older than 3 years of age) one child at a time and no sibling groups.

That future policy would be governed as well by the signing of the Intercountry Adoption Act and The Hague first brought in to effect at this time.

Chart # 1

Adoption Report for Mission of TEARS (Ontario) 1997 (Russian children only all non relative and pre international licensing)

Adoptions completed in 1997	18
Number of Children placed	26
Number of Families that received the children	18
Number of Children age one and under	6
Number of Children one to three years of age	8
Number of Children four to five years of age	5
Number of Children six to ten years of age	3
Number of Children over the age of ten years	4

Incidents in placements were 16% of the total children placed or 4 actual cases 3 of those being with older children over the age of 8 years. It needs to be mentioned here that none of the cases led to a child being at risk but the need was in counseling for behavioral issues. One case was based on a medical indicator. Also, the incident percentage noted here cannot be assumed as the norm since some agencies may have experienced a higher or lower incident rate and the actual rates of incidents and the cause are not publicly given out by governing ministries due to confidentiality.

It should be noted that the overall numbers of children adopted to Canada in this year from Russia and in particular to Ontario were the majority went, totaled 77. Russia was 4th on the sending list of children to Canada in that year behind China 1st India 2nd and Jamaica 3rd. It should be noted that India and Jamaican adoptions consisted mainly of relative adoptions not non-relative. This also indicates the beginning trend in Ontario of relative adoptions that would slowly gain momentum. More interesting is the fact that Romanian adoptions were well down in numbers already at this period of time and the adoptions that had been done earlier as part of the research components to the Ames Report were already becoming dated. The PAR' of the Russian adoptions would have proven timely in reassessing and comparing the Eastern European placements more thoroughly between Russia and Romania

At the same time over 200,000 children worldwide were adopted with the United States receiving almost 16,000 of these adoptive children from around the world.

Based on the growing numbers of international placements to the United States as compared to Canada, it is not surprising that an American researcher Dr. Dana Johnson came to the fore front. Dr. Johnson's material is still widely used today. (*5)

It is understandable then when the numbers are reviewed that Canada had a very pioneer developing international program well behind many other countries. As well it is clear that some influential research beyond the Ames Report was also being used in forming policy for international adoptions in Canada. These materials were not from within Canada but from outside and based on adoption procedures that may or may not in themselves have been well researched or their governing policies considered best practice principles. It is certain that with the diversity coming to Ontario in international adoptions by relative applicants some of the research may not be applicable or relevant.

The Federal Immigration Department would compound this complexity by its own revamping of the immigration regulations governing adoptions. This started in 1997 and was only concluded in May 2006 allowing for adoptive children to receive Canadian citizenship more immediately. To accommodate this pending change, relatives could no longer sponsor minor children related to them but had to adopt them depending on the circumstances affecting the child overseas. One hurdle that was removed by the immigration department was the more rigid regulations governing the medical history of the child. Changing the immigration regulations and allowing for immediate citizenship removed a lot of medical restrictions under the immigration regulations. Now the agency or parents were responsible for assuring careful defining of the medical risks be maintained in the adoption process.

The impact in Ontario was particularly hard as now relative applicants were looking to bring in sibling groups and older children in contradiction to much of the research surrounding the increased risk of such adoptions whether relative or non relative. Ontario was already heading in a more defined direction.

Ontario opted for the licensing of agencies using guidelines for Intercountry adoptions based on The Hague and the Intercountry Adoption Act (IAA) born from The Hague. At the same time Ontario used the research in place at that time to develop policy for child placement, which began to slowly point families to younger children and single placements only. The accepted view that children over the age of two years do not bond as easily and places the adoption at risk became a major future factor for policy in Ontario. As well the thought that more than one child or sibling placement at a time would also raise the risk of adoption breakdown created preference for all recommendations to be for one adoptive child at a time and under the age of three years.

This was the policy that governed the non-relative adoptions but certainly could not be so easily applied to the relative adoptions. The reality of this policy in Ontario has proven itself in the end result that Intercountry adoptions have had a realized drop in major disruptions after the child has been placed here to a family from an international setting.

Today the adoptions at Mission of TEARS (Ontario) reflect this policy based on Chart #2 and detailing the number of placements since Licensing was implemented under IAA guidelines.

Chart # 2

Adoption Report for Mission of TEARS (Ontario) 2000 to 2006 (relative and non relative)

Total number of adoptive applicants	=260
(relative R) 62 and (non relative NR) 198	= 260
Total number of adoptions completed for relative applicants	= 41
Total number of adoptions completed for non relative applicants	= 128
Total number of adoptions classified other*	= 12

Total number of applications still on file for R = 27 and for NR   = 52 = 79

Total of all adoptive applications from 2000 to 2006   = 260

Total number of all children adopted both relative and non relative   = 212

Total number of children adopted by relatives   = 61

Total number of children adopted by non relatives   = 151

Total number of different sending countries (were the children came from) = 28

A fact for changes effecting adoptions can be found when we look at the diversity created between relative and a non-relative applicant particularly as it applies to the sending countries. There were 28 sending countries represented overall for this time frame with non-relative applicants representing the majority of the adoptions completed (198) with the majority of those (183) adopting from only 5 of the 28 sending countries. The remaining 15 applicants that make up the 198 are spread throughout the twenty-eight countries worked in for relative and non-relative placements.

This chart shows that even though the majority of non-relative adoptive applicants still represented fewer countries there was also far more countries open to Intercountry adoptions. The majority of new sending countries were open to serve relative applicants (62) and not because of the few non-relative applicants. This shows the diversity now in place and the growing need in monitoring both relative and non-relative types of adoptions.

For Chart #2 Russia still represents the first country of choice for applicants because it is one of the oldest international programs for Canadians. However two other programs of this agency have actually surpassed Russia for applicants over the last four years and they are Haiti and South Africa. Each of those countries opened to Intercountry adoptions due to different issues. Haiti would open first because of extreme poverty while South Africa due to the HIV/AIDS crisis. Each of those countries share in poverty and HIV/AIDS but the cause and effect of those crises on advancing Intercountry adoptions worked opposite roles of one another as primary factors for those governments to take action. Russia had opened years in advance of most countries for Intercountry adoptions and now in 2008 is slowly trying to ease away from the former cause and effects that created the foreign adoptions in the first place. In particular now that poverty is not as acute or wide spread and the transition in government has brought more stability and opportunity to address social issues such as orphans. Russia now is posed to maintain her children and keep them in country with foster care and domestic adoptive programs funded by the state. Intercountry adoptions are decreasing from Russia.

The above chart does not reflect China' influence on this agency adoption program (this agency was not licensed for China). At this time China is still the overall national #1 country of choice by Canadian applicants. China once the most stable adoptive program has recently moved to begin a more measured pace for adoptions. They as Russia have done, are looking to develop a more domestic based program as well and less foreign placements.

One magazine The Economist in there July 2007 issue speaks to the issue of "How to deal with a shrinking population" and sights several countries now dealing with this problem.

Large countries such as Russia or China are already responding to this real and serious problem and reducing foreign adopters is one way to bring immediate relief.

It should be noted here that older children are being presented more often for adoption in countries such as China who once presented very young children. Not only China but many other countries also now present older children. It has been clearly shown that older children present a higher risk category in adoptions yet the trend is clear in Intercountry adoptions toward the older child. This trend is compounded in the adoptions by the added direction of relative adoptions with also older children and multiple placements at one time.

The figures in Chart #2 show how adoptions have diversified over the years and Non relative applications alone are no longer the dominant factor for bringing children into Ontario. In fact nearly 50% of all children represented here in adoption are relative to the applicant (nephew, niece etc.) which is a complete redirection from ten years ago (see Chart #1) when all applications were for non relative children. For now non-relative applications are still the main driving force in international adoptions but it is clear that is changing.

Another interesting observation can be made from the figures of Chart #2 regarding the policy (in Ontario) in place to guide adoptive applicants. The policy prefers one child for adoption at a time with the age of the child under three years. It is clear from this one agency overview that this also is changing and not just due to relative adoption pressure. If we relate back to the history of were this policy came from and why it was implemented and the obvious successful results from that implementation, we can only assume that either new research has changed thinking toward the policy or new practical aspects to adoption are making former policy redundant. In other words, new policy is replacing old policy or changes are effecting the overall balance to effective policy. The changing curve is clearly there if shown over time even if it is not clear in the immediate. The bases for the perceived change is likely the result of the diversity in the practical aspects and in the number of relative applicants as well the ages of the children in these requests creating the appearance of policy change when in reality none has taken place.

Chart # 2A is Showing Ages of children adopted in Chart #2

Total adopted children in Chart # 2 is 212

Number of children adopted 3 years and under   = 136

Number of children over age 3 up to age 8   = 40

Remaining children over age 8   = 36

Percentage of children over policy age of 3 years 36%

Chart # 2A shows the number of children adopted and the age range in the children represented by those adoptions. All of the relative adoptive children were over the policy age of 3 years.

Number of children adopted by both relatives and non relatives representing multiple placements including twins from the 212 total was 62. However, relative placements equaled 92% or 57 of those children placed from the total of 62.

Percentage of multiple placements represented in the total adoptions overall 29%

The above numbers cover several different countries including Russia. Between the 1997 figures in Chart # 1 and those in Chart # 2 the indication is that the majority of children adopted to non relatives are still age of 3 years or younger. However, all relative children adopted internationally were over the age of 3 years and in most sibling or multiple placements, 92% were relative. There is little research in these relative placements and no required post adoptive reporting to access if the risk factors carry over into this type of adoption as well or if it does is it to the same extent as found by the Ames reports in relative placements. Experienced social workers indicate the risks are there and several incidents have been reported to verify this observation in relative placements.

It should be noted that in Ontario since the year 2000 the Provincial Director under the IAA must license all agencies for international adoptions. This has led to fewer agencies (facilitators) now than in 1997 but more international adoptions are being completed and the growing increase in part can be linked to relative adoptions.

The conclusion is that relative adoptions are becoming more common, are from far more diverse cultures and are usually for older children and more than one child.

Post Adoptive Reports and there use in Russia

A key demand of adoption agencies by countries such as Russia was for mandatory Post Adoptive Reports (PAR') on the adoptive child. These placement reports allowed for excellent information to asses the overall adoption procedures and all the policies governing them. With two reports mandatory in the first year combined with a single yearly report for the next two years, there were four reports in a three-year span. This allowed for credible monitoring of the child' adjustment by the social worker required to make those reports by visiting the family in the home. Sadly not all sending countries demand such follow up and in part it is because no one really utilized this information obtained in the PAR' other than for compliance. For now the main purpose of the Russian PAR' is used for maintaining the legal structure of the agency inside the Russian Federation to keep there status to carry out adoptions. This legal structure is called accreditation.

Although these reports are completed and sent to Russia in the Russian language, it is not clear what use they have in Russia other than in the role of compliance. Certainly they seem not to be used in any way for constructive research and played no role at all inside Russia to dissipate the recent and ongoing negative public overview of international adoptions. Neither have the reports been used to establish the reality that many Russian children of all ages have found loving homes and bright futures through the good and conscientious work of adoption agencies and professional social workers. Reports would have shown that many of the children adopted overcame real medical and institutional handicaps to rise up and accomplish success in many live dynamics including that of the family group. For example, if the figures in Chart #1 and #2 combine to show 100 Russian adoptions that would mean that 300 Post Adoptive Reports were required. If the government has the ability to regulate the compliance of 300 reports from just one agency imagine the thousands of reports from other nations pouring into Russia on the children. The point is that the value of the reports were seen as a legal compliance and used for little else. The question to be asked is could the information inside those thousands of reports been used to define a better and more receptive atmosphere for Russian children to be sent into?

Today in Russia the fingers point at corruption in the money around adoption as the fault for the tragedies that befall some of the children placed.

That certainly needs to be looked at and addressed. But also the wealth of knowledge that has really come from those past adoptions back to Russia is in the research material inside those PAR's. That wealth has been wasted from lack of usefulness. It certainly could have been used to prevent future tragedies by evaluating what went wrong in the former cases.

In particular the PAR' would have shown the knowledge that clearly supports the research undertaken in Russia and contained in this book regarding orphans. The fact is that an orphan child when reunited with a mother figure either domestic or foreign is in a far better developmental environment with a more optimistic and determined future. PAR' would also have shown the reality in parental education and preparation for the development of that environment and most certainly highlighted any weaknesses from any adoptive case.

PAR' and Accreditation

In 2004 rumblings out of Russia were growing louder about the corruption in the adoption program there and how so many Russians were becoming wealthy working in international adoptions. This created the perception that Russian officials were allowing the children of their nation to be basically sold of to foreigners. At the same time, several real and shocking cases were highlighting the front-page news stories in Russia of children being killed by foreign adoptive parents or severally abused by them. It is also true that Russia has the highest cost base for foreign parents in service fees over all other countries. Service fees are what parents pay for accommodation, drivers, translators etc. while in a foreign country. Again, the state looked like it was allowing Russian children not only to be sold to foreigners but also to be placed in real danger.

Doing the right thing amidst the public out cry from within Russia, the Russian Federation began a re-accreditation program for all agencies and an overview of the adoptive policies in place. Throughout 2005 most international adoption actively in Russia slowly ground to a halt. A constant theme in most Russian TV, Radio and Newspaper stories on international adoptions during this time was the same. Russian children were being lost to rich foreigners and placed in real danger by every adoption completed. The perception was well planted within the public conscientiousness but would that perception hold up under scrutiny and in particular what did the research show? Was there any documentation that could confirm that by far the majority of children adopted from Russia to foreign lands were doing well?

The answer is yes, Russia had at her finger tips the volumes of PAR' to validate that thousands of former orphans were thriving in there foreign families and that the negative evaluation of international placements were based on a very small number of cases. It is true that no cases should end up at all in such horrible circumstances as some of the Russian ones did. But why was there never any reference during this time to the fact that Russia had in 1996 implemented a very capable program of Post Adoptive Reporting to monitor the children leaving the states protection?

Furthermore, have these reports played any part in the restructuring of the accreditation program of the foreign agencies for the future other than again being used as a compliance requirement. No, the PAR' have not been utilized only as in the past for compliance.

Now many adoptions are examined only if they encounter a problem and that is certainly understandable. This leaves the examination of the many other placements that have had no immediate problems but an apparent successful conclusion unexplored as to why it succeeded. It is important from a research perspective for the reason of success to be examined as well as the reasons for failure in adoptions. The proper assessment material and the case numbers to make the research valid are already held in the files of each adoption and PAR. A more accurate establishment of the actual risk of an adoption can be better pre determined by the review of this material based on the applicant's life circumstances even before a child should come into the scenario.

It is clear that most research that has affected adoptive policies in Ontario has been mainly child centered. Unlike the early work in the Ames report that also defined the best adult applicants for adopting a child, the later research has targeted the problems as child centered. New reviews in this area are underway and most recently the Ontario government is implementing a universal training program for international applicants used now in domestic adoptions. It is not clear if any of the training programs will be based on the actual post adoptive reports now being completed in a significant number of all international adoptions.

Post Adoptive Reports and there use in Ontario

So what is the use of this crucial material here in Ontario been? Again, most reports are simply filed away as a part of adoption compliance rather than being used for fostering credible information on the development of adoptive children into Ontario.

It is understood and needs to be mentioned that no funding for such research is available in the government level and the public sector is simply unaware of the need. Only adoptive professionals realize the lack in this area. As well the sensitive issue of confidentiality is at stak and no one seems anxious to move into the research due to this factor or if they desire to try they are met with resistants based on confidentiality.

Practical research has been less available to balance the other forms of research in international adoptions because most case research is done when a problem arises in a placement. The information is readily available today within the PAR' but is as yet not fully utilized to further develop more understanding on what indicators can be pre adoptive aids in defining suitable applicants as well as proposed children.

The fact that PAR' will hold even more significant' in monitoring the long-range results in adoptions is a reality. This is understood and put into practice by the Ukraine' demand for a PAR up to the adoptee' 18th year of age but the weakness in this demand on adoptive parents as with the Russian program is no legal enforcement. Logically if sending or receiving governments demand such reports and then legally enforce them to take place the expectation would be that either better use should be made of the reports contents and that some form of subsidy to the cost of these should be made to ease that burden from the parents. As no governing body is likely to do more than continue the use of the PAR' for compliance regulations the real value of the important information within these reports and its influence on adoptions may never be known. On the reverse side of this issue is an even more frustrating fact. For example the Ukraine PAR at one time could be simply done by a parent and that is accepted. It is good that it is done at all but the fact it is done by the parent to avoid the cost of the professional social worker doing the PAR leaves the content of the report more subjective for any future research.

Parental Preparation

The Home Study

Each perspective parent must go through a home study process, which in itself is fairly uniform in the requirements of the applicants.

The home study formerly was considered a two-fold process between the prospective adoptive parents and the professional social worker conducting the study. The elements of the process involved educational and assessment components with each party giving and receiving information. The home study process is to help the adoptive applicants identify their strengths, limitations and readiness for adoption and allows the social worker conducting the home study to asses the capacity and readiness of the perspective parents. The outcome of the home study for the parents is to develop knowledge, understanding and acceptance to help meet the needs of a child not born to them. For the social worker the outcome will be concluded at the end of the written home study in a clear recommendation of the parents and of the type of child they look to adopt.

Home studies include in part some of the following material on the parent;

1/ Interviews by the social worker (at least 4 or 5 one must be in the home)

2/Adoption Medicals for the parents

3/Police Checks, local, federal (RCMP in Canada) and Interpol or other international checks

4/Personnel References

5/Finnacial Information

These are just a few of the main factors in the home study but there was never a mandatory requirement for Intercountry applicants (until recently in Ontario) for parental education or orientation. In the early adoptive times there was little educational support for international adoptive parents unless provided for by the agency, social worker or the parents found assistants on there own. One reality that seems to come consistently from perspective parents both relative and non-relative, is the lack of solid information in adoption procedures that can be sourced from one location, organization or person. This is true even though it has become better over the last few years in finding agencies and social workers that are well experienced in adoptions from multiple countries. It needs to be kept in mind that licensed agencies have only been in Ontario since 2000 and even then to be licensed does not mean an agencies knowledge goes beyond more than one country while others may. It still requires the perspective family to search out the right agency to assist them, which means that a family may have to visit several different organizations doing adoptions. Even if they are working in the same countries those agencies will likely all have a different approach to how and whom they will work with.

There are some very good organizations such as the Ontario Adoption Council or the National Adoption Council of Canada but even they struggle to have sourced materials able to keep up with the complex international changes and the constantly growing numbers of countries now allowing their children to be placed in foreign families. Just as the adoptions have grown from a few per year to thousands so have countries now offering there orphan children. For example Africa has only begun to open its doors in the last four years to serious structured adoptions for their children.

Mission of TEARS (Ontario) at present holds five permanent licenses for this continent of Africa and has worked in almost all the countries in Africa with relative adoptions.

The point is that research in the laws for adoption have certainly opened up channels of security for many formerly reluctant nations to now feel confident in involving themselves.

Research in establishing realities in medical backgrounds on children have grown so much now that we have a Canadian Adoption Clinic in Toronto just for reviewing medicals on proposed children. The advances in HIV/AIDS research and testing have allowed adoptions to be developed in a more secure environment in the face of this global health crisis. Research has created security in policy, licensing and other adoption procedures but there is very little specific and localized information for adoptive parents to draw their initial information from.

Parental Preparation was another early component in most research recommendation. This has been an understood lack in the adoption process both at home and abroad for as long as this agency has been serving families. In 1997 in a meeting with the Educational Department of the Russian Federation, the idea was discussed and considered then of Russia starting its own training program for foreign adoptive parents. It was clear then as it still is today that parents need education specific to their chosen country and on the developmental issues facing orphans. If parents also receive education in the risk factors as based on the research to date regarding adoption, this would further help in the placement.

Ontario is planning to implement a mandatory and universal program for all perspective international applicants consistent with their domestic training program.Mission of TEARS (Ontario) always tried to have Informational Seminars to prepare perspective families for adopting overall not just adopting through our services.

This mandatory education has developed in part because of the dysfunctional work of agencies not developing strong educational components to their programs. In part the assumption by agencies that social workers were preparing parents for there specific country was unfortunate. Some excellent training and educational programs have been developed by both agencies and social workers early on to fill this void but again the lack of any support funding for this type of educational component was not able to make these credible efforts more universal.

Since the government has acknowledge this lack and is determined to address this issue of parental education they must find a credible source that they feel comfortable sending all families too. The families will cover the cost and will need to take the time to complete the course before going on to adopt.

Will this training in an environment comfortable to the regulators of Intercountry adoption in Ontario allow for more parental choice over the age of the child and if they can adopt more than one at a time? Again only time will answer this question. The mandatory educational change is to be scheduled starting for all applicants in 2008.

What are some of the observations that can be made to better the system overall by the individuals who must go through this process for international preparation to adopt?

- Funding of research through adoptive agencies is a must to utilize the PAR'

- Development of a Canadian base International Adoption Institute to govern all adoptive policies and there effect, to collect and dissipate materials and non bias information for parents and to work to inform all sending countries of the success ratios of the adoptions would be a tremendous advancement (this organization could also be utilized in PAR' for research rather than agencies noted above)

- Mandatory PAR' universally for all international placements and the funding for them if required.

- To address the concerns of abuse in adoptive systems foreign countries could easily restrict numbers of children to be adopted to a particular country or through a particular agency reflecting past performance and adherence to regulations or laws governing adoptions as well setting standard fee guidelines for services assisting foreign adopters

- Parental Training for specific countries (covers specifics beyond the upcoming mandatory Ontario parent education)

- Development of funding for agencies who then would have time to apply known research to encompass structuring more quality adoptions for parent and child rather than focus on quantity of adoptions

In Conclusion;

Setting of numbers of adoptions out of one country and received into another would also allow for better monitoring of adoptions based on research now in place Examples of this are in existence now were for instance Ontario has a policy of one child at a time under age three or Ukraine has limited the numbers of children to be adopted to a particular country based on past post adoptive reports or Russia who has limited the number of adoptive agencies operating in Russia for better governing of the international process. Each of these individual efforts is certainly understandable based on research from real circumstances and a good start. The problem is in the reality of enforcement, which leads in most cases to an almost restrictive or very limited opportunity for the orphan to find a family early in the formative months or years of life. Because of the lethargic state that international adoption then takes, children become effected even more by longer term stays in orphanages leading to further developmental delays and institutionalization or other effects related to bonding and adjustment not to mention the compromise in medical care. The reality in enforcement of governing bodies trying to protect birth mothers, their children and their rights is the formation of inflexible policy or stringent law. The end result there is the creation of increased numbers of dependent children coming into a system that is overburden and has no plan or place for kids to go. This results in either no foster care structure or if so one that does not allow for the permanent placement of a child for there own mental and social development. Even more so international adoption becomes so bogged down that it cannot function efficiently to address placements early enough in the child's formative years to gain maximum advantage for the child.

The obvious result is the inability to avoid the known pitfalls of older children needing placement. The catch twenty two syndrome is obviously not working as most Eastern European countries have more orphans now than after World War Two and now Africa and other nations are being devastated by Aids destroying families and creating more orphans. The orphan child problem is now far more global an issue than even twenty years ago. Then most of the adoptions being completed internationally were limited to specific regions of the world and numbers were far less. Today the numbers are greatly increased and adoption is far more diversified and definitely more global in representation.

Research presents opportunity and in the case of adoption for orphan children this opportunity today is the difference between life and death. That much research has already proven.

REFERENCE

1. The Development of Romanian Orphanage Children Adopted To Canada by Elinor Ames Ph.D. January 1997 (known as the Ames Report) was mandatory reading for all adoptive parents in Ontario until recently. *1*4

2. A Follow up Study of Adopted Children from Romanian by Victor Groze Ph.D. and Daniela Ileana MSSA December 1996 (review of American children adopted from Romania) *2*4

3. International Adoptions: Implications for Early Intervention by Dr. Dana Johnson MD PhD and Kathryn Dole MS OTR (1999)*3*5*4

4. International Adoption: New Kids, New Challenges Dr. Dana Johnson MD PhD. (2001)*5*4

5. Long Term Medical Issues in International Adoptions by Dr. Dana Johnson MD PhD (2001)*5*4

6. Risks of Adopting the Institutionalized Child by Dr. Dana Johnson MD PhD (1996)*5*4

7. Understanding Adoptions: A Developmental Approach source Canadian Pediatric Society (1998)*4

8. Impact of Adoption on the Child sourced from Canadian Pediatric Society*4

9. Health Issues in Adopting from Russia article by Dr. Eric Downing*4

10. Fetal Alcohol and Complete Medical Review When Adopting from Eastern Europe by Dr. Carol Ham (2004) *4

Lightning Source UK Ltd.
Milton Keynes UK
UKOW040708130113

204806UK00001B/35/P